# An Arts Therapeutic Approach to Maternal Holding

Little research has explored the everyday, simple and long-term experience of maternal holding, particularly after the first year of a child's life. The research that has been undertaken commonly examines holding through the lens of attachment with a focus on the impact of holding upon the child. Employing an arts-based collaborative inquiry approach, participants' stories of holding, as well as the author's own, convey the significant maternal experiences of holding their children over individual arts therapeutic sessions. Optimal moments of holding included strange, powerful and meaningful experiences of expansion into self-in-relationship. Attention is drawn to the ways in which holding can alert us to the current state of mother/child relationships; how we understand, story and structure those relationships; and the ways in which we can attend to holding in order to develop deeply satisfying experiences of a mother/child 'us'.

*An Arts Therapeutic Approach to Maternal Holding* aims to draw attention to the intersubjective qualities of the mother/child relationship, explore why holding matters, and offer suggestions for therapeutic practice. This book is essential reading for therapeutic practitioners and those in allied health fields who work with mothers and children.

**Ariel Moy** is a Teacher and Research Supervisor in therapeutic arts practice at The MIECAT Institute in Melbourne, Australia and has a private practice focusing on mother/child relationships.

# An Arts Therapeutic Approach to Maternal Holding

Developing Healthy Mother and Child Holding Relationships

**Ariel Moy**

**Routledge**
Taylor & Francis Group

LONDON AND NEW YORK

First published 2022
by Routledge
2 Park Square, Milton Park, Abingdon, Oxon OX14 4RN

and by Routledge
605 Third Avenue, New York, NY 10158

*Routledge is an imprint of the Taylor & Francis Group, an informa business*

© 2022 Ariel Moy

*British Library Cataloguing-in-Publication Data*
A catalogue record for this book is available from the British Library

*Library of Congress Cataloging-in-Publication Data*
A catalog record has been requested for this book

ISBN: 978-0-367-61094-4 (hbk)
ISBN: 978-0-367-61095-1 (pbk)
ISBN: 978-1-003-10409-4 (ebk)

DOI: 10.4324/9781003104094

Typeset in Bembo
by Taylor & Francis Books

This book is dedicated to my husband John, my son Owen and my Nan Ilma for all of their love, thank you.

# Contents

# Figures

# Boxes

# Acknowledgements

I wish to thank Rosanna, Leni and Kitty who gave so generously of their time and energy to this inquiry. Their enthusiasm and willingness to dig deep with me made this research possible. Thank you so much.

Many, many thanks to my supervisor Dr Jan Allen for consistently providing invaluable insight, encouragement, guidance and nurture. I've loved the endlessly creative ways she approached this process. Arriving later in the inquiry, but with much appreciated advice and support (and an acute attention to detail), I also wish to thank my supervisor Dr Stacey Bush.

Over many get togethers, Annette Lowe and Katie Callery contributed to this inquiry with curiosity, humour, knowledge and care – your friendship means a great deal to me and thank you both for reading the final effort.

To my awesome husband John for accepting and holding me through the ups and downs of such a long process, and my beautiful son Owen for providing constant inspiration and moments of holding. Thanks also to my nan Ilma Sinclair who held me when I was young and meant the world to me.

And finally, a huge thank you to Alicia Cohen without whom this would not have been possible.

I'm also grateful for the time spent with our dog Monte throughout the inquiry, we miss him every day.

# Introduction

My child was born in 2006. The next day I wrote about us:

> ## Box 0.1 Ariel Moy, Diary Entry 2006
>
> I hold you in a room of light; two walls are made of glass so that we are suspended in the sky. So full of painkillers I shouldn't feel a thing, I still feel the warmth and weight of you, my son. A shape and weight I'm not yet used to.
>
> Only hours ago, you were held in my womb and now you are in my arms. I look at you wrapped in mint wool and see every possible future and for a moment the room topples into blackness, our world in chaos. A friend said: "Once you have a child, you will always worry". It is not until you sigh and press into my chest that I return to us: your attention demands mine. If not for holding you, I might live in fear forever; a world so far from the fact of your ten wrinkled toes, your hearty cries. Perhaps having held you for so long inside, any distance between us now is too much, too soon?
>
> I touch your black hair for the first time, I feel the strange jerks of your left arm, smell the milky newness of your skin and listen to your gurgles. What happens in the next few hours, happens to *us* as you lie in my arms.
>
> I tell you your eyes look like storm clouds and you become still. I look away from you and the windows ripple with rain. I look back and you have slipped into sleep. Your face caressed with the warm pleasure of a spring day, perhaps you are dreaming the sun. I hold you when you feed, I hold you when you fret, I hold you when visitors come, and I hold you when you sleep. I will hold you as you meet a bigger and bigger world, and my world is exquisitely larger now that you're in it.

At the time of writing, I didn't know that I would choose to spend years exploring holding through my doctorate in Therapeutic Arts Practice. There was something compelling about it that intrigued me then and still does today. Writing "what happens in the next few hours, happens to *us* as you lie in my arms", I remember wondering how I might put into words this strange and fleeting feeling of no longer being the self I'd known. I was not less than, I was

DOI: 10.4324/9781003104094-1

not my son, I was not 'a mother' either. In that moment, I was something *more* but that was as much as I could articulate. I wondered if others felt that way too.

After this first diary entry, I continued to write about holding, cherished photos of it (see image below) and collected images and words in magazines and newspapers. I asked others about holding and listened to stories about new-born and adult children being held; rocking infants to sleep, restraining tantrums in the carpark, holding a dying child and holding a daughter as she gave birth. In these moments of holding every emotion came into play, there was pride, resentment, oneness and boredom. Holding appeared to tell us something about the mother and child relationship entire.

In this book I share the story of an inquiry into mother's experiences of holding their children using an arts therapeutic approach as well as provide a guide for therapists who might wish to adopt some of these methods and ideas for work with their clients. I draw attention to the powerful ways in which holding can alert us to the current state of mother/child relationships; how we understand, story and structure those relationships; and the ways in which we can attend to holding in order to develop deeply satisfying experiences of a mother/child 'us'.

In 2015, neuroscientist Rebecca Saxe captured the first fMRI scans of a mother holding her child (Figure 0.1). She "curled up together" with her infant son Atsushi inside the MRI machine and remained still while it collected images. For Saxe it represented a "very old image made new. The Mother and Child is a powerful symbol of love and innocence, beauty and fertility" (2015, para. 6). She wanted to take that symbol and create something more representative of her experience; combining traditional maternal symbolism with values "usually viewed in opposition … inquiry and intellect, progress and power" (para. 6). The resulting images brought together some of Saxe's experiences as a woman working in science with her experience of holding her child.

Saxe's desire to explore and represent themes of identity and mothering reveal the many curiosities and tensions involved in the seemingly simple act of maternal holding.

Ruth Feldman (2011) writes:

> Touch is the most basic mammalian maternal behavior. As soon as an infant is born, mammalian mothers begin to engage in the species-typical repertoire of maternal behavior, and these postpartum behaviors consist primarily of close physical proximity and the provision of maternal touch. Being such a widespread mammalian behavior, early maternal touch must carry important implications for survival and adaptation and contribute to the growth and development of the young.
>
> (p. 373)

Attachment behaviours (such as maternal holding) are vitally important for the development of an infant with long-term ramifications for their relational styles, well-being and health (Bowlby, 1958; Ainsworth, Blehar, Water & Wall,

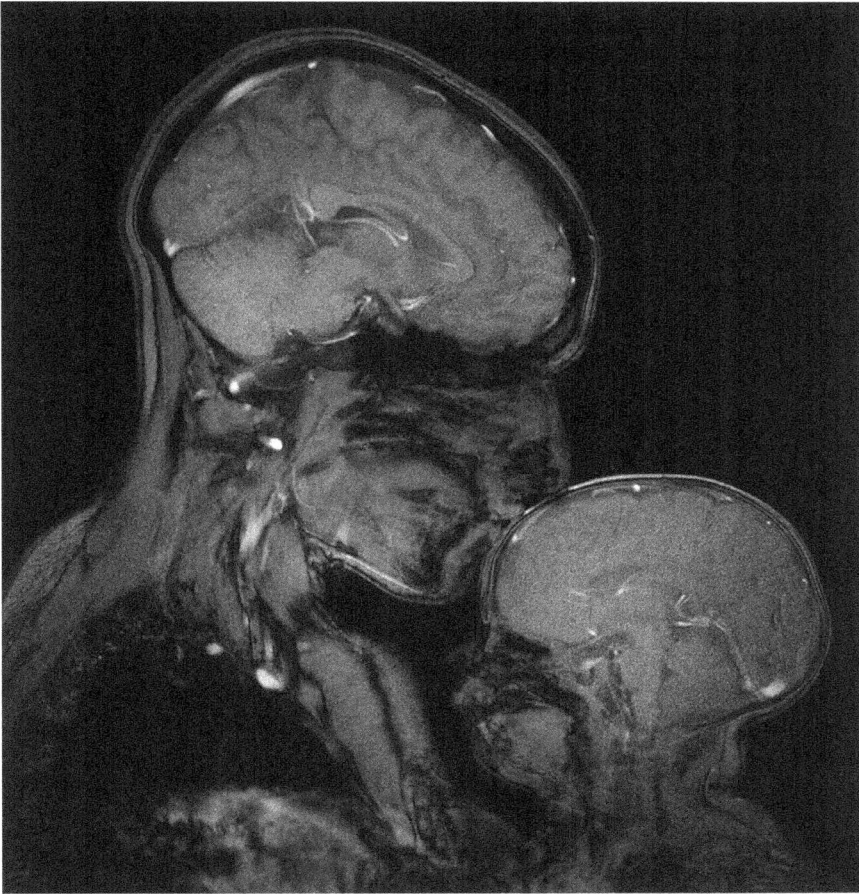

*Figure 0.1* fMRI image of mother holding her child (permission granted by R. Saxe).

2005). Attachment research however has focused on the significance of the mother/child relationship for the child.

I chose to research maternal experiences of holding because I wanted to know if it mattered as much to mothers' understanding and development as it does to children. I did not examine holding through the lens of attachment, but I did wonder if what was so vitally important for a child might not be just as important for the mother. Both mother and child play active roles in the relationship during holding. For example, a child who is in pain will cry, alerting his mother to his needs, and when she holds him, she responds to him, and he responds to her. She is more than her carrying arms, she is a vital human being in relationship with her child, a human being that feels just as much as her child.

I have defined maternal holding as an everyday, long-term, frequent, initially embodied and evolving relational behaviour shared between mother and child. Holding can be generous, supportive and loving, it can also be chaotic, controlling and cruel. A mother's experience of the contours and atmosphere of holding are the subject of this inquiry.

Novelist Jeff Vandermeer (2014) writes:

> The first astronomers to think of points of light not as part of a celestial tapestry revolving around the earth but as individual planets had had to wrench their imaginations – and thus their analogies and metaphors – out of a grooved track that had been running through everyone's minds for hundreds and hundreds of years.
>
> (p. 113)

In light of this quote, I wondered: What might we see differently if we view holding through the lens of maternal knowing? This question has shaped my inquiry journey.

Given the personal significance of holding for me, I constructed my research inquiry around three guiding values (described in depth in Chapter 1). I valued an intersubjective way of being with others, multimodal ways of knowing and an attention to the present moment.

In collecting material for my research, I worked with three mothers who I have renamed for anonymity, Rosanna, Kitty and Leni, in a collaborative relationship over a number of one-on-one sessions (four to eight per participant). Participants were all previously known to me. We had all experienced challenging relational patterns with our own mothers; we were all curious, and deeply concerned about our relationships with our children.

Data was generated based on re-construction of participants' memories of maternal holding and was explored in a collaborative, responsive, open and artistic way. We worked together in cycles of amplification and reduction of material to develop understanding about what maternal holding meant for each of us. I then collected this to look for meaning in common across participants, re-engaging with participants at certain points, but also bringing the data into dialogue with other voices from literature and the arts. All of these approaches articulated by Lett (2011) constitute my particular use of the 'MIECAT Form of Inquiry' (detailed in Chapter 1). Importantly, this form of inquiry is adapted to both research and therapeutic work.

I recognise that all explorations in this inquiry were undertaken within relationships with others, with materials, with spaces and times. As I sat in my living room trying to consolidate and clarify meaning of particular holding experiences, I remained in relationship. Sometimes I recalled the familiar weight of my son's body, at other times, memories of participants' words and gestures arose, I re-engaged with personal therapeutic relationships, healing understanding that arose in sessions, philosophical voices popped into mind, and imagery flittered across my consciousness.

I have taken inspiration in my approach from Kenneth J. Gergen (2009) who writes:

> By using multiple 'voices' in the text, my hope is that the reader will come to appreciate the many relations from which 'I as author' have sprung. Moreover, in using these various voices, my hope is to open a relationship with a broader range of readers.
>
> (p. xxv)

Exploring the 'very old image' of mother and child through a maternal lens and via the simple, frequently engaged act of holding, provoked a surprising and intriguing re-conceptualisation of the mother/child relationship with meaningful implications for therapeutic work with mothers and children.

The words and pictures contained in this book describe the processes participants and I went through as we co-explored and co-developed what we thought we knew about holding and how this knowing changed over time. Woven throughout the book are personal and participant's stories of holding that ask the reader a central question: how might we explore and attend to holding for the benefit of the mother/child relationship? The answers have taken me back to those first moments of holding my son when I realised that what happened to me and what happened to him when we were together happened to *us*. Our shared experiences would always be a part of us, and I came to understand that what happened to us could be affirmed, challenged and changed not by myself or my son alone, but by us.

In a mother's relationship with her child, physical, emotional and psychological holding matters because it provides a moment, however brief, where the deeply interconnected qualities of real relationship move into awareness; enabling both mother and child to strengthen, question, develop and enrich their relationship, or what I refer to as the mother/child *us*.

In Chapter 1, I describe and explore the values that guide the inquiry and how these values were enacted. I convey how exploration of an intimate yet everyday relational experience like holding can benefit from an adaptable, multimodal and relationship focused approach both in research and therapy.

In Chapters 2, 3 and 4 I describe each journey participants and I shared as we inquired into and made meaning of holding experiences. These sessions were exploratory in nature but inevitably included therapeutic insights and meaning making.

In Chapter 5 I briefly describe the three key findings of this inquiry.

In Chapters 6, 7 and 8, I develop each of these findings in dialogue with academic and artistic voices and imagery and make suggestions about ways of working therapeutically with clients to benefit and develop healthy mother/child holding relationships.

While I have written about and direct my writing to women's experiences, I recognise that experiences of maternal holding and mothering are not limited to those born with female bodies and the term 'mother' also includes those who identify as female in a caregiver role with children.

# References

Ainsworth, M. D. S., Blehar, M. C., Water, E., & Wall, S. N. (2005). *Patterns of Attachment: A Psychological Study of the Strange Situation*. New York, NY: Routledge.

Bowlby, J. (1958). The nature of the child's tie to his mother. *International Journal of Psychoanalysis*, 39, 350–371. Retrieved from www.psychology.sunysb.edu/attachm ent/online/nature%20of%20childs%20tie%20bowlby.pdf.

Feldman, R. (2011). Maternal touch and the developing infant. In M. J. Hertenstein & S. J. Weiss (Eds.), *The Handbook of Touch: Neuroscience, Behavioral and Health Perspectives*. New York, NY: Springer Publishing Company.

Gergen, K. J. (2009). *Relational Being: Beyond Self and Community*. Oxford, UK: Oxford University Press.

Lett, W. R.( 2011). *An Inquiry into Making Sense of Our Lives*. Eltham, Victoria: Rebus Press.

Saxe, R. (2015, December). Why I captured this MRI of a mother and child. *The Smithsonian Magazine*. Retrieved from www.smithsonianmag.com/science-nature/ why–captured-MRI-mother-child-180957207/.

Vandermeer, J. (2014). *Authority: The South Reach Trilogy*. London: Harper Collins Publishers.

# 1 How we inquired into maternal holding

## An arts and values informed, collaborative approach

**Box 1.1 Journal Entries 2009, 2010, 2014**

My three-year-old son sits on me as I help him with his colouring book. He's breathing heavily; he has a mild cold. He crunches his apple loudly in my ear. I feel his tummy against my left hand, inhaling, exhaling, as he chats with me about why I chose the red pencil – 'because it's your favourite colour'. It's raining outside and the warmth of his tummy is comforting, I think about how familiar and safe this kind of holding is.

My four-year-old son asks me what I want to do today. I say: "first I want a cuddle". I hold him and he quickly makes himself comfortable so that the holding is for both of us. He wriggles to get into position and then goes quiet. His head is nestled under my chin and my hand holds his bottom as he curls into me. He feels heavy and perfectly shaped; I feel content.

My eight-year-old son leans into me at school to say goodbye for the day. We are in his classroom and he puts his arms around me and rests his head on my chest. The other kids are around, and he doesn't say anything. He's started doing this lately, just initiating a hug as he says goodbye, it's still a surprise to me, I expected him to be reserved – that is how I was as a child – but he has never been that way. His hair is warm beneath my hands as I caress his head. I let go when I feel him letting go.

Moustakas (1994) writes that in research: "the question grows out of an intense interest in a particular problem or topic. The researcher's excitement and curiosity inspire the search" (p. 104). As the above journal entries show, holding my son has been, and continues to be, significant and meaningful for me; on reflection these holding experiences ignited my curiosity and desire to know more.

While my journal entries reveal an 'intense interest' in the topic, they also illuminate some of the values that structure my experiencing with my son. These include: a hope that my son feels supported and important to me within our relationship; a deep satisfaction and sense of who he is as I hold him; an awareness of the many ways in which I experience holding him and our

DOI: 10.4324/9781003104094-2

relationship together; the ways my own expectations affect my experiencing; an appreciation of the moment and the ways in which our relationship constantly evolves.

This book is based on my doctoral research, and the approach and guiding values, described in this chapter, are highly relevant to therapeutic practice. The MIECAT Form of Inquiry I adapted for this research was created by the MIECAT Institute in Melbourne, Australia, an education facility providing graduate courses in arts therapeutic practice and research.

Dr Warren Lett, along with Dr Jan Allen, Dr Jean Rumbold and Andrew Morrish formed the MIECAT Institute in 1998. Their approach is a kind of "bricolage – a crafting of adaptable inquiry methods to co-construct a preferred spirit and sense of lived experiences" (Lett, 2011, p. 277) designed for both research and counselling.

The approach is based upon a collaborative model where researchers and participants (or co-inquirers) recognise the ways in which their relationships contribute to the research and work together to co-construct inquiry procedures, structure and meaning making. In a therapeutic context, the MIECAT approach reframes clients as co-companions. Though researchers and therapists have different ways of working and different intentions, the underlying values inherent in the MIECAT approach are the same. The approach in its research or therapeutic applications *privileges relationship* and attention to the *present moment.*

It has been widely found that the therapeutic alliance or relationship is often the most significant contributor to positive therapeutic outcomes (for example, Lambert & Barley, 2001; Lynch, 2012; Stamoulos, Trepanier, Bourkas, Bradley, Stelmaszczyk, Schwartzman, & Drapeau, 2016). This is in keeping with the MIECAT approach to inquiry and therapy.

Though the goals for this inquiry were exploration with the possibility of an enriched understanding of maternal holding, we did experience therapeutic outcomes. Participants and I did not intend to engage in therapy per se but the act of exploration toward understanding, on a deeply intimate and meaningful topic using the MIECAT approach, resulted in the generation of new information, new perspectives, acceptance and enactment of new understanding in our everyday relationships with our children.

Lett (2011) writes that the MIECAT Form of Inquiry is:

> A collage of coherent procedures, to be used creatively in the emergent search for the meanings of human experiencing and potential of these meanings to be used reflectively in preferred ways of being. It is adapted into practice, both as research and therapeutic companioning.
>
> (p. xii–xiii)

The experience and orientation of the researcher/inquirer in the MIECAT approach frequently allies with the that of the therapist, both oriented toward beneficial meaning making by working in ways that value relationship, emergence and adaptivity. The term 'companioning' is used to capture a way of being with clients or participants that "no matter what the context, there are motivations, hopefully supported by will, to make meaning of things that matter to the inquirers" (Lett, 2011, p. 277) be they researcher, therapist, co-inquirers or clients.

I examined various research approaches and methodologies in order to consider the ways in which I might utilise and adapt the MIECAT Form of Inquiry to explore maternal holding. I recognized that my search for consonant approaches referred back again and again to my own experiences and values. In the same way that a counsellor's values inform their choice of therapeutic approach alongside a sense of their client's needs, I elected to privilege values, so that my fundamental orientation to the inquiry and procedures would revolve and evolve around my selected values. Similarly, when choosing particular therapeutic approaches, a counsellor's values come into play as well as their assessment of client needs.

Traditional positivist research approaches denied the presence and influence of values (Lincoln, Lynham, & Guba, 2011, p. 101). Inquirers were able to and indeed aimed to find objective and generalizable truths and discover value-free facts about phenomena. In the early 20th century researchers acknowledged the inevitable presence of values, particularly in the social sciences, but maintained a desire for value neutral findings. Christians (2011) described how sociologist Max Weber recognized the inevitability of values in the "discovery phase" (p. 63) at the beginning of an inquiry but that once findings were ready to be presented researchers "should hang up their values along with their coats as they enter their lectures halls" (p. 63). This presupposes that we can strip our inquiry process and findings of values and that it is indeed important to do so.

New inquiry paradigms have emerged acknowledging to varying degrees the presence and influence of values in research and practice including Critical Theory, Constructivism and Participatory Approaches (Lincoln, Lynham and Guba, 2011). In recent years this awareness of the influence of values has developed to include, as Barad (2007) writes, the "inescapable entanglement of matters of being, knowing and doing, of ontology, epistemology and ethics, of fact and value" (p. 3).

As Lett (2011) notes there is an "integrative flow" of values, ways of being and ways of knowing (p. 278). Our lived experience reflects an ongoing interaction between what we believe can be known, how we come to know it, the tools we use to come to know, the values that inform these and ultimately, what we do with what we know. As such, "the role of axiology (values) in human inquiry is … seen to be inherent, essential and unavoidable" (Lett, 2011, p. 267).

All inquiry and therapeutic approaches are supported by underlying values whether these are implicitly or explicitly stated. As Barad (2009) writes "values are integral to the nature of knowing and being" (p. 37). Acknowledging and privileging my values in this inquiry has implications for my process, my relationships, my understanding and presentation of findings.

My guiding values are:

- Intersubjective being – privileging relationships
- Multimodality – accessing and working with different forms of knowing
- Attentiveness to the present moment.

One overriding value, discussed in more detail in the *Valuing Multimodality* section later in this chapter, concerns the use and benefits of arts-based approaches to experiencing and knowing. This book is focused on maternal holding, and so I do not linger on arts-based therapy or research theory, many others have written more knowledgably on this topic (see Allen, 1995; Barone & Eisner, 2012; Cole & Knowles, 2008; Leavy, 2015; Lett, 2011; Malchiodi, 2012; McNiff, 1998) However, I hope that through showing how participants and I inquired into maternal holding with the arts as a form of research, therapy, meaning making and presentation, that I meet and generate curiosity on behalf of the reader.

Before exploring my three guiding values, and how they were enacted, I'll provide a brief biography of each participant and an overview of how a typical session with participants proceeded including descriptions of MIECAT terms used. With a feeling for the ways we worked together, and how sessions progressed, I hope to provide a context for the practical applications of my guiding values.

As Finlay (2011) writes: "if you are evaluating a piece of research, it helps to do so within the frame of its own terms and values" (p. 261). By clearly describing the values around which my inquiry and practice constellate, I hope that you will feel invited into a shared space of curiosity and enriched understanding about mothers' experiences of holding their children and that you may then consider employing some of these value orientations and their practical enactments into your therapeutic practice.

## Inquiry participants

Rosanna:

> A mother of four adult daughters Elaina, twins Olivia and Lillian, and Deanna. Rosanna's children had left home by the time we started our sessions. Deanna had already had a child, the participant's first grandchild. As our work together progressed, Olivia as well as Elaina gave birth to their own children.
>
> Rosanna is a practising therapist and has also experienced therapy as a client. Deeply curious and compassionate about human experiencing, Rosanna works to help others discover and develop their strengths.

Leni:

> A mother of two children, Lucy (9) and Alexander (6) at the time of our sessions. In her early 40s, Leni had been a family day-carer for pre-school

children and infants and was moving into an administrative role. She separated from her husband when the children were 6½ and 4 years of age. She has remarried since the completion of our sessions.

Emigrating from the UK and marrying an Australian, Leni had no family living nearby when she had her children and had limited social supports. She experienced post-natal depression and was hospitalized with her son in a Mother-Baby Unit when he was three months old. This is where I met her. She participated in an outpatient program after leaving the unit that included an art therapy component.

Leni was wary of painful emotions but committed to exploring her experiences of holding her children. We had known each other for around six years at the beginning of the inquiry.

Kitty:

In her early 40s, Kitty has one daughter Harley, five years of age when we begin our sessions. Kitty was, at the time, a stay-at-home mother though she is now in the education sector.

Kitty studied psychology at university and worked in the federal public service for 18 years rising to executive level before she gave birth to her daughter. She had participated in volunteer work from the age of 15 to the present with a focus on social and environmental issues.

During the time of this inquiry, Kitty went through unsuccessful trials of IVF and an attempt to conceive with a donor egg, experiencing a deep sense of loss with each; her daughter was experiencing post-traumatic stress disorder and anxiety and Kitty also experienced the loss of her grand-mother, her only familial support.

We met at university 24 years ago.

## General session structure

The participants and I engaged in between four to eight sessions each of vary-ing lengths. Rosanna (eight sessions) and Kitty (seven sessions) participated in sessions of around two hours each while Leni's four sessions were of a longer duration (up to three hours or more). All sessions were audio recorded for later transcription and photographs were taken of all art making.

While my description of the progression through sessions may at times appear linear, the processes we employed were held loosely and were respon-sive to what felt mutually important in the moment of our exploration. Each step involved engaging with previous steps and anticipating/contributing to future steps. Each process was shaped and re-shaped in response to what developed in the shared space of the inquiry over time.

We would begin with a 'warm-in'. Warm-ins were exercises oriented toward experiences of maternal holding but with a non-conceptual focus. I would deliberately draw our attention to and engage with our physical and emotional experiencing. For example, in each participant's first session we closed our eyes and moved with warmed heat-packs in order to facilitate reconnection with experiences of what it felt like to our children when they were infants.

It helped to have an object, image, a memory, feeling or sensation to serve as an access point into a selected experience.

> **Access** point: This describes a choice made about what to bring into focus in that moment. It may be the selection of a key quality (visual or verbal), an object brought along to inquiry, a memory, an emotion, image or sensation arising in session.

For some sessions, materials (like soft toys or photos) were pre-selected by participants, brought to the sessions and served as access points. At times, the warm-in provided an access point to the experience participants wished to explore. Sometimes a new experience would be chosen for inquiry from the access point that emerged as important for participants.

I would then invite participants to re-engage with and explore their selected experience in session. When re-engaging with an experience I would suggest participants close their eyes and allow themselves to immerse in their memories, paying attention to images, emotions, sensations, movement, temperature, textures as they arose. The focus was on their embodied experience over the conceptual experience at this stage.

Explicitly telling me about their chosen experience was not requested but all participants chose to do so either before making a representation, during or afterward. We would then return to the *embodied* experience of their recollections again and again to stay with what was not yet fully conceptually known.

I provided art materials for participants including drawing and painting materials, objects for installations, plasticine and materials for sculptures and images in postcards/magazines etc for collage. Movement or 'body statues' were also offered as a means of representation (I had a video camera available if participants wished to record movements, but we did not end up using this). All sessions were undertaken in spaces that were large enough for us to spread out and move about, these spaces were quiet, warm and private.

After an initial re-engagement with an experience, participants were asked to make a representation.

> **Representation**: A MIECAT representation is a multimodal creative expression. It may be, for example, a drawn artwork, an installation, a gesture or movement, a song or poem or sculpture. A representation is only limited by materials at hand and imagination.

When participants felt that they had taken their representation as far as they wished to, that the expression held something of significance for them, we began our exploration of it together. Importantly, the process of making the representations, the sharing of experiences, and the ways in which we worked with those experiences and the representations together were all considered informative source material.

We explored our material in multiple ways:

- Via the use of *phenomenological description*: Focusing on what we saw in the representation while attempting to at first note, then put aside, assumptions and conceptual knowing. This encouraged looking at our representations 'as if for the first time'. Phenomenological description and bracketing are important terms that required examination in light of my value of intersubjectivity, they are discussed in more detail in the *Valuing Intersubjectivity* section.
- Approaching the representation from multiple visual frames of reference.
- Employing imaginative variation. Asking questions like 'what would it feel like if X were removed/changed or if this image/shape had been a different colour, big, smaller etc?'
- Exploring the what, how, when, where and who of the representation and their relationship with the experience explored;
- Engaging in a dialogue with the representation and parts of the representation: asking questions, clarifying, summarizing, embodying, amplifying and reducing to significant qualities or key elements (described below).
- Bringing in my resonances to participant's work as well as our encounter as we co-explored their experiences. These were termed ISRs (intersubjective responses, described in the *Valuing Intersubjectivity* section). These might include what I was curious about, an image or feeling that arose for me, a representation in words, embodiment or art materials made for the participant;
- Imagining and role-playing what, if anything, the participant would tell their child about the representation and its making;
- Exploring participant's experience of the process of making the representation and our relationship as we worked together;
- Exploring what participants felt they might now know that they did not know before.

Participants and I acknowledged that working with friends had potential disadvantages. As our relationships were already established and would continue on after the inquiry was complete, there was the possibility of concerns around what they might wish to share within our friendship and what they might wish to keep private. As Kitty commented at the end of our session work: "At first, I didn't know how we'd go, because of having a long relationship and sometimes that's hard to be honest but it's been very easy, you've done very well". A number of decisions helped navigate these concerns: we openly focused on *content in process* during sessions, attending to and navigating tensions and curiosities in our relationship as they arose. This content in process also served as informative material for the inquiry.

> **Content in process**: Paying attention to and choosing to work with the process of *how* content emerges in relational engagements as it arises.

Having explored our representations and work to our mutual satisfaction, we would then find ways to reduce that information so that we might come to an *approximation to meaning*.

> **Approximation to meaning**: Recognising the evolving, relational and contextual nature of meaning, the term 'approximation' is employed in the MIECAT Form of Inquiry to reflect that meaning changes.

Reducing our material involved identifying *key elements*, bringing those elements together into *clusters* and then exploring those clusters to reduce them to simple sentences, paragraphs or imagery that described the essence of what they now understood about their experiencing (including a single word or titles, *themes* or *depictions*).

> **Key elements**: Key elements are words or images spoken about or represented during sessions. These words or images were identified by participants and/or myself as powerful, important, meaningful, or intense; they may have been accompanied by gestures or expressions; they might have been repeated; they might have raised questions; been emphasized or accompanied by a change in vocal tone or followed by a long pause. They are a reduction of inquiry information toward sense-making or meaning.
>
> **Clustering**: In a further act of reduction, clustering brings key elements together in meaningful ways. Key elements are clustered based upon a sense of connection between elements.
>
> **Themes or Thematic statements**: A 'theme' is a succinct statement that captures a representative pattern of being, about which something is becoming known. It conveys how an important pattern functions for participants.
>
> **Depiction**: Like a theme, a depiction aims to capture a participants' pattern of knowing/being in a succinct but story-like way. A depiction may be described as a creative snapshot of mutually valuable knowing co-created between participants and I. Depictions in this inquiry took the form of a paragraph length 'story'.

It was important to take the inevitably large amount of material and reduce these to simpler statements of understanding. These significant and meaningful qualities of experiencing could be further reduced but also developed by the making of a *creative synthesis* (an artistic representation showing our approximation to meaning). This is a recognition that there are things that art can say and evoke that straight forward language cannot. Understandings manifest in various different forms – as embodied sensations, as creative expressions, as conceptualisations and as patterns of being with others and our environment.

A form of reduction like a key word, cluster or title might also serve as an access point into a new exploration. In this way, the approach can work in cycles of exploration, amplification and reduction of data to meaning.

We engaged with these processes and terms in relationship with the three guiding values described in depth below.

## Valuing intersubjectivity: privileging relationships

> Intersubjectivity is at the heart of being human.
>
> Zlatev, Racine, Sinha, & Itkonen (2008, p. 2)

> We found existing human patterns of being – relationally and socially con-structed and available to reconstruction – through procedures of inquiry and dialogues of intersubjectivity, held in values of compassionate reciprocity and mutuality.
>
> Lett (2011, p. xiv)

There are times when I experience a profound sense of relationship, it might be with other people, animals or objects, spaces, music or weather. The sand beneath my feet feels a part of me, a shared moment of laughter with a friend feels more than just mine. Until I began engaging with arts-based inquiry and practice, despite a degree in philosophy and psychology, I did not have a word to describe these 'intersubjective' experiences.

In keeping with my arts-based approach, I represented what intersubjectivity felt like for me in a non-conceptual way as I began my research by taking a series of photographs of two flames closely intertwining and then examining these from an imaginative point of view.

Representing intersubjectivity was particularly important as applying language to this term is difficult, steeped as our society is in fundamental conceptualisations of self and other rather than an intersubjective self-in-relationship.

I could have chosen to conceptualise and value intersubjectivity as an epiphe-nomenon, an intriguing by-product emerging from the reality of our subject/object divide. Instead, I have taken this experience, so precious and curious to me, aflame with vitality, and elevated it to a guiding value for this inquiry. To experi-ence intersubjectively is to become aware of the many relationships at play in any one moment, it is a three-dimensional experience that does not lend itself easily to two-dimensional language.

One might ask why this would matter in a therapeutic space and I would respond by saying that the way we view ourselves in relationship with others, our environments and materials impacts how we interact, it shapes what we think is possible and valuable in our interactions and what our goals might be.

An approach to working with clients that values intersubjectivity will look different to an approach, for example, employing Cognitive Behavioural Therapy (or CBT, Beck, 1964). In CBT, notions of dysfunction and function, or illness and wellness, reside primarily within the individual and their personal attitude to an objective reality. If we can help the client reorient themselves to the world in an objectively 'healthy' or functional way, then we have achieved our goals. This would appear to be a very satisfactory outcome for any therapeutic approach.

However, by recognising the ways in which we are in constant interaction with the world, that is, by valuing an intersubjective reality, we are able to explore and potentially enhance our significant relationships with others, our environment and materials. We pay attention to the many ways in which we *co-construct* our reality in relationships rather than visualise a problem as residing solely within ourselves as a static 'irrational' attitude that requires fixing.

Similarly, approaches that separate mind and body suggest that our rational being can shape our experiencing. While our thoughts are powerful contributors to our behaviours and feelings, they are but one form of knowing (further explored in the second guiding value of *multimodality*). A respect for the ways in which we are always in relationship and how these relationships interact with our thoughts, our bodies and emotions provides more information about our presenting and underlying concerns.

It might be argued that valuing intersubjectivity reduces personal agency by displacing or dispersing responsibility onto something external from one's self. I suggest that valuing intersubjectivity extends our responsibility across relationships, it promotes *relational* agency.

Existential psychologist Jacobsen (2007) writes: "human beings are always in relationships...probably we are nothing other than the combined sum of our relationships" (p. 5) even though our felt sense of existence is often as a separate, bounded and private individual.

Gergen (2009), like Barad (2007) suggests a radical intersubjectivity, that all of us are "multi-beings" always in co-existence and co-action. He states:

> In whatever we think, remember, create, and feel – in all that is meaningful to us – we participate in relationship. The word 'I' does not index an origin of action, but a relational achievement.
>
> (p. 133)

He explains that: "within any relationship, we also *become somebody*" (p. 136) for example, 'with my mother, I come into being as a child'. This kind of multi-being, as Stepnisky (2014) describes may be considered "ecstatic" but also "terrifying" (p. 245).

Different qualities of intersubjectivity may be focused upon including 'embodied intersubjectivity' (Di Paolo and De Jaegher, 2015; Fusaroli, Demuru, & Borghi, 2009) or 'intercorporeality' (Fuchs, 2016; Merleau-Ponty, 1945; Dreyfus, 2002; Weiss, 1999) and 'interaffectivity' (Fuchs & Koch 2014, Fuchs, 2016). For example, Weiss (1999) writes that "to describe embodiment as intercorporeality is to emphasize that the experience of being embodied is never a private affair but is always already meditated by our continual interactions with other human and nonhuman bodies" (p. 5).

The relationship between maker and materials is also intersubjective. Byrne (2014) writes of the "mutuality that seems to exist within the relationship I have with art" (p. 220). This 'mutuality' between materials, maker and emerging art is described in Wang and Green's (2017) article, where Wang explains:

> I lock myself in my studio and focus on sewing on canvas – which is quite a frustrating process for me. The canvas is thick and tough. It reminds of the fabric of the chair which I was sitting on in that embarrassing staff meeting. Every stitch hurts my fingers. Every stitch makes an unpleasant sound.
>
> (p. 29)

As the article progresses, the materials selected and engagement with the making contribute significantly to what comes to be known about Wang and Green's experiences.

Franklin (2012) writes of the arts: "they do not describe experience, they directly manifest experience" (p. 90). In relationship with his art, Franklin found that "I kept moving my awareness in as we re-created each other" (p. 90) noting that there is a "self-referential mutuality between objects and artist" (p. 90). So, too, Quail and Peavy (1994) describe the relationship between client and materials/art during therapy sessions:

> The client's experience of increasing awareness and dynamic energy in the making phase in art therapy seems to demonstrate that there is a field, a space between the art object and client where meaning arises, a spatiality from within her to outside of her.
>
> (p. 56)

This speaks to Van Manen's (1990) lived space; a sense of the space we are in shifting as we engage with it. This engagement with space and objects may be unavailable to our conscious awareness and yet it still shapes the environment and relationships we are in. Holding a child in a warm, softly lit room is a very different experience to holding them on a cold, windy train station platform.

De Quincey (2000) provides different definitions of intersubjectivity in terms of their strength or weakness. He would label the kind of intersubjectivity I value in this inquiry as a "strong-experiential" (p. 138) where "my experience of myself shows up qualitatively differently when I engage with you as a reciprocating center of experience" (p. 238). Importantly, De Quincey notes that this stronger kind of intersubjectivity does not equate with agreement between those in relationships: "the vitality of this form of intersubjectivity is that it is often heightened by authentic disagreement and exploration of differences" (p. 239). Intersubjective experiences are not about *sameness* of experience, they are about mutual encounter.

One might argue we are subjective beings first, and occasionally engage in or become aware of intersubjective interactions. I agree with De Quincey's 'strong' intersubjectivity': "the being of any one subject is thoroughly dependent on the being of all other subjects, with which it is in relationship. Here, intersubjectivity precedes subjectivity" (De Quincey, 2000, p. 139). That is, I come to know my Self in relation *with* you, to others, to my environment and the objects within that environment.

This definition allows for the possibility that our felt sense and culturally and linguistically dominant conceptualisation of a self/other divide may be a matter of where we focus our attention. If we are intersubjective beings that does not preclude experiences of selfhood. A felt sense of separateness from other people, for example, does not necessitate a felt sense of separateness from the space we inhabit or the objects in that space. Experiencing separateness is also a relational product; what I felt connected to I now feel separate from. A relationship still exists but it may feel strained, diminished or unimportant, for example. This lived quality of separateness emerges from intersubjective being-in-the-world.

As De Quincey (2000) writes: "we tend not to notice the second-person perspective because it is right in front of our noses every day. It is the medium in which we most naturally live" (p. 147). We partake in a "fish-in-water' syndrome" (p. 147). We don't notice our intersubjectivity because it is always, already present. As Stern (2004, p. 78) notes, we co-exist within an "intersubjective tissue" (p. 78).

Dynamic Systems theory provides a perhaps more easily digestible description of fundamental interrelatedness. Originally devised to explain mathematical problems, this theory was later employed to describe infant development by psychologists Esther Thelen and Linda Smith. They published *A Dynamic System Approach to the Development of Cognition and Action* in 1996 and their theory has progressively influenced fields as diverse as philosophy, education, neuroscience, biology, counselling and artificial intelligence (Galloway, 2013).

Their approach moved away from traditional, linear and dichotomous nature or nurture explanations (and problems) of development to provide a theory that acknowledged multiple sources of mutual influence, complexity and fluidity. They explored how "structure and patterns arise from cooperation of many individual parts" (Thelen & Smith, 1996, p. xiiv). They also "categorically reject machine analogies of cognition and development" (p. xix) in recognition of the "enormous sensitivity and flexibility of behaviour to organise and regroup around task and context" (p. xix).

Thelen and Smith (1996) recognized emergent processes rather than concepts of pre-ordained design, multimodal sources of information, processing and expression and the co-operative relationships present amongst these sources. In doing so, their approach is consonant with my three guiding values. As Thelen & Smith (1996) wrote:

> All mental activity is emergent, situated, historical, and embodied, there is in principle no difference between the processes engendering walking, reaching, and looking for hidden objects and those resulting in mathematics and poetry.
>
> (p. xxiii)

Dynamic systems theory proposes a 'porous' individual, one that participates in an ongoing "give and take with (our) physical, emotional and cultural experiences" (Fausto-Sterling, n.d., para. 2). An interplay occurs between qualitatively felt 'internal' and 'external' worlds extended beyond the boundaries of skin.

This approach represents a "gestalt shift" (Clark, 1998, p. 16) conceptualising humans as incarnated, contextual, co-operative and extended in the world. From the theoretical position of embodied or extended mind, John Teske (2013) describes cognition, for example, as "scaffolded, embedded, and extended" (p. 768) with both the body and our environment.

Andy Clark (1998) writes that we might now explore the "use of external media as both additional memory and as potent symbol-manipulating arenas" (p. 19). He goes on to provide the example of 'John', an academic writing a paper (Clark, 1995). In summary, he shows that John may like to credit the finished paper to his 'brain' but the paper is really the product of "the brain and body operating within an environmental setting" (p. 19), John is an "agent-in-the-world" (p. 19). His thinking and understanding includes the aid of reference books, papers, pens and saved files on computers. He cycles through iterations of meaning-making that "reach out into the environment" in order to organise and re-organise information and understanding. John functions within various intersubjective relationships with non-human entities.

The entanglements between humans and technology are now a significant area of inquiry into what it is to be and know, along with our relationships with other humans, environments and entities. Heffernan (2016) notes that our relationship with the Internet "is entrenched. It's time to understand it … as the latest and most powerful extension and expression of the project of being human" (p. 21). Dynamic systems as well as extended mind approaches encourage us to pay attention to the many evolving relationships that we participate in and how we shape and are shaped by relationships in an ongoing flow of experiencing.

## Intersubjectivity in action

Valuing intersubjectivity requires a research approach that focuses on and transparently communicates significant relationships at play and their contributions to shaping the inquiry. Finlay (2011) notes that "rigorous and transparently" conveyed research is "what we look for when evaluating other people's work" (p. 261). Lincoln, Lynham and Guba (2011) write about "validity as authenticity" (p. 121) one criteria of which is "fairness … all stakeholder views, perspectives, values, claims, concerns and voices should be apparent in the text" (p. 122). I have attempted to clearly convey the varying relationships present in different stages of the inquiry. I have also provided 'stakeholder' quotes and representations throughout including my own, participant, literary and artistic voices. If I have shown to the best of my ability, where and to what degree participants and I have contributed to information generation and findings then readers have the opportunity to evaluate whether the analysis is "both plausible and justified" (Finlay, 2011, p. 265).

I have acknowledged my presence throughout the inquiry with participants and readers, including reflexively considering my own and others role at different points of the research; providing 'ISRs' for participants (see below), talking openly with participants about what relational dynamics appear salient in the moment of sessions (content in process) and providing examples of creative representations that contributed to choices I made particularly around the formation of findings and the engagement of findings with literature.

> **ISR or intersubjective response:** A MIECAT term. When I experienced a strong or compelling resonance with a participant's words or artwork, I offered them a personal response. This response could include, for example, words or physical gestures; visual art works or poetry. At times these ISRs were spontaneous, emerging in a shared moment between participants and myself; at other times I went away to consider my response and offered my ISR in a later session or via correspondence. ISRs provided participants and I with information about the qualities I felt were, for example, significant or intriguing as they emerged in our relationship. At times ISRs served to amplify a point of resonance and at other times they asked questions about resonant moments (including consonant or dissonant moments). These ISRs also enabled me to look back at my own process throughout the inquiry to reconstruct and re-examine my responses to relationships between myself, participants, materials and the inquiry, then and now.

Reis (2011) writes that a "reflexive methodology requires a constant dialogue with research 'participants' to continually reframe the researcher's own understandings of what is being studied" (p. 4). Valuing intersubjectivity in research and therapy requires an attention to and description of the many relationships that are involved in the inquiry or therapeutic process at different stages including relationships with our environment and the objects within it (for example, art materials and our representations).

Cole and Knowles (2008) note that:

> A researcher's presence is evident in a number of ways throughout an art-informed research 'text' (in whatever form it is presented, and by implication, throughout the entire researching process). The researcher is present through an explicit reflexive self-accounting; her presence is also implied and felt, and the research text (the representational form) clearly bears the signature or fingerprint of researcher-as-artist.
>
> (p. 66)

An approach that values intersubjectivity requires transparency and reflexivity on behalf of the researcher/therapist and participant/client, both on reflection and in the present moment (explored in *Valuing Attentiveness to the Present Moment*).

One of the first research decisions I made was to work with three participants who were also previously known to me, in this way our relationships were already salient for us. I elected to work with these mothers without their children present. I hoped that by working with friends, with rapport already established, we might feel safer to sit with the not quite known and/or uncomfortable material that might arise. This also contributed to my/our decision to work with a small number of participants over an extended period of time.

Working without children present meant we explored mother's re-constructed memories of maternal holding rather than exploring maternal holding as it occurred. This decision was made for practical reasons and so that participants felt free to express all that was occurring for them as they re-constructed holding their children. I wanted them to feel free to explore and express without concerns around what they wanted their children to hear or not hear. Given the sensitive subject matter of maternal holding, I offered participants, and they accepted, full confidentiality (each of them chose their own pseudonym). This too encouraged freedom in what was explored and expressed.

Together, participants and I co-created material and understanding during our sessions. Lincoln, Lynham and Guba (2011) propose that "the *way* in which we know is most assuredly tied up with both *what* we know and our *relationships with our research participants*" (p. 123) one aspect of which is "reciprocity, or the extent to which the research relationship becomes reciprocal rather than hierarchical" (p. 123).

Rowan (2006) also proposes the guiding value of researching "as if people were human" (p. 114). He states: "this means that as researchers we do not hide behind roles ... we do not exclude ourselves from the research process" (p. 114). Working with friends in an intensive manner across a number of sessions required sensitivity to our experiences of consonance and dissonance both in session and also in our friendship. Decisions were continually made about what to bracket in or out in service of the inquiry as well as our friendship.

A shared enthusiasm for learning more about maternal holding helped guide and support our relationship during the inquiry. By showing participants my own enthusiasm and curiosity, I hoped to contribute to the creation of a safe space and relationship conducive to co-exploration. Lett (2011) describes the relationship of co-inquirers (in research as well as counselling):

> It is assumed that a deep intersubjective connectedness will be created. This connection would have qualities of strong trust, resonance and respect of the importance of the content in the process of their relating.
>
> (p. 4)

When valuing intersubjectivity, the researcher's knowing and being is an important factor as at every stage of inquiry, the researcher is always present and in relationship. Again, this requires transparency and reflexivity on the part of the inquirer/therapist.

Sawyer (2007) refers to the "myth of the lone genius" (p. xv) and writes that "even insights that emerge when you're completely alone can be traced back to previous collaborations" (p. xii) echoing Gergen (2009) and Barad's (2009) radical intersubjectivity. What may appear to have emerged from a relationship between myself and the materials or findings, is more of a *focus* upon that relationship while gently holding the presence of other relevant relationships in mind (for example, my relationship with participants and my own relationship with my son).

Participants also brought into our inquiry their own significant relationships particularly with their children, but also with their partners, friends and their worlds. For example, I frequently invited participants to imagine/articulate how they might speak to their children about their representations, it was a great way of accessing different information and also noticing the textures of our different relationships. One of the sessions was explicitly structured in order to work with the concept of 'Relationship as Host' (Lett, 2011).

> **Relationship-as-host**: The notion of 'relationship-as-host' invites the conceptualisation and experience of relationship as a third entity in, for example, the mother/child dyad. This provides inquirers with the opportunity to dialogue with the relationship in order to explore how the intersubjective space may feel and what that intersubjective space may have to say about the bond between mother and child.

Valuing intersubjectivity was woven throughout the entire inquiry process. I continued to check in with participants once our sessions were complete and I entered into different relationships with the materials generated. We discussed the change in relationships with materials and findings as the inquiry progressed; dialogue between us remained open, I sent each mother their individual findings as I worked with them and they provided feedback on what I represented of their maternal holding, I then reworked those findings. It was important that their individual findings felt valid and authentic to them.

At the next stage of working with materials across participants to come to more general findings, I remained mindful of each mother's feedback as I developed my relationship with their data further.

It was important to acknowledge that participants' relationships with their children and myself evolved over time, and their experiential, creative, conceptual and practical forms of knowing changed in relationship with our inquiry. We agreed that the research work, and presentation, would stay with what was important to them at the time of the sessions. As the inquiry progressed, it would also increasingly reflect the ways in which my knowing as researcher changed within various relationships including my relationship with each mother but also with other written and artistic voices and imagery.

I invited participants to provide creative or written reflections on maternal holding after our sessions were complete. This gave us the opportunity to include their changing voices as well as my own as the inquiry evolved over time. Finlay (2011) proposes 'resonance' as an evaluative measure for research: it was important that participants were able to resonate with the inquiry findings at the time of their sessions, but it also felt important to me to give them the opportunity to share their knowing once the sessions were complete.

The entanglement of multiple relationships at play might have posed a difficulty in this inquiry if our aim was to delineate 'cause-and-effect' relationships and definitive knowing, however our search aimed for insights into maternal holding as it manifested for each mother and I, at a particular moment in time.

It is important to note that intersubjective relationships are often outside of our awareness and yet still active in the moment. For example, as I wrote up the *Dialogue with Literature* in Chapters 6, 7 and 8, I was holding within me my relationships with participants, processes, data, findings, art materials, shared spaces, my own maternal experiencing and other voices. These relationships arose in and out of awareness but always informed my writing.

> **Dialogue with literature**: This is a way of bringing findings to other voices in academia, literature and the arts in order to develop and understand those Findings further. By engaging with other voices with respect and curiosity, it is hoped that a co-creative dialogue might illuminate, support, question and/or hone the inquiry's Findings.

Valuing intersubjectivity encourages curiosity and the potential for excitement during inquiry as what is co-created cannot be predicted in advance. As Springgay (2005) writes: "encounters do not reveal; they create" (p. 44). This meant paying particular attention to content-in-process. For example, if either of us noticed something occurring between us, we made choices about whether to explicitly bring it into the shared space (say with words, facial expressions or movements) or to 'bracket it out' (explored below).

As with therapeutic relationships, paying attention to the textures of our encounter and how these unfolded during sessions provided more information about what we were exploring together. For example, I might notice a change in the relational atmosphere and ask questions about what had arisen for the participant in that moment, or what had arisen for me.

It was often challenging to slow down and notice the many different and changing relationships at play at any one point. Emotional 'colours', relational threads, different materials and our shared space as well as prior knowing and ways of being intermingled constantly. Paying attention to and valuing other forms of knowing (described in the following *Multimodality* section), was immensely helpful in the process of making decisions about which relationships to explicitly engage with and explore at different stages in the telling of this inquiry.

Valuing intersubjectivity had implications for how I defined findings. Individual participants findings comprised statements of significant knowing about maternal holding termed *themes*. These were given to participants and are available in Chapters 2, 3 and 4. However, I elected to work further with individual participant themes to see if there were any commonalities across mothers. I was intrigued by the possibilities of relationships between participants experiences of holding. Within the scope of this inquiry, it was not possible to explore every single participant theme in dialogue with relevant literature and arts (there were 29 themes generated overall). By looking at commonalities across participants, the development of findings became manageable but also gave me the chance to engage with other voices in depth. In so doing, it was my hope that these findings might be considered relevant and significant to a wider audience (Finlay, 2011; Barone & Eisner, 2012).

Moustakas (1990) writes that phenomenological research: "requires a passionate, disciplined commitment to remain with a question intensely and continuously" (p. 15). The process of this inquiry involved over five years of a focus on maternal holding – my knowing about holding my son changed over that time particularly as he grew into a young man. My relationships with participants, their relationships with their children, my relationships with my supervisors and many other academic, literary and visual voices changed over time as well. What I felt I knew about maternal holding was challenged, reinforced, changed and expanded over the years as I stayed with my curiosity about it. Questions abounded at each 'stage' of inquiry, answering one had a ripple effect on others, on what I knew then, on what I know now.

Sometimes, in research or therapy, remaining with a question is difficult. Questions can challenge us. Sometimes there were droughts in experiences of holding, at other times life events eclipsed little moments of intimacy. Still, participants and I acknowledged these strains on inquiry and relationships and stayed with the question. I hope that as readers my privileging of relationship makes sense and that the consequences, limitations and benefits of this value in inquiry and therapeutic practice are clearly communicated.

### *A note on phenomenological 'bracketing' and intersubjectivity*

Phenomenology as a philosophical and social science practice proposes that we inquire into experiences as part of a relationship *with* the phenomena. As soon as we are aware, we are aware of something and we bring to that something our awareness. In order to gain knowledge, I must attempt to become as conscious as I can of the various lenses through which I perceive and interact with the world. I do this by 'bracketing' out my preconceptions. The MIECAT Form of Inquiry includes this process in research and therapy.

Like positivist research approaches, early (Husserlian) phenomenology assumes a subject/object divide (Carman, 1999, p. 206) but draws our attention to how we view or interact with others through our own subjective filters. Transcendental phenomenology suggests the use or attitude of 'bracketing' in order to get to the essence or objective truth of the phenomenon (Moustakas, 1994). Moustakas writes: "the world in the bracket has been cleared of ordinary thought and is present before us as a phenomenon to be gazed upon, to be known naively and freshly through a 'purified' consciousness" (p. 85).

Bracketing asks us to put aside our prior knowing and values and attend to the 'thing itself'. In order to come to what appears essential and unchanging about a phenomenon, one must diligently note one's pre-conceptions and 'clean the lenses' through which we observe. Phenomenological bracketing however does acknowledge that:

> We can never exhaust completely our experience of things no matter how many times we reconsider them or view them. A new horizon arises each time that one recedes. It is a never-ending process ... the possibility for discovery is unlimited.
>
> (Moustakas, 1994, p. 95)

Valuing intersubjectivity may seem at odds with this traditional notion of bracketing because the process assumes a subject-object divide. If I suggest that our reality is always co-constructed with someone/something else, then any human ability to strip relationships of themselves in order to see the "essence of a phenomenon ... a universal" (Van Manen, 1990, p. 10) is not possible. The 'thing itself' is for us always in relationship with us, and thus we are a part of the phenomenon.

However, Heidegger (1988), a German philosopher who developed Husserl's ideas of phenomenology, considered our intersubjectivity to be innate and prior to consciousness or thought; we are beings-in-the-world or 'dasein' (Heidegger, 1988, p. 6). Before I am an experiencing thing that makes conscious sense of my experience, I am a thing that exists in a world and cannot exist without the world. This orientation recognizes and values intersubjective being. In Heidegger's 'dasein' the knower and known are constantly and irrevocably "co-constituting each other and unable to exist without the other" (Laverty, 2003, p. 27).

Being present to the moment by bracketing out what one thinks one already knows is valuable in inquiry and therapy. It draws attention to, and allows for exploration of, the values and assumptions each mother and I already brought to what we thought we know about maternal holding. As Démuth (2013) writes: "if we want to learn something about the reality we meet, we should know something about the way we capture it or how the meeting with reality is constructed" (p. 7).

In her book examining the lives and philosophies of famous existentialist and phenomenological thinkers, Bakewell (2016) provides a description of what the writer Flaubert is said to have written to fellow writer Maupassant:

> There is a part of everything that remains unexplored, for we have fallen into the habit of remembering, whenever we use our eyes, what people before us have thought of the thing we are looking at. Even the slightest thing contains a little that is unknown. We must find it. To describe a blazing fire or a tree in a plain, we must remain before that fire or that tree until they no longer resemble for us any other tree or any other fire.
>
> (p. 103)

This reflects a profound phenomenological bracketing. However, it also recognizes the possibility of continuing to stay in relationship with that tree or fire and notice, in the present moment, something different, unanticipated, something that might manifest experientially as we try again and again to put aside the lens of our preconceptions.

In exploratory phases we can attempt to bracket out what we, in relationship with maternal holding, already bring to it in order to be present to what *is* in the moment. This does not strip maternal holding of integral parts of its being (that is, the phenomenon for us as humans) but encourages us to look at maternal holding from multiple points of view.

Quoting Saint-Exupery, Merleau-Ponty (2014) writes: "man is a knot of relations, and relations alone count for man" (p. 483). Valuing intersubjectivity means that it may not be possible or even desirable to come to a fixed essence of an experience somehow stripped of its context and relationships, but we may formulate Lett's (2011) approximation to meaning, a sense of knowing that feels significant and important for now.

The MIECAT use of bracketing is not an attempt to divine a fixed, objective truth. It promotes an *attitude* of bracketing at various stages in the inquiry to allow for openness and/or amplification of what is not quite known but may be emerging into awareness. This encourages the possibility of changing what we think we already know. Lett (2011) writes that bracketing in research and therapy:

> Manages the companion's ability to stay with the tide of reciprocal experiencing so as to avoid interpretation, bringing favoured opinions or judgements into play, to allow the inquiry to proceed as it seeks construction of meaning within the experiential data.
>
> (p. 268)

Recognising a fundamentally intersubjective mode of being asks us to examine over and over again the various relationships entangled and active within an experience. By deliberately and temporarily putting aside what is already known, we give ourselves the chance to find out more about experiences, to be surprised, and perhaps to modify or question what we think we know.

### Reflections on intersubjectivity

I have written about valuing intersubjectivity from a conceptual point of view but my experience of it is multifaceted and deeply felt. Ultimately, the inquiry employed intersubjectivity in action, just as therapeutic work does. I hope that my words have done justice to the benefits of noticing and valuing this way of being and knowing.

Re-reading my journal I discovered this 2011 entry:

**Box 1.2 Ariel Moy, Journal Entry 2011**

My son has been outside in the garden with my husband. He walks inside and comes over to me as I sit on the couch. He tells me: "I have to be careful with this arm" in a voice that seems calm but purposeful. I ask him why. He then shows me his arm with a long red scratch on it. My facial expression (creased brow, downturned mouth), my posture (leaning forward near his arm), my tone of voice (concerned, worried) and words ("oh no, where did you get that from?") communicate that his injury is important and that I feel it might be painful. His entire demeanour changes. He casts his head down looking at the floor, his voice trembles as he replies: "I don't know" and then a few seconds later, "can I have a Bandaid?" Now there are tears in his eyes and he wants a cuddle.

## Valuing multimodality

> We are, each one, the carrier of enormous amounts of undigested, multimodal experiences stored in the trillions of circuits on our brains, in forms beyond verbal language, able to be accessed and connected into more conscious awareness.
>
> Lett (2011, p. 13)

Valuing multimodality means paying attention to and engaging with the many ways in which we know including knowing through art making and expression. How we know and come to know is fluid and responsive to the relationships we are engaged in and the ways in which we are engaged with them at the time. For this research, I relied on Heron and Reason's (1997, 2001, 2008) proposed four interdependent ways of knowing: experiential knowing, presentational knowing, propositional knowing and practical knowing each of which I will discuss in more detail shortly.

Valuing multimodality invites us to deliberately attend to, bring into awareness and work with the different modes of knowing available to us. Heron and Reason (1997) propose that the effort to develop *congruence* between different ways of knowing supports: "the primary purpose of human inquiry"; that is, "practical … action in the service of human flourishing" (p. 288). Bringing our four different ways of knowing into awareness and relationship with one another gives us richer information about what we feel we know, enables us to develop what we know and provides us with increased agency in our lives.

There is a congruence between valuing intersubjectivity and multi-modality. The way we know is not limited to internal conceptualisations but rather includes our relationships as well as our immediate experiencing, artistic or symbolic knowing, and our practical knowing by doing. Heron and Reason's (1997) Participatory Inquiry approach recognises our innate intersubjectivity. They note that the "mind and the given cosmos are engaged in a cocreative dance" (p. 279). Our participative awareness is played out "within an intersubjective field" (p. 280).

Astrophysicist Janna Levin (2016) writes that with Einstein's theory of spacetime we discovered another means of inquiring into space. We had looked up at the night sky but now we had the option of 'listening' to it (for the sound of gravitational waves). In part, listening to the universe was made possible with technology only developed in recent decades but what also made it possible was the generation of a new theory that expanded how we understood space and therefore how we might come to know it. Similarly, if we expand our definition of knowing, if we choose to value experiential, artistic, practical as well as conceptual knowing, then we have a much larger scope for approaching inquiry in research and therapy. As embodied beings, intersubjectively embedded in the world, with the capacity for emotion, thought, imagination, creative expression and action our knowing can be carried by all of these modes.

Below I describe some of the relationships between Heron and Reason's (1997) multiple ways of knowing, MIECAT's 'multimodality' and voices from the arts-based and extended mind research communities as they manifest in this inquiry including the benefits of working multimodally.

### Experiential knowing

Our first mode of knowing is through embodied being, through "direct encounter" (Heron and Reason, 1997, p. 280) with the world as we resonate with and shape the world through our relationships with it. This is a form of co-creative knowing within the multitude of relationships possible for us. It includes sensation and emotion; it is embodied; it is pre-reflective, tacit, it is not *about* an encounter, it is *being in and with* an encounter as it happens. Experiential knowing plays a foundational role within this inquiry and Heron and Reason's other three forms of knowing. Maternal holding begins as a profoundly physical act so asking our bodies what they might know about holding might provide us with direct and rich information otherwise glossed over if we focus on conceptual knowing.

Experiential knowing is "feeling and imaging the presence of some energy, entity, person, place, process or thing" (Heron and Reason, 1997, p. 280). It is "profoundly real – solid, sound and vibrant at the moment of experience". Importantly "to experience anything is to participate in it, and to participate is both to mould and to encounter" (Heron and Reason, 2008, Experiential knowing, para. 4). Experiential knowing involves the knower and the values they bring to what is known, it is what we understand in the moment of experience, pre-thought.

As Damasio (2000) writes: "all emotions use the body as their theatre" (p. 51). Rothschild (2000) describes the relationship between embodied knowing and conceptual knowing and the benefits of attending to physical sensations: "awareness of body sensations can be a superhighway to the past, a tool for helping the client connect not only with forgotten traumatic memories but also with forgotten resources" (p. 118). When, for example, a client finds their throat closing up as they explore a memory, that bodily reaction will tell client and therapist something about that prior experience.

Western culture has tended to value conceptual knowing over and above experiential knowing (Heron & Reason, 1997; Seeley & Reason, 2008) but voices championing experiential knowing have increased over the last hundred years. Many theorists and researchers across a broad range of academic fields including cognitive science, linguistics, philosophy, artificial intelligence, psychiatry and phenomenology (Adams, 2010; Clark & Chalmers, 1998; Di Paolo, 2018; Froese & Fuchs, 2012; Shapiro, 2011) refer to what might broadly be described as an embodied, embedded, extended and/or enactive theory of knowing (usually referred to as 'mind'). These orientations hold the common idea that our ability to articulate or know reality is intimately and dynamically shaped by our body (including but not limited to the brain) *with* our environment (Wilson, 2002, p. 625). As Clark (1998) writes:

> If brains are best understood as controllers of environmentally situated activity, then might it not be fruitful to locate the neural contribution as just one (important) element in a complex causal web spanning brains, bodies and world?
>
> (p. 16)

Modern ideas of embodied mind acknowledge and explore the ways in which "the ideational and the material are intimately linked" (Reynolds, 2017), the ways in which knowing arises from more than just the brain, and the ways in which we know intersubjectively.

Merleau-Ponty (1945) spoke of knowledge as derived from the body's experience of the world. To know something is to "return to this world prior to knowledge, this world of which knowledge always speaks, and this world with regard to which scientific determination is abstract, signative, and dependent" (p. xxii). He places the highest value on what our body communicates to us, what we know, as we experience.

The MIECAT approach to education, inquiry and therapy values experiential knowing by drawing attention to and staying with what the body tells us in sensation, emotion and relationship at any one moment. We develop openness and familiarity with our embodied, non-verbal vocabulary, noticing what our direct non-conceptual experiencing and encounters have to tell us.

### Presentational knowing – artistic and creative shaping of experience

Building upon experiential knowing, Heron and Reason's (1997) presentational knowing represents knowing that is *about* our felt sense of being in the world. This knowing about is an expressive, symbolic and imaginal knowing without reference yet to categorization, rational judgment and intellectual fixedness. They describe it as an "intuitive grasp of the significance of our resonance with and imaging of our world, as this grasp is symbolized in graphic, plastic, musical, vocal, and verbal art forms" (p. 281). This knowing gives us insight into what an experience means for us pre-conceptually but in a way that builds upon and shapes direct experiencing, as well as providing direct experiencing in the process of making the art.

Seeley and Reason (2008) describe four component themes to presentational knowing: 'Sensuous encountering', 'Suspending', 'Bodying-forth' and 'Being informed' (p. 7). The first and last describe the transition into and out of presentational knowing. The second theme of 'suspending' describes a 'staying with' and an openness to the "complexity and unknowing" (p. 11) that arise when the intellect is temporarily put aside. It is the "foundational element of presentational knowing" (p. 12). It involves a "whole body response[s] to experience" (p. 12). This is followed by the 'bodying forth' theme. In this stage of presentational knowing an artistic shaping or forming of knowing occurs that can "round my experience off" (p. 14).

Seeley and Reason (2008) affirm an open, intuitive, whole bodied and allowing encounter followed by a shaping and expression of that encounter into a form that holds it *symbolically*. The "sensuous encountering" (p. 12) and forming of presentational knowing provides a rich grounding for conceptual (propositional) knowing. Attending to this kind of knowing also helps mediate a tendency to skip or leave 'undigested' experiential knowing:

> Poised at the edge of the realm of experiential knowing where our senses and imagination meet, we run the risk of the intellect prematurely rushing in with a show of certainty, planning, and a quick answer to dispel the anxiety of dwelling in complexity and unknowing.
>
> (p. 11)

Further, Lett (1993) writes that: "so much experience is not encoded verbally, and the explication of stored meanings is usually more complex than verbal skills alone can convey" (p. 16). The MIECAT approach allows space for the qualities of our experience to emerge into consciousness before they are fixed or confirmed via conceptualisation. Words can be brought to both presentational and conceptual knowing but our relationships with those words are different. Working with presentational knowing is an attempt to symbolise and express with an attitude of wonder, the other attempts to contain and understand with an attitude of clarity.

McNiff (1998) defines art-based research as the "use of the arts as objects of inquiry as well as modes of investigation" (Preface, para. 20). We come to know something as we make art and we also come to know something when we engage with the art made in an artistic way. Levine (2009) writes: "images possess energy, and they demand that we respond to them with the energy of our own imagination. If we try to think the image, we must find an imaginative, energetic way of thinking" (p. 2). We can jump straight into conceptualisation about our art once it's made but staying with it in a non-conceptual way gives us the chance to find out more about both the experience represented and our experience of making and encountering the representation.

Philosopher Alva Noë (2015) suggests that art and philosophy are practices that afford us a glimpse into how we reorganise our being and knowing. Art includes a "looping structure" (p. 32): it "is a practice for bringing our organisation into view; (and) in doing this art reorganises us" (p. 29). Seeley and Reason (2008) concur: "presentational knowing is an experience in itself, informing experiential knowing as well as being informed by it" (p. 19). This recognizes the fundamentally intersubjective relationships between art, artist and audience, how art both represents and in the process of representing provides us with an experiential knowing as well. Capacchione (2001) describes her experience of art-making: "while creating these drawings it felt as if my hand had taken over and was doing all the work. My conscious mind had stepped aside; it was like dreaming on paper" (p. 32). That dreaming also tells us something about what we're representing. In research or therapeutic practice, paying attention to presentational knowing as we make something and then as we engage with it gives us more information about what we are inquiring into.

Working with presentational knowing allows for ambiguous, dissonant, confusing and pre-reflective knowing to emerge into awareness. Levine (2009) writes that arts-based "research takes place in the liminal space of the imagination in which contradictions can co-exist" (p. 9). It offers us the chance to be with and shape our knowing before it is "swallowed up by abstracted propositions and theories about it" (Seeley & Reason, 2008, p. 3). In therapeutic practice it is so important to be able to 'sit with' what arises and allow for some expression of that experiencing; to be able to cope with not yet quite knowing how we feel or think or want to be; to allow that non-conceptual knowing to breathe and develop. To let that drawing or movement or installation to speak for itself first before we begin speaking for it.

Art making is not just an expression of an experiential knowing but a *development* of and *response* to that knowing. Van Manen (1990) writes that art is not "just representational or imitational of some event in the world. Rather, it transcends the experiential world in an act of reflective existence… the artist recreates experiences by transcending them" (p. 97).

Presentational knowing captures experiencing in a way that conceptual knowing does not. This is eloquently described in both written and visual mediums by Sousanis (2015) when he writes/draws:

> The verbal marches along linearly, step by step, a discrete sequence of words, 'strung one after another, like beads on a rosary'. The visual on the other hand … presents itself all-at-once, simultaneous, all over, relational.
>
> (p. 58)

Making and working with art are intersubjective encounters – with materials, with space, with others. Barad (2003) writes that we should "allow matter its due as an active participant in the world's becoming … it is vitally important that we understand how matter, matters" (p. 803). Working with art tools and materials shapes experiential knowing into presentational knowing and in engaging with the made artwork in whatever form it takes we are provided with further information about our experiencing. Sousanis (2015) points to the benefits of working with presentational knowing when he wonders: "what can be made visible when we work in a form that is not only *about* but is also the thing itself" (p. 59).

When we shift between different art modalities, we also invite the possibility of a shift in what we may come to know. Engaging with dancing and making music, sculpting or drawing invite different embodied, emotional and imaginal qualities. What movement might present to us about what we know may be quite different to what sculpting may bring to us. When the written word is used in service of presentational knowing it shapes knowing differently than drawing or painting. No one modality is more or less than the other, they are different but equally valuable "texts of experiencing" (Lett, 2011, p. 12) and expression.

If we shape experiential knowing via presentational knowing and if conceptual knowing is grounded in and "carried by presentational forms – the sound or visual shapes of the spoken or written word" (Heron & Reason, 1997, p. 281) then encouraging this kind of knowing is incredibly valuable if we wish to mine our experiences to come to meaning conceptually and practically (Barone & Eisner, 2012; Finley, 2008; Franklin, 2012; Leavy, 2015; McNiff, 1998; Rolling, 2013; Sullivan, 2005). Levine (2009) notes: "Art is a way of knowing…knowing by making…to base our research in the arts means to engage the imagination" (p. 5).

Bringing expressive arts into research and therapeutic spaces allows us to access and develop knowing in a way that accepts contradiction and ambiguity, that allows not quite knowing to evolve, and forming to take place. In doing so, it allows for surprise. When we ask ourselves to inquire into something like holding but attempt to put aside what we already know, by engaging our bodies and materials and allowing our busy thinking selves to step back, however briefly, we encounter our imaginal selves, we shape experiencing in unexpected but informative ways. We have the chance to discover something new.

Similarly, when experiencing is expressed artistically, we create an 'object' that can be shared and examined outside of oneself and by another. These 'objects' can powerfully evoke feeling and imagination, they offer a direct experience to us inviting engagement without telling us what to feel or think. They give us space to respond, to notice, to linger and to question, so important in therapeutic work. And they allow for the 'object' of the art to be externalised so that therapist and client can explicitly, together, explore what it has to share.

## Propositional knowing – conceptualisation

All forms of knowing are means of "articulating reality" (Heron & Reason, 1997, p. 281). Propositional, or as I term it, conceptual knowing, articulates reality with the use of language in service of concepts, to "know in conceptual terms" (p. 281). It is the most typically represented form of knowing in research and many therapeutic approaches as it has often been considered "an end in itself" (p. 287). However, grounding conceptual knowing in experiential and presentational knowing enables us to access and understand our experience in a fuller way; in ways that are "both more liberating and more fundamentally informative" (Heron & Reason, 2008, Propositional Knowing, Para. 2).

Conceptual knowing brings information we have gleaned from other modes of knowing into a more typically shared language of understanding. There are rules to language that enable us to communicate with one another efficiently and quickly but never completely. As John Berger (2016) wrote: "a spoken language is a body, a living creature, whose physiognomy is verbal and whose visceral functions are linguistic. And this creature's home is the inarticulate as well as the articulate" (p. 5). Even a shared language cannot universally fix understanding.

I took the photo in Figure 1.1 to represent how I understood conceptual knowing. My hand touching the frame felt like an iteration of my son's hand

*Figure 1.1* Ariel Moy, *Invitation*, digital photograph.

touching the door. There was the experience of holding my son, the representation taken in a photograph and then there was myself reflecting on it, considering it, putting the experience into words, 'putting my finger on' what it all meant. When I took these multiple modes of knowing into how I next held my son, I was in engaged in Heron and Reason's last form of knowing described below.

### Practical knowing – knowing how to be in the world

Heron and Reason (1997) write that "practical knowing is knowing how to do something" (p. 281). This is a knowing how to be in the world given awareness of, grounding in and congruence between the three other forms of knowing. It results in a highly 'skilled' and informed being-in-the-world or knowing "how to choose and act" (p.287).

Practical knowing explicitly takes place within the world of other human beings. It sits at the apex of Heron and Reason's forms of knowing precisely because it describes how we might be with others in a way that leads to human flourishing, considered an end in itself. Practical knowing serves: "to enhance personal and social fulfillment and that of the eco-networks of which we are a part" (p. 287).

This kind of knowing is knowing-in-action, it is purposeful, it manifests in the ways we behave, respond, interact, and create with the world. It is "knowing in its fullness (that is) consummated in and through agency" (Heron & Reason, 2008, Practical knowing, Para. 2). As Lett (2011) writes "when understanding occurs and is accepted, it needs to become meaningful in the life of the persons … in the practice of living" (p. 24). If a therapeutic goal is for increased client agency, for an enhanced ability to satisfactorily engage with others and their world, then practical knowing represents the desired outcome of the work that goes on in session.

## Multimodality in action

Valuing multimodal ways of knowing means paying attention to and actively engaging experiential, presentational, conceptual and practical knowing at each stage of research and therapeutic work. Before moving into various stages of inquiry, I clearly and repeatedly reminded participants and myself about the many modes in which we know. This shaped how we worked together, what we imagined was possible, the kinds of knowing that emerged as valuable at different points, the ways in which we took this knowing into our mother/ child relationships and the way in which I developed and presented findings.

I began each session by engaging with experiential knowing. I crafted specific activities to bring us into sensations and emotions particular to maternal holding (like warmth, weight and movement). These activities were co-developed across sessions with participants so that they fit with what was happening for us at that moment in time. This 'lit up' our experiential knowing, inviting it into participants' chosen re-engagement with memories of maternal holding.

Moving into our exploration of maternal holding, I made sure we had enough space and a wide range of materials and tools to engage presentational knowing (as well as experiential knowing in the making of and working with representations). These ranged from pastels and paints to plasticine and collage, soft toys and blankets to found objects and music.

Once representations were made, we co-explored and worked with them multimodally engaging experiential and presentational knowing as well as conceptual knowing. For example, to inquire into the expression or artwork we spoke with and embodied different 'characters' within the representation. We imagined what it would be like to move within the representation, noting what spaces were open and what spaces were filled. We explored where we felt aspects of the representation within our bodies and what emotions these sensations might carry. We described representations phenomenologically while attempting to bracket out our conceptual knowing. We approached the representations from multiple angles and distances. We imagined taking representations out to our children and talking with them about our art. At times we focused in on a particularly intriguing or powerful quality within the representation and amplified it by making another representation.

I also developed and gave form to resonances with participant's experiencing, representations and or our interactions in session by offering multimodal inter-subjective responses (ISRs) as previously described. Sometimes during a session, sometimes between or after sessions, these ISRs were not always explored explicitly between us, they were offerings of a non-conceptual knowing that could be received by participants in any way they felt comfortable with.

We loosely held an inquiry structure during sessions including re-engagement with/re-construction of past holding experiences followed by a representation of these and then an exploration of the representation. However, employing a multimodal approach to exploration of maternal holding, making and working with representations, allowed for spontaneity. We were able to go with what felt fitting or possible in the moment. By regularly checking in with participants (and myself) about the 'feel' of the techniques and tools we were able to continue working together in a way that was uniquely co-constructed between us while at the same time staying with the topic of the inquiry. This meant we regularly moved, as one does in life, between different forms of knowing; for example, being in the experiential now, touching on an emerging image or metaphor, formulating an idea and engaging with one another in cycles of being and knowing.

Once I began working with our data post-sessions, I noticed that if I was stuck on a cluster of materials and wanted to know something more about it, I might interrogate my conceptualisations, but I could also engage with them and the materials in different ways. I could 'talk' with this data, I could draw it, I could embody it or my confusion around it. Again, how I interacted with data was only limited by my imagination.

In this presentation of my research, honouring multimodality has been challenging. While limited to the written word and image, I have endeavoured to engage or draw attention to other modes of knowing. At times I have described participants and my own references to experiential knowing (sounds, tastes, textures, movements, scent, relationships), I have provided imagery of our presentational knowing and included, I hope, evocative descriptions of our process and findings, and I've made references to practical knowing (outcomes shared between participants/myself and our children). I recognise that conceptual knowing still takes centre stage, but I hope that the writing and imagery included in this book invite multiple forms of knowing and engagement for the reader.

Barone and Eisner (2012) suggest "evocation and illumination" (p. 153) are essential evaluative criteria for arts-based research. We come to know something when it evokes a response in us. Different writing styles and language are used for different audiences – each academic discipline has its own lexicon which consists of worded shortcuts to complex concepts, an understanding of which is earned through learning within that academic field. Each style reflects different intentions, but all serve to evoke a response in order for their audience to come to know something more about what the author wished to convey. By engaging with maternal holding in multiple ways, I hope that readers become curious about, discover new information, approaches or ideas, feel moved, and/or pay a new kind of attention to their clients' and their own holding experiences. Ultimately, I have attempted to "democratize" my way of communicating (Van Manen, 1990, p. 119) in order to provide the best possible chance of relevance and resonance for researchers, practitioners and mothers.

### Reflections on multimodal knowing

> **Box 1.3 Ariel Moy, *The Feeling of Holding*, Diary Entry 2016**
>
> I sit on the couch with my son resting on top of me. I have my arms around his body, and he lays his head back against my chest and neck. I can feel the length and angles of him as he adjusts himself to 'get comfy', I let out a soft protest "ugh" and we both laugh. I recall how light he used to be: it's harder to breathe with his ten-year-old weight and that makes me conscious of my chest rising and falling. I can smell the shampoo he used and feel the tickling softness of his onesie. I wonder what it would feel like to be held like this. I close my eyes and listen to him talk; I love listening to him, and as I focus solely on listening, I discover that I too, am held.

Park (2001) writes:

> There has been a long tradition in the West of dichotomizing intellect and emotion, and more generally, mind and body, associating knowing with the former...There is only one expression in Chinese, symbolized by one

character, which means both mind and feeling … in Chinese we know with
our head and heart simultaneously, with our mind and with our body.

(p. 88)

---

**Box 1.4 Ariel Moy, *Knowing and Words*, poem.**

I know with words,
But wait, that's not it.
I might show you instead,
Colours and shapes,
Or maybe it's the way,
They move that matters.
And then there's,
Sensations bubbling up,
Pressure, texture, temperature,
A kaleidoscope of difference,
World upon world opening,
But I could just tell you with words …

---

The goal of coming to multimodal knowing about maternal holding
experiences has an important caveat: what is known now, what is meaningful
now, is always open to change as knowing changes over time within relationships. This speaks to my final value explored in the next section.

## Valuing attentiveness to the present moment

> The only time of raw subjective reality, of phenomenal experiencing, is the
> present moment.
>
> Daniel Stern (2004, p. 3)

If you've ever seen a dog let off leash for a run at the beach, you've seen a
creature utterly in the present moment. It appears that the dog does not consider the person they've left behind, they're not planning their nap at the end
of the day; they're smelling the sea, pounding the sand and sighting new
friends. For me, a dog embodies the 'now'.

If, as Stern (2004) writes, the only time of subjective reality is 'now' then our
knowing about our past and our access to it is only available in the present
moment. The present shapes our knowing about our past and the past shapes our
knowing about the present. Without past knowing we would not be able to
engage in ongoing relationships for example, or speak or drive a car, everything
would always be brand new. The dynamic relationship between past and present is
lived by each of us every day. As Barad (2007) writes: "the past is never finished. It

cannot be wrapped up like a package, or a scrapbook … we never leave it and it never leaves us behind" (p. ix).

This inquiry explored maternal holding experiences by working with memory. Some holding experiences had occurred that morning, others had happened weeks, years and decades earlier. In each of our explorations, memories of holding were re-constructed and re-engaged with in the present moment. Valuing the present moment meant paying attention to and staying with what arose in the 'now' from within the many active relationships between the mothers, myself, materials, the space, the imagined presence of our children and our past.

Below I explore the entangled relationship between the past and present, the experiencing and remembering selves, the reconstruction of memories, the ways in which attending to the present moment enables access to experiential knowing, and the complementarity between valuing attentiveness to the present moment and valuing intersubjectivity. I suggest the only way one can 'return' to a past experience is in the present moment. Stern's 'raw subjective reality' speaks to Heron and Reason's (1997) experiential knowing – the ground upon which all other forms of knowing are built. Paying attention to memories and knowing as they are experienced in the moment provides us with important information about both the past and the present, information that is further elaborated in artistic, conceptual and practical knowing.

### The relationship between the experiencing and the remembering self

> No memory or mental image exactly replicates the constellation of nerve impulses associated with the initial sensation.
>
> Coyle and Fischbach (1997, p. x)

As Coyle and Fischbach (1997) note, what is experienced in the present moment when we recollect a memory is not the same as what we experienced at the time the memory was made. And yet, it is our only means of accessing our past. Working with memories to understand experiences requires us to pay attention to the ways in which we experience those memories in the present moment, the ways the present moment shapes those memories and is shaped by them.

All stages in the process of encoding, storing and retrieving memories are "fragile and powerful" (Schacter, 1997, p. 20). Memories are shaped by experiencing at the time of memory encoding, processing and storage and also shaped by experiencing on retrieval. Remembering occurs through the lens of our perceptions, prior understandings and our current context.

Kuhn (2002) writes: "memory is a process, an activity, a construct" (p. 298) and refers to the performance of "memory work". Lohmeier and Pentzold (2014) highlight the purposefulness inherent in memory-work: "in which the past is expressively and consciously represented, interpreted, reflected and dis-cursively negotiated" (p. 779). Environmental and relational factors contribute to the expression of memories 'retrieved'. We bring effort to memory encoding and retrieval, but the work is not fully under our conscious control, much of it is undertaken beneath consciousness. A retrieved memory might be better described as a *re-constructed*, re-imagined or even re-negotiated memory and this re-construction occurs in relationship with our embodied being, our presentational and conceptual knowing, and our action in the world. Memory reconstruction is an intersubjective process.

There have been many inquiries undertaken into the factors that contribute to memory reconstruction. Since the 1970s researchers have explored the reliability of eyewitness testimony noting the ways in which verbal cues can re-shape and add to memories (Loftus & Palmer, 1974). Loftus went on to explore how false beliefs about memories and even false memories can be created. These false memories can have serious consequences (Berkowitz, Laney, Morris, Garry, & Loftus, 2008).

Standing, Bobbitt, Boisvert, Dayholos, & Gagnon (2008) explored whether social cues (like experimenter clothing and the presence of bystanders) and contextual cues (like music) present during the learning phase of a memory recall study, influenced memory recall performance. They found that memory retrieval improved if these cues – not relevant to the learning exercise – were present during learning and at retrieval. Schacter (1997) notes that: "salient information in the present retrieval environment (subject's current attitudes) helps to distort their recollections of what they once believed" (p. 16). That is, contents that may appear to have nothing to do with a memory can affect encoding and retrieval.

Memory recall can also be influenced by aging and visual distractions (Wais, Martin, & Gazzaley, 2012); the difficulty of the tasks encountered and the individual's level of executive functioning including self-regulation, planning, and flexible thinking (Angel, Bastin, Genon, Salmon, Fay, Balteau, Maquet, Luxen, Isingrini, & Collette, 2016); and resting heart rate variability (Gillie, Vasey, & Thayer, 2014). Rubin and Umanath (2015) suggest that while we might consider a memory for an event as a single occurrence it is "most often constructed from general (i.e. allocentric) knowledge of the scene abstracted from exposure to multiple perspectives" (p. 2). Memory retrieval can include an amalgam of similar experiences.

Memory is malleable. Gisquet-Verrier & Riccio (2012) note that reactivation of a memory not only serves to "restore the accessibility of the memory", it also serves to "induce the malleability of that memory, both of these aspects being essential for updating processes" (p. 407). When a memory is retrieved or re-activated it becomes labile, that is, new information may alter the memory (Alberini, 2011). The networks of associations from which memories are accessed throughout the brain become richer, extended and more complex each time they are re-activated by retrieval. This updating improves our ability to "adapt to the changing environment" (p. 8).

Memory is adaptive. Dunlap, McLinn, MacCormick, Scott, & Kerr (2009) proposed that "memory generates a variance in payoff" (p. 1102), for example, retaining memories is more helpful in familiar stable environments where the retrieval of a memory about how to behave toward or understand something is more likely to be correct. Retaining memories can be less helpful in changeable, unreliable environments where the memory may be of no benefit to survival.

If we speak *about* past experiences, even milliseconds later, the experiences are already re-constructed in the present moment. Remembering may be conceptualised as an articulation of other forms of knowing *about* experiential knowing. Importantly, the relationships between experiencing and remembering are "interdependent" (Heron & Reason, 1997, p. 280).

While always in relationship, different forms of knowing can be used "in association with, or dissociation from, each other" (Heron & Reason, 1997, p. 280). What we know in the present moment may be tacit and pre-reflective, but it includes prior learning and experiencing, it includes other forms of knowing, and it includes the remembering self. What we know of the past is the result of what was experientially known *then*, what is experientially known *now*, and what we know *about* this experiential knowing in the present moment.

Flaubert's problem of 'falling into the habit of remembering' (Bakewell, 2016, p. 103), of seeing what we already know, may be reconceptualised as a problem of wanting to capture the sensorial immediacy of experiential knowing but instead seeing only what we already know *about* that experiential knowing. However, limiting what can be known to the domain of reflection and remembering ignores our experiential knowing in the present moment. Experiential knowing may be implicit but is nevertheless active in the now.

Studies suggest that what we experience as the present moment lasts around three seconds (Gerstner & Goldberg, 1994; Nagy, 2011; Poppel, 2004; Stern, 2004). Colwyn Trevarthen is quoted as saying that the experience of the present moment is "something flexible and highly expressive.... It's biological. It's mental. It's spiritual. This is the timing of the human spirit" (Kessler, 2011, para. 9). There is a felt sense and meaning to what is considered a present moment beyond the number of seconds it is comprised of. As Stern (2004) writes "psychological present moments must have both a duration in which things happen and at the same time take place during a single, subjective now" (pp. 25–26).

Daniel Stern pioneered techniques that inquired into the present moment and the benefits of doing so. Hoping to discover more about mother/infant interaction along with Terry Brazelton and Colwyn Trevarthen (Beebe & Steele, 2013), Stern used an approach he called microanalysis. He filmed mothers and infants together in "natural interactions" (Stern, 1977/2002, p. 1). These interactions were then analysed for "behavioural units" (p. 3) including, for example, "gaze aversions, small shifts in arousal and so on" (p. 3).

Stern (2004) notes that "seeing the world at this scale of reality changes what can be seen and thus changes our basic conceptions accordingly" (p. xiv). He viewed the split-second moments captured between mother and child as "the basic building block of relationship experiences. Abstractions such as generalisations, explanations, and interpretations, or higher-order phenomena such as narratives, are made up of these basic, primary, psychological experiences" (Stern, 2004, p. 245). He captured in film tiny moments of mother/child experiencing.

This privileging of the present moment was coupled with Stern's deep interest in intersubjectivity. At this level of analysis, it was possible to see how mothers and infants participated in interactions that showed them simultaneously "changing with" (Beebe & Steele, 2013, p. 238) one another. Their relationship is enacted as a "dance" (Stern, 1977, p. 133) rather than a series of stimulus-response patterns; "together they evolve some exquisitely intricate dyadic patterns" (p. 133). Stern sees intersubjectivity as "an innate, primary system of motivation" (2004, p. 97) and our sense of self is generated and maintained by fulfilling intersubjective needs: "we need the eyes of others to form and hold ourselves together" (p. 107).

We can gain raw and significant new information about our past experiences and current experiential knowing if we carefully attend to the present moment. Staying with and noticing the 'now', what is felt/seen/smelt/tasted/heard/touched and shared with others as it is occurs, gives us a better chance of articulating our experiential knowing. While tacit and pre-reflective, we are *aware* of experiential knowing, we notice it in ourselves and others. If experiential knowing is the grounding upon which all other forms of knowing are built, then staying with as much of that experiential knowing as possible is highly valuable for research or therapeutic inquiry.

## Attentiveness to the present moment in action

Attending to and remaining open to the present moment demands a flexible inquiry approach. As Lett (2011) writes: "the use of procedures of inquiry emerges through the interactions, and creates a methodology suited to their particular concerns. There is no predetermined or fixed form of inquiry" (p. 8). What emerges as significant at any point in time, is noted and attended to. It can provide important information about what particular focus or way of working might be most helpful in that moment. Valuing the present moment had many implications for the inquiry as it unfolded.

Some processes and activities were organised in advance of our sessions but were readily put aside if other approaches were better suited to the material that arose in our shared space. This required participants and I stay attuned to our experiencing. We had a specific topic to explore but we did not feel beholden to sticking to a plan about how to explore it. We agreed we would enact the values of intersubjectivity, multimodality, and attentiveness to the present moment and we agreed that maternal experiences of holding were our focus but what emerged in the moment as our relationship unfolded alerted us to what did or did not hold value and import for us. Sometimes, if we stayed with what emerged, something that appeared to be a ramble down a side-track revealed itself to be powerfully informative, at other times those rambles were simply moments of straying, exploring intriguing distractions or gaining space from our topic.

Valuing the present moment and an emergent, responsive approach meant that enacting and then describing our inquiry was not easy; things did not progress in an entirely linear way but rather jumped back and forth, informed by and informing, our knowing, much as remembering and experiencing are entangled. In light of these challenges, this approach to inquiry required reflexivity which "refers to the researcher's self-awareness and openness about the research process" (Finlay, 2011, p. 265). In writing up this inquiry, I have attempted to clearly convey what occurred, and when, in a linear fashion but wish to acknowledge that the experience of the inquiry's unfolding felt more like a constant gathering and shifting of tiny moments of vitality coalescing, vanishing, appearing and always moving.

Like presentational knowing, staying with the present moment involves acceptance of ambiguity, ambivalence and the not quite known, it is not always comfortable. A certain trust is involved in working this way, in allowing the only partially formed knowing to be held in the intersubjective space of the inquirer/ participant or therapist/client relationship in such a way that we can explore it in the moment without yet conceptualizing what it is *about*. This requires attention to the relationship as it unfolds; to cues of discomfort or curiosity, eagerness or reticence emerging within the relationship. It asks us to acknowledge these emotions and choose when to stay with them and when it may be more fruitful to, for example, take a reflective stance or change a modality of exploration.

There are two significant challenges when valuing the present moment in inquiry. As previously described, the first is that a constant negotiation takes places between what holds energy in the moment and what serves the inquiry. The second challenge speaks to the risk that the inquiry never ends. As our knowing constantly evolves, we cannot fix meaning forever but we can approximate meaning in time. To negotiate these, I selected a general number of sessions, and I was given a general timeline within which to complete the research, and both of these supported the containment of the inquiry. Participants were also comfortable with accepting that what meanings they came to during sessions, and afterward while I worked with their material to come to individual themes, were a product of their time.

Maternal holding particularly draws attention to changes in knowing as participants lived with their growing children in an everchanging relationship. What participants knew about their holding changed at a number of timepoints: after our sessions were complete, after I worked with our material and after I had taken that material and worked with it to come to some general findings. I checked in and shared with each mother particularly as I worked with their 'individual' material but as the inquiry progressed, I privileged my different forms of knowing in relationship with the material, findings and other voices/imagery.

Merleau-Ponty (1953/1988) wrote that:

> The philosopher is marked by the distinguishing trait that he possesses *inseparably* the taste for evidence and the feeling for ambiguity…what makes a philosopher is the movement which leads back without ceasing from knowledge to ignorance, from ignorance to knowledge.
>
> (pp. 4–5)

As I inquired into maternal holding and presented this research, I attempted to hold both my desire for evocative and meaningful statements about knowing and a recognition of the often non-linear, dynamic way in which knowing evolves over time and in relationship. I have tried to transparently convey the inquiry journey while acknowledging its complexity. In the ongoing dance of experiencing and reflection, attending to the present moment was my attempt to honour different forms of knowing so that each one might speak to maternal holding experiences as richly and honestly, for now, as possible.

### *Reflections on attending to the present moment*

> She had a kind of genius for being amazed by the world and by herself, all her life she remained a virtuoso marveller at things.
>
> Bakewell on Simone de Beauvoir (2016, p. 109)

A memory from 2017:

---

**Box 1.5 Ariel Moy, Diary Entry, 2017**

I hold my son while we wait for coffee in our favourite café. He stands in front of me and I have my arms around him with my head resting on his. At first, I simply feel the pleasure of his warmth and body resting against mine, then I notice the movement of others around me and that I should pay attention to when the barista calls out my coffee order. And then I return to the joy of holding him. I move in and out of these two experiences for the minute or so before the coffee is made. I move between feeling joy and warmth and the awareness that this moment will soon be over.

---

A poem from 2018:

---

**Box 1.6 Ariel Moy, *Knew, Knowing, Now*, poem.**

An explosion of now and then,
The present a lens through which,
I see and taste and tell,
What I knew, what I know and what I don't quite know yet.

---

### *Conclusion – holding the inquiry*

In order to explore maternal holding I adapted the MIECAT Form of Inquiry by privileging values; working with and paying attention to intersubjective being, multimodal knowing and the present moment.

Working in this way has been challenging and deeply engaging. When I first explored my guiding values and imagined how they might play out in the inquiry I made a number of drawings. I noticed a sense of accretion, of layering, of questions and answers that weren't always conceptually clear but were intensely felt.

I returned repeatedly to my guiding values throughout each stage of the inquiry, to check if I was working in a way that was congruent with them. Sometimes congruence was not always easy to determine or enact. It also required transparency about my work at each stage, a reflexive stance and ongoing engagement with Heron and Reason's (1997) four forms of knowing.

Initially I could only imagine how my values might play out in the research. As I began working with participants, I noticed and reflected upon how *we* navigated these values together. When I began working with individual and across participant material 'alone', and then developed findings in dialogue with other voices, the navigation of guiding values was different again. These values were alive and responsive at every stage of the research process and required constant attention and care. In the image and poem below, I have attempted to convey the feeling of these values and their enactment at this inquiry's end.

---

**Box 1.7 Ariel Moy, *Enacting an Axiology*, poem.**

A new corridor each time,
For a while the patterns on the walls are familiar,
but on return, another layer revealed.
Doors open and close,
Appear and disappear,
Smells, sounds, colours and temperatures fluctuate.
There is a house for these in-between places,
A structure loosely held,
Letting the labyrinth shape and reshape endlessly.

---

I believe that exploration of an intimate yet everyday relational experience like maternal holding can benefit from an adaptable, multimodal and relationship focused approach, an approach that lends itself well to a therapeutic relationship.

Below I make some suggestions about how you might integrate some of this inquiry's approaches into your practice when working with mother/child relationships.

**A note on representations:** Most representations made by participants and I were constructed in a short amount of time. Through the making of these creative expressions we hoped to access knowing about whatever questions we held in body and relationship at that particular moment. None of us have artistic training but like everyone, we have the desire and ability to express ourselves in non-conceptual terms. These representations were raw, immediate, surprising and deeply informative for all of us.

## Suggestions for therapeutic work: exploring maternal holding

- Orienting to the work: To ease into exploration, start with an embodied 'warm-in' exercise to orient clients into an experiential space. This might include holding heat-packs as I did with participants but really is only limited by what you and the client feel is relevant to holding. Other clients might feel more comfortable telling you the story of their memory first, followed by a warm-in exercise. The main take-away is that prior to making any kind of representation, attending to embodied, present experiencing engages non-conceptual knowing, knowing that is often bypassed in our eagerness to 'contain' or understand experiencing.

- As with any therapeutic space, offer your client enough privacy and room to express themselves without concern over others hearing or seeing them. Provide a range of creative materials, enough space to spread these out and move around in. Though we didn't use these in the inquiry, a sand tray with a good selection of objects and figures can also be incredibly helpful when making representations and exploring these.

- You might suggest that your client choose a holding memory that arises for them right now or one they've selected earlier: holding their infant child, holding their toddler, holding their tween, teen or adult child. Each of these experiences emerge from a different mother/child relationship in a different context, at a different point in time. They may bring an object (like a photo, item of clothing, soft toy etc) to serve as an access point into memory.

- Encountering memories: When your client is reconstructing their memory, encourage attention to bodily sensations, emotional atmosphere and flow, imagery and words that arise and fall away, changes in space and time, smell, textures, sounds, temperature. Paying attention to these qualities in a holding moment provides richer information about what holding is like. It allows deeper access into the lesser known and as yet unarticulated moments of holding, something easily put aside or diminished when attending to the more obvious, every-day and known qualities of holding. Your client may spend time quietly reconstructing their memory or they might do so as they make their representation.

- Making a representation: The focus here is on representing without conceptualisation, putting aside what they think they already know, to see, feel and make what emerges. This is often surprising and can be uncomfortable as we are not yet at a stage of clarity, containment or agreement with what is emerging. We're providing a safe space for ambiguity, ambivalence, discord and not knowing.

- Co-exploring and recording: When the client feels they have made enough for now and the representation has been recorded (if an 'art object' hasn't been made, for example, with a body sculpture, movement or sound) you can enter into exploration of the representation. See what words, gestures, expressions emerge for your client as they initially speak about the representation. Try to steer clear of conceptualisations at this starting point. Focus on what can be seen and felt without explicit interpretation. You can note down any words or phrases that feel significant within the relational space (noted, for example, by repetition, intensity of vocalisation, facial or body expression etc). You may ask: What colours, shapes appear? How is the space filled up – are there busy areas? Empty areas? Loud or quiet areas? What are the relationships between the shapes? Are there textures? Can you move parts of the representation? Are there temperatures to different parts of the representation? Is there movement or is the representation fixed? You can also ask about what the process of making the representation was like.

- You can then move onto questions that invite more conceptualisation: What do you see when you look at the representation? What associations arise for you? What is surprising about the representation? What makes sense and what are you curious about? If any parts of this representation had a voice, what would they say? If you could change any part of the representation, what would it be? What feels valuable?

- Reduction of information: One way of clarifying and synthesising understanding can be to gather words/phrases that you've recorded throughout the session and reduce these down to an important word, sentence or theme that captures the essence of what you have come to understand or of a quality of knowing that stands out for you both right now.

- From here you might choose to use one of these words/phrases or images as another access point into your ongoing exploration of maternal holding and enter the cycle of inquiry again.

- As a way of finishing off a session you might ask: Is there something that you've discovered today that you might bring to your next holding moment? Or, is there something that you would like to inquire into further in our next session? Is there something that felt particularly powerful for you today? Or, what, if anything, would you describe to your child about what you've come to know today?

- At any stage of this co-exploration (including between sessions) you might choose to offer an 'intersubjective response' that feels helpful to your client and your client/therapist relationship. This could be a word, a phrase, a curiosity or a creative representation and see where that takes you both. It may simply be received without comment; it may be rejected and give rise to clarification around a client's current understanding or it may end up being explored in later sessions. It is valuable to be able to 'speak' with the client in this presentational way, creative expression and artistic knowing are powerful tools for exploration, generating knowing and meaning making not only for clients but for practitioners.

- The above suggestions are also applicable to exploring our own responses as therapists or inquirers to client material both in session and outside of session.

- As with any work that invites lesser understood and 'controlled' material (in the form of experiential and presentational knowing) it is important to stay present to your client's as well as our own embodied cues and utilise techniques to help ground them if the work appears to be triggering.

## References

Adams, F. (2010). Embodied cognition. *Phenomenology and the Cognitive Sciences*, 9(4): 619–628. doi:10.1007/s11097-010-9175.

Alberini, C. M. (2011). The role of reconsolidation and the dynamic process of long-term memory formation and storage. *Frontiers in Behavioral Neuroscience*, 5(12). doi:10.3389/fnbeh.2011.00012.

Allen, P. (1995). *Art is a Way of Knowing*. Boston, MA: Shambhala.

Angel, L., Bastin, C., Genon, S., Salmon, E., Fay, S., Balteau, E., Maquet, P., Luxen, A., Isingrini, M., & Collette, F. (2016). Neural correlates of successful memory retrieval in aging: Do executive functioning and task difficulty matter? *Brain Research*, 1631, 53–71. doi:10.1016/j.brainres.2015.10.009.

Bakewell, S. (2016). *At the Existential Café: Freedom, Being, and Apricot Cocktails with Jean-Paul Sartre, Simone de Beauvoir, Albert Camus, Martin Heidegger, Karl Jaspers, Edmund Husserl, Maurice Merleau-Ponty and Others*. New York, NY: Other Press.

Barad, K. (2003). Posthumanist performativity: Toward an understanding of how matter comes to matter. *Signs: Journal of Women in Culture and Society*, 28(3), 801–831. http://www.jstor.org/stable/10.1086/345321.

Barad, K. (2007). *Meeting the Universe Halfway: Quantum physics and the entanglement of mater and meaning*. London: Duke University Press.

Barad, K. (2009). Matter feels, converses, suffers, desires, yearns and remembers: Interview with Karen Barad. In R. Dolphijn and I. van der Tuin (Eds.), *New Materialism: Interviews & Cartographies*. Retrieved from https://quod.lib.umich.edu/o/ohp/11515701.0001.001/1:4.3/–new-materialism-interviews-cartographies?rgn=div2;view=fulltext.

Barone, T., & Eisner, E. W. (2012). *Arts Based Research*. Thousand Oaks, CA: Sage.

Beck, J. S. (1964). *Cognitive Therapy: Basics and Beyond*. New York, NY: Guilford Press.

Beebe, B., & Steele, M. (2013). How does microanalysis of mother-infant communication inform maternal sensitivity and infant attachment, attachment and human development, *Maternal Sensitivity: Observational Studies Honoring Mary Ainsworth's 10th Year*, 15(5-6) doi:10.1080/14616734.2013.841050.

Berger, J. (2016). *Confabulations*. London: Penguin.

Berkowitz, S. R., Laney, C., Morris, E. K., Garry, M., & Loftus, E. (2008). Pluto behaving badly: False Beliefs and their consequences. *American Journal of Psychology*, 121(4), 643–660. doi:10.2307/20445490.

Byrne, L. (2014). Excavating evidence from experience. *Journal of Applied Arts & Health*, 5(2), 219–226. doi:10.1386/jaah.5.2.219_1.

Capacchione, L. (2001). *The Art of Emotional Healing*. Boston, MA: Shambhala.

Carman, T. (1999). The body in Husserl and Merleau-Ponty. *Philosophical Topics*, 27(2), 205–226. Retrieved from http://www.complextrauma.uk/uploads/2/3/9/4/23949705/carman_body.pdf.

Christians, C. G. (2011). Ethics and politics in qualitative research, In N. K. Denzin, & Y. S. Lincoln (Eds.), *The Sage Handbook of Qualitative Research*, (pp. 61–80). Thousand Oaks, CA: Sage.

Clark, A. (1995). I am John's brain. *Journal of Consciousness Studies*, 2(2), 144–148. doi:10.1017/S1477175608000134.

Clark, A. (1998). Where brain, body, and world collide. *Daedalus: Journal of the American Academy of Arts and Sciences (Special Issue on the Brain)*, 127(2); 257–280. doi:10.10007/978-0-387-74711-8_1.

Clark, A., & Chalmers, D. (1998). The extended mind, *Analysis*, 28, 10–53. Retrieved from http://consc.net/papers/extended.html.

Cole, A. L., & Knowles, G. J. (2008). Arts informed inquiry. In G. J. Knowles, & A. L. Cole (Eds.) *Handbook of the Arts in Qualitative Research: Perspectives, Methodologies, Examples and Issues*. Los Angeles, CA: Sage Publications.

Coyle, J. T., & Fischbach, G. D. (1997). Preface. In Daniel L. Schacter, Gerald D. Fischbach, Joseph T. Coyle, Marek-Marsel Mesulam, & Lawrence E. Sullivan (Eds.) *Memory Distortion: How Minds, Brains and Societies Reconstruct the Past*. Cambridge, MA: Harvard University Press.

Damasio, A. (2000). *The Feeling of What Happens: Body, Emotion and the Making of Consciousness*. London: Vintage.

Demuth, C. (2013). Ensuring rigor in qualitative research within the field of cross-cultural psychology. In Y. Kashima, E. S. Kashima, & R. Beatson (Eds.), *Steering the Cultural Dynamics: Selected Papers from the 2010 Congress of the International Association for Cross-Cultural Psychology*. Retrieved from https://scholarworks.gvsu.edu/iaccp_papers/109/.

Di Paolo, E. A. (2018). The enactive conception of life. In A. Newen, S. Gallagher, & L. de Bruin (Eds.), *The Oxford Handbook of Cognition: Embodied, Embedded, Enactive and Extended* (pp. 71–94). Oxford: Oxford University Press Retrieved from www.ezequieldipaolo.net.

Di Paolo, E. A., & De Jaegher, H. (2015). Toward an embodied science of intersubjectivity: Widening the scope of social understanding research. *Frontiers in Psychology*, 6: 234. doi:10.3389/fpsyg.2015.00234.

De Quincey, C. (2000). Intersubjectivity: Exploring consciousness from the second-person perspective. *The Journal of Transpersonal Psychology*, 32(2), 135–155. Retrieved from https://pdfs.semanticscholar.org/5e82/60991d22fa36011c9ec904d308ef7443f6a.pdf.

Dreyfus, H. (2005). Hubert L Dreyfus interview: Conversations with history. Institute of International Studies, UC Berkeley. Retrieved from http://globetrotter.berkeley.edu/people5/Dreyfus/dreyfus-con5.html.

Dunlap, A. S., McLinn, C. M., MacCormick, H. A., Scott M. E., & Kerr, B. (2009). Why some memories do not last a lifetime: Dynamic long-term retrieval in changing environments. *Behavioral Ecology*, 20(5), 1096–1105. doi:10.1093/beheco/arp102.

Fausto-Sterling, A. *Dynamic Systems Theory*. Retrieved from http://www.annefaustosterling.com/fields-of-inquiry/dynamic-systems-theory/.

Finlay, L. (2011). *Phenomenology for Therapists: Researching the Lived World*. Chichester, UK: Wiley-Blackwell.

Finley, S. (2008). Arts-based research. In G. J. Knowles & A. L. Cole, (Eds.), *Handbook of the Arts in Qualitative Research: Perspectives, Methodologies, Examples and Issues*. Los Angeles, CA: Sage Publications.

Franklin, M. (2012). Know thyself: Awakening self-referential awareness through art-based research. *Journal of Applied Arts & Health*, 3(1), 87–96. doi:10.1386/jaah.3.1.87_1.

Froese, T., & Fuchs, T. (2012). The extended body: A case study in the neurophenomenology of social interaction, *Phenomenology and the Cognitive Sciences*, 11, 205–235. doi:10.1007/s11097-012-9254-2.

Fusaroli, R., Demuru, P., Borghi, A. M. (2009). The intersubjectivity of embodiment, *Journal of Cognitive Semiotics*, 4(1), 1–5. doi:10.1515/cogsem.2009.4.1.1.

Fuchs, T. (2016). Intercoporeality and Interaffectivity. *Phenomenology and Mind*, 11, 194–209. doi:10.13128/Phe_Mi-20119.

Fuchs, T., & Koch, S. C. (2014). Embodied affectivity: On moving and being moved. *Frontiers in Psychology*, 5, 1–12. doi:10.3389/fpsyg.2014.00508.

Galloway, J. C. (2013). Review of the book *A dynamic systems approach to the development of cognition and action* by E. Thelen & L. B Smith. *Adapted Physical Activity Quarterly*, 30(1), 85–87. doi:10.1123/apaq.30.1.85.

Gergen, K. J. (2009). *Relational Being: Beyond Self and Community*. Oxford: Oxford University Press.

Gerstner, G. E., & Goldberg, L., J. (1994). Evidence of a time constant associated with movement patterns in six mammalian species. *Ethology and Sociobiology*, 15(4), 181–205. doi:10.1016/0162-3095(94)90013-2.

Gillie, B. L., Vasey, M. W., & Thayer, J. F. (2014). Heart rate variability predicts control over memory retrieval. *Psychological Science*, 25(2), 458–465. doi:10.1177/0956797613508789.

Gisquet-Verrier, P., & Riccio, D. C. (2012). Memory reactivation effects independent of reconsolidation. *Memory and Learning*, 19, 401–409. doi:10.1101/lm.026054.112.

Heffernan, V. (2016). *Magic and Loss: The Internet as Art*. New York, NY: Simon & Schuster.

Heidegger, M. (1988). *The Basic Problems of Phenomenology, Revised Edition*. Indiana, USA: Indiana University Press. (Original work published in 1975).

Heron, J., & Reason, P. (1997). A participatory inquiry paradigm. *Qualitative Inquiry*, 3 (3), 274–294. doi:10.1177/107780049700300302.

Heron, J., & Reason, P. (2001). The practice of co-operative inquiry: Research 'with' rather than 'on' people. In P. Reason and H. Bradbury (Eds.) *The Handbook of Action Research* (pp. 144–154). London: Sage Publications.

Heron, J., & Reason, P. (2008). Extending epistemology within a co-operative inquiry. In P. Reason and H. Bradbury (Eds.) *The Handbook of Action Research*, 2nd ed. London: Sage Publications. Retrieved from http://www.human-inquiry.com/EECI.htm.

Jacobsen, B. (2007). *Invitation to Existential Psychology: A Psychology for the Unique Human Being and Its Application in Therapy*. Chichester, England: John Wiley & Sons.

Kessler, R. (2011, January 28). Hugs follow a 3-second rule. Retrieved from www.sci encemag.org/news/2011/01/hugs-follow-3-second-rule.

Kuhn, A. (2002). *Family Secrets: Acts of Memory and Imagination*. London: Verso.

Lambert, M. J., & Barley, D. E. (2001). Research summary on the therapeutic relationships and psychotherapy outcome. *Psychotherapy: Theory, Research, Practice, Training*, 38(4), 357–361. doi:10.1037/0033-3204.38.4.357.

Laverty, S. M. (2003). Hermeneutic phenomenology and phenomenology: A comparison of historical and methodological considerations. *International Journal of Qualitative Methods*, 2(3), 21–35. doi:10.1177/160940690300200303.

Leavy, P. (2015). *Method Meets Art: Arts-Based Research Practice*. New York, NY: The Guilford Press.

Lett, W. R. (1993). *How the Arts Make a Difference in Therapy: Papers from a Conference at La Trobe University, January 1992*. South Melbourne, Victoria: Australian Dance Council.

Lett, W. R. (2011). *An Inquiry into Making Sense of Our Lives*. Eltham, Victoria: Rebus Press.

Levin, J. (2016). *Black Hole Blues and Other Songs from Outer Space*. New York, NY: Alfred A. Knopf Publishing.

Levine, S. (2009). *Researching Imagination – Imagining Research. Trauma, Tragedy, Therapy: The Arts and Human Suffering*. London: Jessica Kingsley Publishers. Retrieved from http://expressivearts.egs.edu/fileadmin/Resources/Public/Downloads/Researching_Imagination_-_Imagining_Research.pdf

Lincoln, Y. S., Lynham, S. A., & Guba, E. G. (2011). Paradigmatic controversies, contradictions, and emerging confluences, revisited. In N. K. Denzin, & Y. S. Lincoln (Eds.), *The Sage Handbook of Qualitative Research* 4 (pp. 97–128). Thousand Oaks, CA: Sage Publications.

Lynch, M. M. (2012) Factors influencing successful psychotherapy outcomes. Retrieved from https://sophia.stkate.edu/msw_papers/57.

Loftus, E. F., & Palmer, J. C. (1974). Reconstruction of automobile destruction: An example of the interaction between language and memory. *Journal of Verbal Learning and Verbal Behavior*, 13(5), 585–589. doi:10.1016/S0022–5371(74)80011–80013.

Lohmeier, C., & Pentzold, C. (2014). Making mediated memory work: Cuban-Americans, Miami media and the doing of diaspora memories. *Media, Culture & Society*, 36 (6), 776–789. doi:10.1177/0163443713518574.

Malchiodi, C, A. (2012). *Handbook of Art Therapy*. London: The Guilford Press.

Merleau-Ponty, M. (1953/1988). *In Praise of Philosophy and Other Essays*, Everston, IL: Northwestern University Press. (Original work published 1953).

Merleau-Ponty, M. (1945/2014). *Phenomenology of Perception*. New York, NY: Routledge.

McNiff, S. (1998). *Art-Based Research*, London: Jessica Kingsley Publishers. [Kindle Edition]. Retrieved from Amazon.com

Moustakas, C. (1994). *Phenomenological Research Methods*. Thousand Oaks, CA: Sage.

Nagy, E. (2011). Sharing the moment: The duration of embraces in humans. *Journal of Ethology*, 29(2), 389–393. doi:10.1007/s10164-010-0260-y.

Noë, A. (2015). *Strange Tools: Art and Human Nature*. New York, NY: Hill and Wang.

Park, P. (2001). Knowledge and participatory research. In P. Reason and H. Bradbury (Eds.) *The Handbook of Action Research* (pp. 84–93). London, UK: Sage.

Poppel, E. (2004). Lost in time: A historical frame, elementary processing units and the 3-second window. *ACTA Neurobiologiae Experimentalis*, 64(3), 295–301. Retrieved from http://citeseerx.ist.psu.edu/viewdoc/download?doi=10.1.1.197.5551&rep=rep1&type=pdf.

Reis, A. C. (2011). Bringing my creative self to the fore: Accounts of a reflexive research endeavour. *Creative Approaches to Research*, 4(1), 2–18. doi:10.3316/CAR0401002.

Rowan, J. (2006). The humanistic approach to action research. In P. Reason and H. Bradbury (Eds.) *The Handbook of Action Research* (pp. 106–116). London: Sage.

Rubin, D. C., & Umanath, S. (2015). Event memory: A theory of memory for laboratory, autobiographical, and fictional events. *Psychological Review*, 122(1), 1–23. doi:10.1037/a0037907.

Quail, J., & Peavy, V. (1994). A phenomenologic research study of a client's experience in art therapy. *The Arts in Psychotherapy*, 21(1), 45–57. doi:10.1016/0197-4556(94)90036-1.

Reynolds, J. (2017). Maurice Merleau-Ponty (1908–1961). In J. Fieser and B. Dowden (Eds.), *Internet Encyclopedia of Philosophy*. Retrieved from www.iep.utm.edu/merleau/.

Rolling, Jr, J. (2013). *Arts-Based Research Primer*. New York, NY: Peter Lang.

Rothschild, B. (2000). *The Body Remembers: The Psychophysiology of Trauma and Trauma Treatment*. New York, NY: W.W. Norton & Company.

Sawyer, K. (2007). *Group Genius: The Creative Power of Collaboration*. New York, NY: Basic Books.

Schacter, D. L. (1997). Memory distortion: History and current status. In D. L. Schacter (Ed.) *Memory Distortion: How Minds, Brains and Societies Reconstruct the Past* (pp. 1–46). Cambridge, MA: Harvard University Press.

Seeley, C., & Reason, P. (2008). Expression of energy: An epistemology of presentational knowing. In P. Liamputtong, & J. Rumbold (Eds.) *Knowing Differently: Arts-Based & Collaborative Research*. New York: NY: Nova Science Publishers Inc.

Shapiro, L. (2011). *Embodied Cognition*. New York, NY: Routledge (Taylor & Francis Group).

Sousanis, N. (2015). *Unflattening*. Cambridge, MA: Harvard University Press.

Springgay. S. (2005). Thinking through bodies: Bodied encounters and the process of meaning making in an e-mail generated art project. *Studies in Art Education: A Journal of Issues and Research*, 47(1), 34–50. Retrieved from http://www.jstor.org/stable/25475771.

Stamoulos, C., Trepanier, L., Bourkas, S., Bradley, S., Stelmaszczyk, K., Schwartzman, D., & Drapeau, M. (2016). Psychologists' perceptions of the importance of common factors in psychotherapy for successful treatment outcomes. *Journal of Psychotherapy Integration*, 26(3), 300–317. doi:10.1037/a0040426.

Standing, L. G., Bobbitt, K. E., Boisvert, K. L., Dayholos, K. N., & Gagnon, A. M. (2008). People, clothing, music, and arousal as contextual retrieval cues in verbal memory. *Perceptual and Motor Skills*, 107(2), 523–534. doi:10.2466/pms.107.2.523-534.

Stepnisky, J. (2014). Social psychology from flat to round: Intersubjectivity and space in Peter Sloterdijk's *Bubbles*. *Journal for the Theory of Social Behaviour* 44(4), 413–435. doi:10.1111/jtsb.12060.

Stern, D. (1977). *The First Relationship: Infant and Mother*, 2002 ed. Cambridge, MA: Harvard University Press.

Stern, D. (2004). *The Present Moment in Psychotherapy and Everyday Life*. New York, NY: W. W. Norton & Company.

Sullivan, G. (2005). *Art Practice as Research: Inquiry in the Visual Arts*. Thousand Oaks, CA: Sage Publications.

Teske, J. A. (2013). From embodied to extended cognition. *Zygon: Journal of Religion and Science*, 48(3), 759–787. doi:10.1111/zygo.12038.

Thelen, E., & Smith, L. B. (1996). *A Dynamic Systems Approach to the Development of Cognition and Action*, reprint ed. Cambridge, MA: MIT Press.

Trevarthen, C. (2009). Embodied human intersubjectivity. *Journal of Cognitive Semiotics*, 4(1), 6–56. doi:10.1515/cogsem.2009.4.1.6.

Van Manen, M. (1990). *Researching Lived Experience: Human Science for an Action Sensitive Pedagogy*. Ontario, Canada: State University of New York Press.

Wang, I., & Green, D. (2017). Stitching east and west. *Creative Arts in Education and Therapy – Eastern and Western Perspectives*, 3(1), 26–43. doi:10.15534/CAET/2017/1/4.

Wais, P. E., Martin, G. M., & Gazzaley, A. (2012). The impact of visual distraction on retrieval in older adults. *Brain Research, 1430*, 78–85. doi:10.1016/j.brainres.2011.10.048.

Weiss, G. (1999). *Body Images: Embodiment as Intercorporeality*. New York, NY: Psychology Press Routledge.

Wilson, M. (2002). Six views of embodied cognition. *Psychodynamic Bulletin and Review*, 9(4), 625–636. doi:10.3758/BF03196322.

Zlatev, J., Racine, T. P., Sinha, C., & Itkonen, E. (2008). Intersubjectivity: What makes us human? In J. Zlatev, T. P. Racine, C. Sinha, & E. Itkonen (Eds.), *Shared Mind: Perspective on Intersubjectivity* (pp. 1–14). Amsterdam: Benjamins. doi:10.1075/celcr.12.02zla.

# 2 Holding one is holding all

## Rosanna, Elaina, Olivia, Lillian and Deanna

At the beginning of our work together, Rosanna decided that she wanted to honour each individual relationship with her four daughters by exploring them separately. Our sessions were structured in a way to support this. Sessions comprised of a part A – involving an initial exploration of a holding experience; and part B – a development of our understanding of the selected holding experience to come to an approximation to meaning.

There was a profound interweaving of relationships in our work as memories and understandings of one mother/daughter relationship sparked those of her other relationships. Our last two sessions brought our work together to capture what was similar and consistent across her experiences of holding her daughters.

We shared eight sessions. The initial exploratory sessions (A sessions) took place at my home, some of the data reduction sessions (B sessions) took place at a local café across a large table we shared in a booth that afforded us privacy. Below, I have structured the sessions around each daughter.

### Deanna: not holding, pain, memory and holding across generations (Sessions 1A and 1B)

> It's almost like part of holding her, is the experience of *not holding her.*

My first session of working with participants threw both my procedural and content pre-conceptions to the wind. I planned to start by working with a non-verbal artmaking, but it turned out that holding Deanna had been a rare, intense and fraught experience for Rosanna. She needed to tell the story of her selected holding experience to provide a context for myself as co-inquirer but also for herself as a way of easing into her memories.

> I'm building the feeling, it's not just about description, I'm building in my own mind and body the sense of what this (experience of holding Deanna) means to me.

DOI: 10.4324/9781003104094-3

Rosanna noted that holding Deanna was 'not simple'; it was intricately entwined with the experience of *not* holding her, and this unexplored terrain was where we needed to begin.

The first holding memory Rosanna chose to explore described the moment when Deanna gave birth to her first child (Frankie); Rosanna's first grandchild. The recollection proceeded slowly and quietly; each moment translated in a stream of consciousness. Rosanna alternated between closing her eyes and pointing at a series of photographs depicting Deanna's labour.

Rosanna felt "profound relief" when her grandchild was born, knowing that Deanna was "safe". This was quickly followed by the memory of Deanna's tears:

> It was probably the first time since she was very young that I had seen her cry, so I didn't know what she looked like when she cried.... She was crying from happiness.

It was important to select memories that included Deanna's child as "I couldn't have done it any other way": holding Deanna included holding Frankie.

Rosanna described the holding moment she had selected to explore though it was not easy to recall:

> I may have felt that it was important that her *mother* held her rather than me ... as a symbolic act.... I don't think it would have mattered to her who it was ... but I may have felt that this is the moment when I'm supposed to hold her.

The labour that culminated in the birth of Frankie, as well as a rare holding moment for Rosanna, also included a significant experience that Rosanna felt was hers alone.

The story of Deanna's labour involved a kind of psychological labour for Rosanna. The birthing took more than 30 hours; Rosanna, Elaina and Lillian (two of Rosanna's other daughters) were all present to support Deanna. In the first 20 hours they had very little staff involvement as the hospital was overwhelmed with birthing mothers. Three quarters of the way through the labour, Rosanna left the birthing centre to have a rest as she felt that things were getting 'better' for Deanna:

> I lay down on the couch and ... just allowed myself to feel what I was feeling from having been with Deanna and holding her and going through this labour.
>
> And I lay there, and I let my mind and my visualisation just do what it needed to do, and it went through every trauma that I'd ever experienced, and I felt like I was experiencing it ... all at once. It felt like every trauma I'd ever had had been reactivated.
>
> I just lay there in shock for a good hour or more and my husband came in and he sat quietly there for a while and eventually I recovered enough

to go back. It was not easy going back. But I was greatly comforted by knowing that my daughters were looking after her so well and the midwife.

Rosanna recalled that:

> My first labour was so traumatic, and I guess I relived that as well, I must have. I went through 37 hours alone (except for the few hours in the delivery room), I didn't have anybody.
>
> I didn't know it was going to be *so* hard, and so *hard* for me, let alone so hard for everyone else. So, by the time I come to this here [*points to photo of Deanna holding baby Frankie*] I am already in a pretty powerful memory state, so that had to have affected the way I was feeling when I was holding her.

When Rosanna returned to the labour room, it felt as if:

> The air is thick, everything is thick, the air is *thick* ... the *feeling* is so thick, it's the only word I can find for it.... I think you must just be over-whelmed by memory, by feeling.

The layering of memories and the present moment emerged as an important theme in Rosanna's experiences of holding her daughters. She had not been held during her own traumatic experiences and watching her daughter go through such a prolonged and dramatic labour triggered Rosanna's traumatic memories.

The experience of allowing those memories to resurface and course through her body accompanied Rosanna as she returned to her daughter in the last stages of labour but rather than separate her from her daughter, they brought her closer to Deanna. Her daughter was now a mother herself. Rosanna held her as they both gazed upon Frankie and a part of that holding included Rosanna's prior experiences.

So too, Rosanna's experience of the intermingling of her children's needs with her own experiencing emerged as a significant theme in her holding experiences. As she noted:

> I've experienced that physically with all of my children, that I don't know whether you've experienced this with (your child), but that if one of them got hurt, I would actually *feel* their pain go right through my body like a shudder.

In the moment of holding Deanna, as she held her baby, Rosanna attended to many things. She was aware of her own needs and the importance of navigating those in order to be present with her daughter, and she was acutely aware of Deanna's needs as she experienced them from within their relationship.

Relational needs required attending to as Rosanna held her daughter; at once a simple brief moment in time and also so full of unspoken experiences shared body to body. This is what Rosanna felt she knew by re-engaging with the photographs and attending to her embodied memories. She then went on to make her representation of holding Deanna.

As she drew, Rosanna described how the desert, with its heat and vastness represented her experience of Deanna, her emotions are "very hot", "violent ... unrestrained" but also captured her "warmth, heat, energy". Deanna's "huge presence" was coupled with a "deep symbol of loss", the "drawing is full of empty spaces, *full* of empty spaces". She said:

> I think that what is the problem in that situation is that at some point you actually forget that you ever did [hold her daughter]. At some point it becomes very set in stone and it took a cataclysm, an emotional cataclysm to shift that.

Rosanna described how her "hands are trying to enclose or hold or comfort, and the energy (of Deanna) is *stopping* the hands from coming any closer". Deanna just "didn't invite any physical touch at all" as she was growing up. This prompted Rosanna to see in her drawing an "evolution from fertility to desert" and she wondered how she might "evolve" and "help" their relationship in the present.

*Figure 2.1* Rosanna, *Holding Deanna*, soft pastel on paper, 420x295mm.

In later sessions and correspondence between us, Rosanna felt it was integral to acknowledge "the pain, and darkness and birth" of the holding experiences she shared with Deanna. This may have prompted the selection of Deanna's labour, such an intense and extended experience of holding, for our inquiry. Part of the pain was the shock of realising she could not remember holding Deanna:

> When I look at the photos and I actually see that I'm standing next to her and I've got my arms around her and I think oh really, wow, I wonder what that felt like? I wonder what she felt? I wonder what we said to each other? There's almost nothing left. And it came as such a shock to realise that. That oh, wait a minute, I've forgotten her entire childhood, it's as if she wasn't there. I remember the family but it's as if she wasn't there. How strange. Really strange.

Holding Deanna involves an "absence of memories" of her childhood but also a depth of feeling – pain, sorrow, strangeness – around that absence. And yet Rosanna's relationship with Deanna also included a "brightness … [a] sunshine quality" displayed in the colours chosen for her representation and Rosanna felt that this was a "very good sign".

Rosanna followed her drawing with an installation:

*Figure 2.2* Rosanna, *Installation with Deanna and Frankie*, digital photograph.

This included Rosanna, Deanna and Frankie in the middle, entwined together with string. Though there was little touch and holding between Rosanna and her daughter, there was a powerful sense of 'touching' in 'the next generation down'. Like Deanna, Frankie is generally 'restrained' in her physical expressions of love, both Rosanna and Deanna consider it a "rare privilege" when they get to hold her. Those rare moments are so "precious" and "connect me to my daughter". The fire behind them captured "love ... the huge warmth of love".

Temperature played a part in Rosanna's holding of Deanna and Frankie: she experienced warmth with Frankie, but that heat ramped up to an intensity that physically repelled when trying to hold Deanna.

Rosanna considered herself "affectionate" with her other daughters but with Deanna, in response to her apparent aversion to being held, Rosanna stopped offering it. Holding changed after a crisis Deanna went through six years earlier and since that time, she allowed Rosanna to hold her and Rosanna began offering to hold as well.

Like the string, Rosanna felt that:

> The whole experience around my relationship with Deanna and the issue of holding her is completely bound up with memory.... It's not the memory of holding her, it's the absence of memory.

After we had finished our sessions working with Deanna, Rosanna shared a story:

> Last weekend Deanna rang me, asking me if I'd like to come over for a visit which I was happy to do. We made some space with Frankie being minded and it was clear that Deanna wanted to have some time alone with me, which is unusual. She talked about her stuff, and I talked about the research project and holding.
>
> "Which daughter did you start with?" she asked. "You," I said.
>
> I didn't go into much detail, but I must have said something because she spoke about the fact that she never felt like hugging me. I asked: "Do you like to hug your sisters?" "No, not much though a little more than I feel like hugging you". She said she only felt to touch her male boyfriends.
>
> It was good to be able to say it, to speak about it openly and I was able to be respectful of this reality and genuinely didn't react with any pain, just an acceptance. Whether this reality of hers is inherent or caused by child-hood experiences I don't know, I suspect it is both. When we were back at her flat and it was time to say goodbye, she came to me and hugged me. As she did this, I responded not with a returning hug that would hold her longer but the words: "I love you" which came out of me organically without a forethought.
>
> Well, I didn't think about it, it just sprang out of me, it just literally sprang out of me, as soon as she was able to do that [hug Rosanna]. So, I was *so* happy about that, so really, that was just wonderful and that was very, very special and that came out of doing this.

Rosanna had, unconsciously, been able to respond to her daughter in a way that she felt showed care for Deanna's reality and needs as well as personal authenticity – love was conveyed and holding was experienced by them but in a different way. She added:

> Well, that's partly because of having done this work [our sessions] it meant that I was in a different state … because I had acknowledged it to myself, I'd let myself feel it and deal with it and so there was a very open space … and she must have felt that, yeah.
>
> And, and since then, she's been warmer. Not huggy, but just come in and giving a kiss or something.

Making her art representations (Figures 2.1 and 2.2 above) captured qualities of Rosanna's experiencing that not only surprised, moved and challenged her, but also generated new knowing about her relationship with Deanna. Rosanna brought this knowing to the next time she had the chance to hold her daughter. She experienced deep gratitude for Deanna's hug and returned that holding with loving words.

The layering of the present moment with memories, and the intensity of the darkness where memories should be, was conveyed so exquisitely, it left me wondering about the many moments of my past that I brought to experiences of holding my son. Whether it's the tensions of an argument had a minute before, or the complete lack of memories of being held by my own mother, I know that I have brought bits of me into our holding, just as my son has brought his own experiences into our shared space. This feels neither good nor bad, it feels honest.

---

**Box 2.1 Ariel Moy, *An ISR for Rosanna's Session 1B*, poem.**

She cries, I am in shock.
Blackened memories appear,
just off the page
on the edge of the desert.
I held her … it could have been anyone.
In the thickness, her mother held her,
so very lonely,
I am windswept dunes beneath an absent sun
Her and her absence, pulsing with energy,
pushing my hands away.
Powerful, beautiful sunshine
Stops my hands from coming any closer
But I cross the space
without memories
I touch, I make memories
And connect.

Paying attention to a mother's personal memories that accompany holding, as Rosanna did during Deanna's long labour, may help us understand and develop our holding experiences not only for ourselves, but for our children. If we can find ways to attend to and explore those qualities of our experiencing we *unconsciously* bring into our relationship, for example, with creative representations and attention to embodiment, we have the chance to change our mother/child relational dynamic.

After these two sessions I gave Rosanna a poem (see Box 2.1). It was composed almost entirely of Rosanna's own words but in my shaping of it, I hoped to respond to her story and explorations. It was a way of meeting her pain and intense love on an aesthetic level.

## Elaina: transitions and psychological holding (Sessions 2A and 2B)

Their needs come first.

Rosanna's experiences of holding her eldest daughter Elaina had recently changed. Elaina had given birth to her first child, and Rosanna described that the holding now felt "freer" and "easier". Elaina's "hugging and holding needs (were now) being met" and both mother and daughter gave and received holding in new ways.

Holding Elaina had previously involved an acute experience of need. Elaina "loved to be hugged and held but in a child way so there was this unmet emotional need". Rosanna was deeply aware of her "responsibility" toward Elaina and all of her daughters.

Rosanna had always valued delicacy and tact when identifying and navigating Elaina's needs. However, she was also clear about how giving Elaina was in their relationship as well as with her other sisters, she possessed "great compassion" for her mother.

Stories of reciprocity in needs navigation with Elaina led Rosanna into making her installation about what it was like to hold her now (see below).

As with Deanna, it felt significant to Rosanna that holding Elaina *included* holding Elaina's child and further, holding her other daughters, their partners and their children. As Rosanna said: "holding one is holding all". This was represented by the warmth and light of the candle at the heart of the installation. Though holding each daughter was particular, qualities of holding across all children implicitly recognised their deep familial connection.

Rosanna conveyed how the physical holding of one daughter expanded into psychological and emotional holding of many. This kind of holding was supported by the use of technology as evidenced by the mobile phone in the installation. Text messages and photos about present moments and feelings could be sent and received in real time. Psychological holding of the family as a whole was not simply a sensation or conceptualisation experienced within Rosanna, but an action she was able to share with the family.

*Figure 2.3* Rosanna, *Session 2A Installation*, digital photograph.

The open Babushka doll bases represented Rosanna's holding experiences over time with Elaina: "When I hold her, I'm holding the past, not just the present". The present moment expanded to include Rosanna's past relationship with Elaina; there was always a recognition of what had been, along with what is now.

The present moment also included Rosanna's memories of other relationships. Awareness of the way Elaina "receives the hold without any … barrier" brought to mind Rosanna's experiences with her own mother. She recognised that holding could be "very boundary dissolving" and that as such, she had never wished to be held by her mother. This was not a resistance to physical affection but rather an understanding, from a young age, that her mother's boundaries were fraught. She said that our inquiry into maternal holding:

> Has clarified for me … that decisions that I've made about how to negotiate the relationship with my mother have in fact … are correct. I knew they were correct, but I didn't know why…. But now it's become much clearer.

I was particularly interested in the relationship between Rosanna's experience of boundaries with her mother and her daughter. It was not surprising to find that what Rosanna had experienced as a child in terms of holding was relevant to how she held her daughters. Rosanna's adverse experience as a child had contributed to her acute sensitivity to the power inherent in the mother/child relationship but she had not repeated that relational style. Unlike her mother, Rosanna treated boundaries with Elaina as tenderly and respectfully as she could, she did not attempt to dissolve or dominate personal boundaries, but rather approached them with care and as much awareness as possible.

This resonated strongly with me and how I held my son. Past attachment patterns had emerged as I held him over the years. I was aware of these patterns and continued to work therapeutically (as Rosanna had) to attend to these as much as possible outside of our mother/son relationship and the moment of holding. I understood that I brought myself and my memories (implicit and explicit) to my experiences of holding my son but, like Rosanna, I also found that holding my child and *his* experiences fed back into my relational styles and understanding.

What Rosanna felt when looking at her installation was a strong sense of how "the relationship (with Elaina) will develop ... adapt ... become fuller" because of changes in needs that Elaina and Rosanna both had experienced. By treating Elaina's needs with care, by taking responsibility for her own power and boundaries, by recognising the presence of the past both shared and her own, and by attending to the ways in which holding her grandchild contributed to holding her daughter and the family entire, Rosanna relayed a strong sense of what holding felt like overall:

> The entirety of the holding. The entirety of ... it's love, really, that's what holds you, that's what binds you and ... that's what the holding is.

As with Deanna, we followed the first session a few weeks later with a second session, allowing time for our work and understandings to simmer. After the briefest of discussions Rosanna launched into a drawing (see below).

Once finished, Rosanna described how this represented a "story I suddenly saw ... [I] condensed [the] story down to just holding". The story spoke to a larger narrative of her relationship with Elaina from infancy through to Elaina's own new stage of motherhood.

Rosanna had tried so hard to meet her daughter's perceived needs as a child and adolescent, but she felt she never quite navigated them successfully, not until Elaina had her own child. These attempts were accompanied with guilt. Then, with the birth of Elaina's baby, feelings of 'emptiness' transformed into 'fullness' for Rosanna. While she initially ascribed these states of being to Elaina, they ultimately described the changes she felt within their *relationship*.

These relational changes resulted in Rosanna's sense that she did not "have to hold her the same now". With Elaina's perceived needs for affection from her mother diminishing now that she had a child, Rosanna felt that she could hold Elaina while also being "free to hold another" – to hold her grandchild, her other daughters and *herself*.

The "bubble" of their holding experiences and relationship "expanded to include others". The fullness noted in Elaina's experience was now also explicitly a part of Rosanna's experience; *she* felt "fuller" within a now expanded,

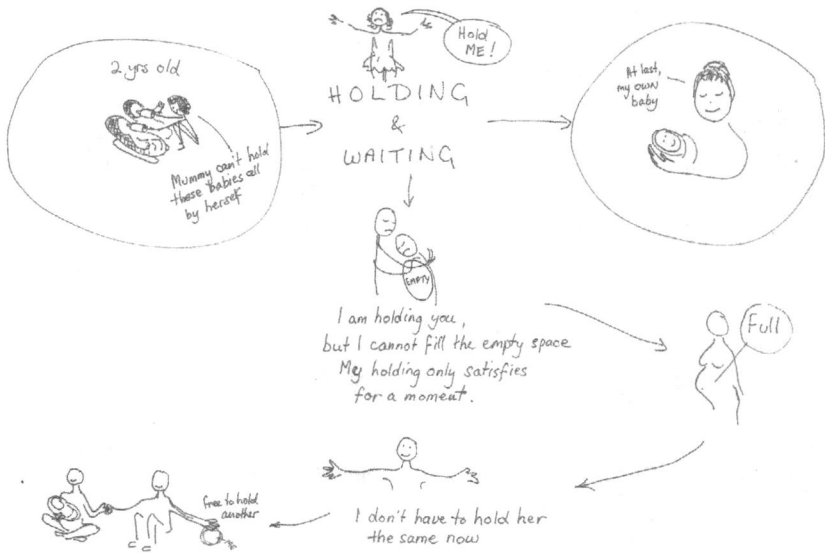

*Figure 2.4* Rosanna, *Representation 2B*, pen on paper, 420x295mm.

"global bubble" of "us". With transitions around needs in one member of the mother/child relationship came changes within the other.

## Olivia and Lillian: uncomplicated holding and stories of us (Sessions 3A and 3B)

> And that's something that's very distinctive ... in the hold, they're open and relaxed but ... not needy.

Exploring what it's like to hold her twins, Rosanna launched into making a representation. She told stories about her daughters as she drew; relaying the textures and timelines of her relationship with each daughter (see Figure 2.5).

She asked if I might "draw too" and so as we talked, I also made a representation (see Figure 2.6).

A feeling for difference and sameness arose, she noted: "You can really only get meaning ... define anything, by its difference" and a powerful sense of who Olivia and Lillian were individually was thematic in our inquiry.

Rosanna experienced the twins as a little different from one another, but as a pair, she experienced a "huge difference" between the twins and what it felt like to hold her other daughters. Rosanna explained this difference in how "holding has always been so much easier" with the twins, holding felt "safer" with them and "uncomplicated".

*Figure 2.5* Rosanna, *First Representation for Session 3A*, soft pastel on paper, 420x295mm.

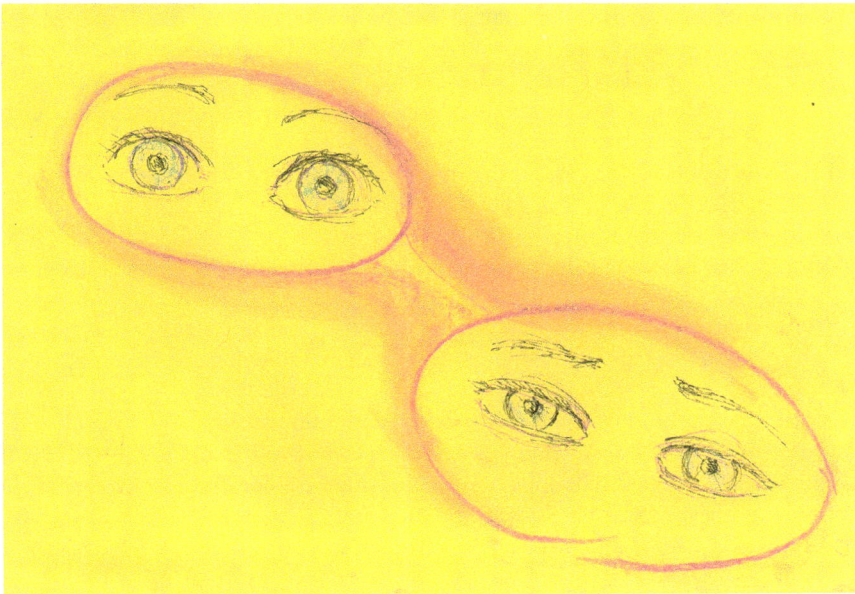

*Figure 2.6* Rosanna, *Second Representation for Session 3A*, soft pastel on paper, 420x295mm.

Physically, the twins resembled Rosanna more than her husband whereas Elaina and Deanna were more like him. Her experiences of their personalities also reflected similarities with her husband – Elaina and Deanna were more "practical" but "their emotional nature is much more volatile and out there".

The stories Rosanna told as she made her representation conveyed shared experiences with her twins. They revealed qualities in common, qualities Rosanna felt she could understand and engage with more easily because of their familiarity.

As her pastels curved along the paper, Rosanna told a story of her relationship with Lillian and a period in Lillian's adulthood that contributed to Rosanna's experiences of holding her:

> Lillian had … a huge problem that she needed to heal from, and I took responsibility … for my part in the problem … and so I said to her: 'I will be here for you any time, day or night, for as long as you need' and she took me at my word.

Both mother and daughter had attended a therapeutic organisation, Rosanna for a brief amount of time, Lillian for longer. Having undertaken her own therapy years prior Rosanna felt she had developed an understanding of what her daughter's therapeutic experiences might be like. She was able to offer Lillian ongoing and specific support.

Over a period of two years, at all hours of the day and night, Rosanna was available for Lillian to come to her, to express her emotions and be held. These shared moments and approaches to psychological healing led to "really deepest holding, holding at the deepest level" and created a profound "bond" between them.

In turn, Rosanna felt able to share some of her own experiences as Lillian understood the "therapy process" and so didn't feel "responsible" or like "she had to fix it or that I was burdening her". This was very important to Rosanna. As with her other daughters, she remained very clear about boundaries and "not wanting my needs met" by her daughters.

With Olivia, Rosanna provided more recent stories as she felt that her daughter:

> Was always more closed, more closed off than Lillian … really the relationship with Olivia and the holding experience has been relatively recent.

As with Elaina, holding and the mother/daughter relationship had changed with the birth of Olivia's child. Rosanna now noticed that Olivia would call her and reach out, talking about her relationship and her child in ways that she had not done previously. Rosanna felt "useful" and a "resource" to her daughter now. She did however note that a few years earlier:

> I was beginning to really actively reconnect with Olivia, and wanting to hold her, and wanting to give her hugs, and she responded completely happily to that, you know, *she* was happy to reconnect with me and … hug me.

Despite her previous distance in her teens and early adulthood, when Rosanna moved toward Olivia, "crossing the space" as she had done with Deanna, she found that Olivia welcomed her holding.

The ease and flow with which Rosanna drew the twins matched her strong sense of how much easier holding them was. This had to do with safety and familiarity. The twins, like her, are:

> People who don't hurt others, or certainly don't want to. They will always tend to withdraw rather than attack and … doing this project, and thinking about the holding, really focused my attention on *how different* the holding is with both of the twins [as opposed to Deanna and Elaina] because it's *safe* for me because they won't attack me.
>
> And that's, you know, being purely self-serving, self-protective, but that's the reality … because your children *can* hurt you, yeah.

Rosanna resonated with the twins' more "internal" artistic natures and the ways in which she felt they were "delicate". The familiarity Rosanna experienced also manifested in embodied qualities of holding and further, "being held by *them*", particularly as adults:

> It's the *way* they … come into the hold; it's the way they stay in the hold; it's the way their arms come around, they're both taller than me so if we're standing … they have to actually lean down slightly and there's a sort of a not a mothering but a *daughtering*, in the way they do it … it's very loving … but not in a needy way.

The element of need was an important factor in this holding, as it had been with Elaina: the ease with which Rosanna held the twins had to do with both her feeling that she did not impose her own needs on them but also, she did not experience problematic needs directed at her. It was not that the twins didn't have needs, it was that whatever needs they had pertaining to Rosanna were met enough; she did not feel any pain, complexity or difficulty.

This familiarity, ease and lack of need brought Rosanna into a strong experience of the present moment when she held the twins.

But Rosanna's representation did not capture her twins accurately enough. It was important to her to show their unique personalities explaining that "something about this one (her drawing) isn't right". She made a second representation (see below).

Selecting sharper ink pens, Rosanna carefully represented her daughter's eyes (Lillian on the left, Olivia on the right) as she talked about how she experienced them. Each one "looked at the world" differently. Lillian approached everything with wonder, she was the subject of many funny stories in the family consisting of strange coincidences, she was captured by her "wide open eyes". Olivia on the other hand was represented with "half-closed eyes". Rosanna sensed a wariness and a desire to step back and observe in her.

Though holding Olivia was a more recent experience, Rosanna felt:

> In fact, in my heart, I'm incredibly close to Olivia.... I think the thing about Olivia is that there's a part of me that *knows* her, she's ... of all my children, she's most like me.

Rosanna conveyed that a large part of holding her twins was her experience of their personalities; the ongoing, essential qualities that described how she saw them engage with the world and with her. This experiencing drew her into the present moment. Conversely, with Elaina, a lot of the earlier holding had to with "past baggage (more than) the present or ... her personality", holding had, as with Deanna, triggered much of their past experiencing.

The dance around need continued as we explored this second representation. Describing the changes in holding Olivia now that she'd had a child, Rosanna felt that "she needed me, probably for the first time in her adult life" and yet this need was not experienced negatively, it did not tug on their relationship or engender guilt in Rosanna as it had done with Elaina. Rather, it was deeply satisfying because the needs that Olivia conveyed were needs Rosanna did not feel burdened by, they were needs for mothering she felt able to meet with and for Olivia.

In our second session, Rosanna described how the twins:

> Both hug me the same, and feel the same, and yet my sense of holding does have a difference which is based on a different shared history.

Shared history shaped Rosanna's holding experiences with all of her daughters. It was important for her to access those shared stories in order to explore and express what holding was like for her.

Curious about the image I had drawn in our previous session (Figure 2.7) while she made her first representation, Rosanna asked me about it. I explained that from her words and the images she made, I felt that holding her twin daughters brought with it a lightness and "ease" to the relationship because of how familiar Rosanna found the twins. She noted, in keeping with the flowers she saw in my representation: "the main thing is, they wouldn't have any thorns". In their shared history, her twins "didn't hurt me".

In these sessions it was clear that Rosanna's understanding of each daughter's personality, or the way she psychologically experienced each daughter, was an important contribution to holding. What Rosanna knew of her daughters was the result of the interactions between herself and them over time and in the present moment. Her stories of their personalities and shared mother/child history spoke of a less complicated holding and familiarity that Rosanna cherished.

After these sessions, I wondered about Rosanna's experiences of her children's personality during holding. I understood how a child that appeared familiar or similar to the mother, might contribute to experiences of holding that felt freer and easier. Feeling that we understand a child's needs or concerns

*Figure 2.7* Ariel Moy, *An ISR for Rosanna for Session 3A*, soft pastel on paper, 420x295mm.

in the moment might result in holding that feels more fitting for the child, and thus more satisfying for both. But something niggled at me.

What Rosanna, and I knew of our children was deeply relational. We only knew them from within our relationship, from the perspective of that relationship. Someone else would know them differently, from within their relationship. Rosanna's use of the words: 'familiarity' and 'daughtering' intrigued me; there was something reciprocal and dynamic that existed within any definitions of the child in relationship with the mother. Soo too, if the child was to describe their mother, they could only describe her from the perspective of their relationship with her. I did not explore this further at the time, but a curiosity around the relational qualities of 'personality' descriptions would arise again when working with Leni and Kitty.

## Holding one is holding all (Session 4)

In our last two sessions we explicitly explored what holding experiences Rosanna might find in common across all of her daughters. She brought a photo of each daughter to the session and built her representation around these. She explained that each photograph was taken by herself and her husband but also processed by them in their own dark room as the children were growing up. These photos were tangible but also psychological reconstructions of significant memories (both discrete and amalgamations); they were the family's "precious record" of their children (see below).

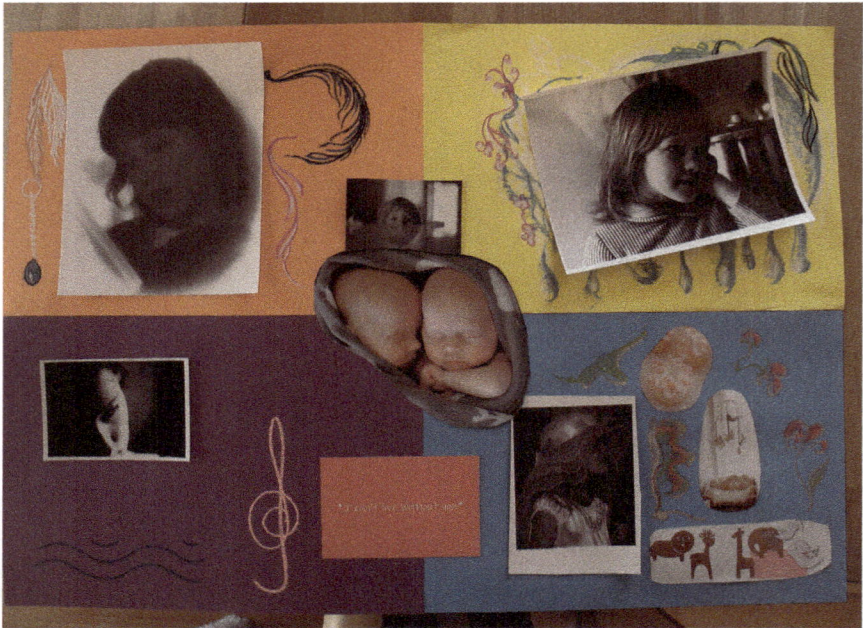

*Figure 2.8* Rosanna, *Representation 4A*, mixed media collage and pastel on paper, 590x420mm.

Throughout our inquiry Rosanna had communicated her holding experiences in the form of stories: stories that conveyed the experiences she shared with her daughters as well as her understanding of each daughter – how they moved in the world and the emotional and psychological qualities she experienced in relationship with them. Holding her children always extended beyond physical holding to include emotional and psychological holding. Sometimes stories of holding did not include shared physical holding at all. As Rosanna explained, we needed to:

> Take into account the nationality of the person. I'm very English … (and) also life experience – dissociation, disconnection from the body. I chose to enter into the project … the experience (of inquiring into maternal holding) in the modality that interested me the most – the psychological.

This allowing space for exploration of the area of holding that interested Rosanna the most reflected our mutual value of going with what held curiosity and energy for the inquirer. We did not shy away from asking about the embodied qualities of holding and Rosanna did explore these but her experience was most felt in the emotional and psychological domain.

The stories that arose in these last sessions involved more than one daughter and at times the whole family. Stories were vehicles for expression as we reconstructed memories but also appeared to be active elements during holding – Rosanna's holding in the moment included her memories and her stories of each child; these stories (how she understood her daughters, how she understood the events of their relationship) informed her holding.

Rosanna recognised and was grateful for the ways that her mother/child stories *evolved* as her children (and she) matured and had children of their own. Each mother/daughter "bubble" continued to expand to include others as well as feelings of simplicity, safety and freedom.

When she had finished making the collage, Rosanna noticed that: "all of the pictures that I chose are pensive". Each daughter had her "concerns" and Rosanna described these with her stories. It was important that their concerns were shown, as awareness of these was embedded in Rosanna's holding experiences.

What emerged as a surprise in this session was the strength of Rosanna's *own* need, shown by the red postcard in the middle bottom of the representation with the words: "I can't live without you".

When I first broached the appearance of the postcard Rosanna responded: "Well, that's just me" and then moved on to more stories about her daughters and the holding of the extended family as they arose in response to her representation. It wasn't until our final session that we explored what it meant to acknowledge the involvement of her own needs during holding.

Rosanna noted that when she selected the postcard, she "wasn't specifically looking for something to represent me, just sifting through postcards". That was precisely the reason we worked with postcards – to see what imagery grabbed us unawares. When I inquired as to what she felt the postcard might say about holding, she explained that she realised the postcard was:

> Actually, about me … like a red light! Oops, I let myself come in there. My daughters would throw their hands up and say: "Of course you have a role!" [and yet] My reaction there (was), I suddenly thought "really, I shouldn't be there", I slipped in there, just a little bit of me.

I reminded her that the inquiry was about her experience of holding to which she responded that, for her, it felt normal that a mother would "tell about the children, not herself".

I wondered if this telling was about a mother's "knowing" of her children, as this knowing had arisen in all of our sessions – a knowing about who she felt her children were and had been as well as the history they had shared, to which she agreed: "I think definitely".

Looking at the postcard, Rosanna felt that: "I shouldn't have put my own needs there".

> ARIEL: Yet children aren't robots, even if your needs aren't explicit, your experience will be sensed by your children, if you're not wanting to be there, if you're enjoying it, if you're preoccupied …
>
> ROSANNA: I imagine it is developed in children as part of their survival, an awareness of their mother's needs … that's part of loving.

Need had been such a significant presence in Rosanna's holding experiences, but the need had always been considered from the point of view of her identifying, navigating and attending to her children's needs. She was acutely aware of the "huge power" she had in the mother/child relationship.

In this, our last session, Rosanna's own needs emerged as integral to her holding experiences. She did not wish to "burden" her children with her needs, but the need to have them in her life, the need to attend to *their* needs, the need to hold them be it physically, emotionally and/or psychologically for them, but also for herself, was ever present.

Rosanna 'held' herself so that she could hold Elaina and her new grandson. Rosanna understood that her 'role', her feelings and needs, her *presence*, were a natural part of the holding experience for both herself and her daughters. Holding was a relational experience, but there were ways of holding herself, and meeting some of her needs when mother and child were apart that she felt were necessary in order to unburden their relationship when they were together.

Another intriguing quality of holding, perhaps contributed to by having four adult daughters, was a sense of 'flow' during intimacy. This flow manifested as an understanding that holding one daughter or granddaughter could expand to a feeling of holding the rest of her daughters and their families as well. This was explored in depth in our work with her eldest, Elaina, but did appear as important across all of her relationships with her children.

The flow experienced during emotional and psychological holding was supported by technology, images of which were explicitly included in her representation of holding Elaina but related to all of her daughters. Rosanna explained:

> And … I was aware of that experience … [that] holding is this … this group text thing … with Elaina (and everyone else in the immediate family). There are … plenty of [text messages], she [Elaina] sends photos, and she sends little video clips every day. Which is lovely, I mean how many kids do that?
>
> We had one of them [group messages] going in the morning, and at night you know and then all the ones in the middle! And the funny thing is that those texts come through on [her husband's] iPad, [his] iPhone, my computer, my iPhone and my iPad so when one comes in it goes "ding, brrr, dee!" all around the room as they all come in!

The joy accompanying the messaging was important, but even more so was the feeling of involvement in her daughters' and grandchildren's lives. She was able to respond in audio, text and video, in real time and within seconds of new events occurring. The ongoing and regular dialogue shared between family members allowed Rosanna to experience different kinds of holding. When she did see her daughters (many of whom now live interstate) there was a continuity of intimate contact that mashed up technological, emotional, psychological and physical holding.

This flow also included a sense of expansion across time – the ways in which Rosanna experienced holding her daughters involved those stories of what holding was like for each mother/daughter dyad in the past. Holding her children now included holding them then. I understood this feeling: holding my son (aged seven at the end of our sessions) often touched on moments of holding from his infancy, from his toddler years or from the day before. Time spread out on an equal plane during optimal moments of holding. I wondered what it would be like to hold my son when he was an adult, how many more memories and stories we might have shared and how these would shape our holding.

Rosanna's words "holding one is holding all" summed up significant qualities of her holding experiences: holding in the present moment included holding stories of the past; holding one daughter or grandchild could include holding others, and holding her daughters could include holding herself and being held, as she termed it, a kind of "daughtering".

## After our sessions

After working with Rosanna's data to come to patterns/qualities of maternal holding, receiving feedback and making changes to the findings, I gave Rosanna my final themes (included at the end of this chapter) and a visual response (Figure 2.9). I hoped that it captured some of the interconnected and expanding bubbles of each mother/child relationship I had sensed were of so much value in her holding (see below).

Rosanna later responded with an image and words (see Figure 2.10 and Box 2.2).

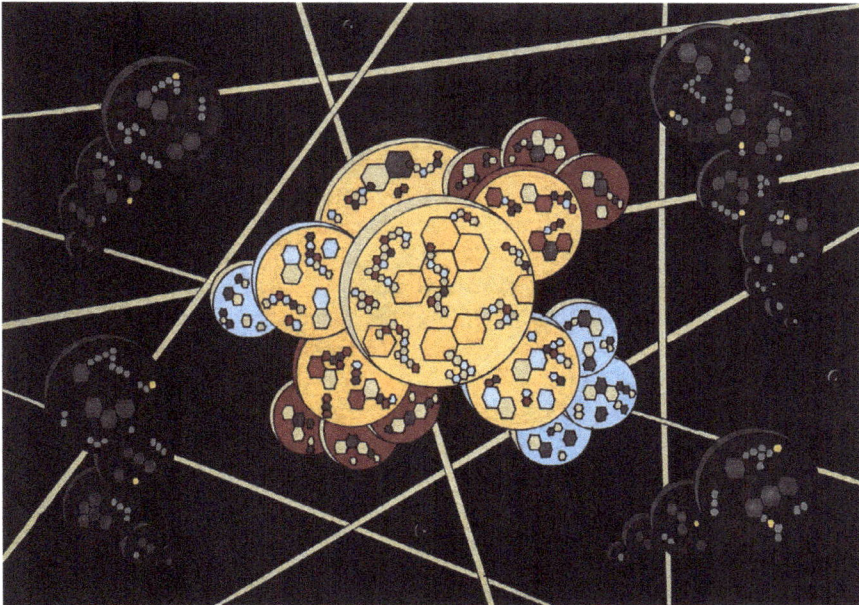

*Figure 2.9* Ariel Moy, *An ISR for Rosanna (after our sessions were complete)*, felt tip pen on paper, 295x210mm.

*Figure 2.10* Rosanna, *Representation Post-Sessions*, felt tip pen on paper, 420x295mm.

**Box 2.2 Rosanna's written response to her representation post-sessions**

I am a Babushka doll. I gave birth to four daughters, one inside the other, down to the smallest. A woman came to me and asked, what is it like to hold your children? I said, I brought them out from where they were stacked inside me, and I lined them up, in a row. I made a picture for each one of them, to tell them how I felt. And I tried to tell them in words, some hearing, some not.

But tell me, said the woman, how do *you* feel about holding them? I feel pain and sorrow through the love, because without them I would not be a Babushka doll, just a plastic doll with thin legs. They are my desert, my wasteland, my salvation and my fire.

The woman wrote it down again – but how do you *feel* when you hold them? So I drew her a picture, because the feeling was transparent, it would not allow itself to be grasped. The picture said what I knew, what I had known for ever so long but would not let myself say.

The Babushka doll is a covering, an outer shell that prevents anyone touching what is inside. I cannot say how I feel about holding my children, because I cannot feel it. I can know it, but not feel it. I can feel love, and I feel it and see it flow out from the covering, like life-giving tendrils that release fertile pollen into the air. This is my touch, but I do not feel it. I can see it inside me, but once it leaves my body, it is no longer mine, it is theirs.

The Babushka doll in my picture has only one hand, and an empty sleeve. The hand holds her tummy, where the children were, the empty sleeve is both concave and convex, it gives and it takes. She has no face, because she isn't really there. Everything she gives will feed her children's children. And then she will be gone.

\* \* \* \* \* \* \*

My littlest babushka doll that came from inside me – went away, and then she came back. She was pushing out her own little doll, and there was no-one else to help her. This was the moment when all the holding that had never happened, happened. And this time I was there. I held her hands, her body, her gaze and her fear, and we held on without breaking for six hours, with no more than thirty seconds between contractions. Fifteen second micro-sleeps, and then we held each other again.

The real holding of love, the real touching of love, these are not romantic, or sentimental. These are primitive, survival-based, practical, and born of necessity. These are tough, determined, and willing to die.

This is nature at its most basic and animalistic, and yet most sublime. Herein is humankind's eternal conflict.

What struck me most was the power of Rosanna's holding experiences; her love flowed from her like lifeblood to her Babushka dolls. Rosanna's holding *is* love for her, she can passionately convey this love in words and imagery, she can "see" and "know" it but "cannot feel" it.

Rosanna's body is a "shell that prevents anyone touching what is inside" and also prevents her from feeling touch in return. This speaks to her childhood experiences as well as qualities of dissociation (mentioned in Sessions 1A, 2B and Session 4B). Nevertheless, she holds within "life-giving tendrils" of love that unfurl and are given to her daughters.

Once the mother has given all she can, she will be "gone". Yet the "hand [that] holds her tummy, where the children were ... gives and it takes". In receiving, Rosanna is concretely present. There is no explicit elaboration on what she takes from holding, but she does describe her daughters as "my desert, my wasteland, my salvation and my fire". Rosanna's fertility, given to her daughters, is returned to her in the form of "salvation and fire" – life-giving properties.

Further, a Babushka doll is defined by the space she has made for smaller dolls within, even when those dolls are out in the world: "without them, I would not be a Babushka doll, just a plastic doll with thin legs". Babushka dolls make sense only in relationship with other real or potential Babushka dolls.

Holding, as a manifestation of love for Rosanna, is described as "survival-based" and this suggests, along with "salvation" that survival is relevant to both mother and child, holding is deeply relational.

I wonder if the love that is given to her daughters is not her daughter's alone, but belongs to the mother/child relationship, to the original *set* of Babushka dolls however far away they may be from one another, this would make sense with Rosanna's sense that "holding one is holding all".

As portrayed in her drawings and words over our sessions, if the *feeling* of holding and love are difficult to articulate, the significance and necessity of it for her children as well as herself was not. An inability to articulate the feeling of maternal holding and love did not mean it was absent; Rosanna showed us the shape of feeling in what she sees and knows. For Rosanna, holding is love, and love is a fire that will not "allow itself to be grasped"; though we cannot hold it, we nevertheless feel its effects.

## Rosanna's themes around maternal holding

Below, I provide a distillation of findings for Rosanna. I have selected two ways of representing these findings (both described in Chapter 1). Themes are a succinct statement describing a pattern of being for the participant during holding. A depiction takes this statement and expands it to invite the reader into the participant's experience. In depictions I deliberately include many of the words and images the participant used; those words and images that comprised the data for the inquiry.

**Theme 1: Holding is sometimes bound up with memory and pain** (Deanna only)

Depiction: My past exists in the present. Holding you can cause such pain though you do not bring that pain. The pain is mine: unspoken and unknown to you. When you gave birth to our first grandchild I remembered – there had been no one to hold me. The air was thick with my past. My own experiences of being held and not held are sometimes bound up with holding you now. A dessert burns under an empty sun. There is warmth in holding you – the emptiness comes from my memories and lack of memories, from my own darkness and pain.

**Theme 2** (with separate sub-themes for each daughter): **Holding you then is a part of holding you now**

Depiction: We created photos that captured our memories of times shared together – of who you were, who we were and who we are now. These precious memories are a part of holding each of you – recalling our relationship in the past, building our relationships in the present and understanding who each of you are now.

Depictions and sub-themes for each daughter:

**Theme 2.1: Deanna, you are a brilliant sun and I have learned how to hold you tenderly**

Depiction: You are a sun – hot, powerful, full of light. You are both masculine and feminine. I do not remember holding you as a child and that fills me with pain, there is an emptiness in our past. You did not want to be held and I did not cross the space, you had the power to burn me. But now I have found how to hold you in the right way – tender, comforting. With the birth of your first child and our first grandchild we are connected again – a rebirth into the warmth of love we share as adults, as mother and daughter.

**Theme 2.2: Elaina, I could not fill the empty spaces inside of you though our loved flowed freely. Now you have had your own child, you are full. As the bubble of us expands, holding you encompasses more than the two of us**

Depiction: When you were younger, I could not fill the empty spaces inside of you. You wanted so much to give and receive love. There is pain in our past, memories seared into me – I was not enough for you then. Now you have your own child and you are finally full. Your warmth and softness shine from within. We are free to hold one another and ourselves. You have let me know that I gave you both roots and wings. Now our love is encompassing – the bubble of us has expanded.

**Theme 2.3: Lillian, you are delicate but assured. You never broke our connection and we share a deepest holding**

Depiction: We share a history as adults and our holding is deeper for it. You never broke our connection. Between us, there are no games. You are delicate but assured. Holding you is simpler, easier than holding your sisters.

**Theme 2.4: Olivia, I know you deeply as we are most alike, holding you is familiar. And you hold me too, your endearing and fascinating mother**

Depiction: You are most like me, I know you deeply. You withdrew when you were younger, kept your pain within but as you mature, our relationship matures. Now that you have a child you see me differently, there is a different reason for our relationship. Holding you is familiar; you hold me too. I am endearing and a bit fascinating to you. You chose of your own accord to reconnect with the good parts of your childhood, like your sister you are delicate but also assured.

**Theme 3: The huge warmth of love – holding one is holding all**

Depiction: Holding each one of you is to know you and us but now it expands as energy flows from holding one to holding all. I do not hold just you, but also your relationships – your partner, your partner's family, your children. Our love is fuller and encompassing now, as huge as the universe, *it fills my universe*, the huge warmth of love.

**Theme 4: The emotion that goes with holding my daughters is the most important part of holding for me, not the physical aspect of holding them**

Depiction: The emotion that goes with holding my daughters is the most important part to me, not the physical holding. The psychological and emotional qualities of holding are what interest me most. Traumatic life experiences have also led me to feel that perhaps I hold something back in a bodily sense when I hold my children. I know I can hold my daughters emotionally.

**Theme 5: As the story of us changes how I hold you shifts and adapts**
Depiction: You are adults now and you have experienced different relationships, hardships, joys and the birth of your own children. You see me and us in
a different way. How I hold you adapts, the story of us changes, the bubble of
us expands.

**Theme 6: As your mother I am aware of the huge power I have in
our relationship. I make sure I do not burden you with my needs: your
needs come first. But you do know that I cannot live without you and
knowing I need you is a part of loving**
Depiction: As your mother I am aware of the huge power I have and *have had*
in our relationship. I do not wish to burden you with my needs; your needs
come first. So, I make sure there are appropriate boundaries in place. How I
hold you adapts to your changing needs – as you get older and find a partner,
I have to let you go, your partner now holds you. But I can't live without
you, that's a little bit of me that slips in to Us. Part of loving is awareness of
the other and so, though I don't put my needs first with us, you are aware of
them.

**Theme 7: I am full of empty spaces; I do not remember holding you
as a child. There is darkness and pain. Now, I build memories of
holding you in the right way – the way you wish to be held** (about
Deanna only)
Depiction: I am full of empty spaces. Memories of you growing up, of me holding
you, are absent. I remember not holding you. There is darkness and pain. But now
that you have had your own child, we have changed. I remember to cross the
space and connect with you: I build memories of holding you again, in the right
way, the way you wish to be held, when you want to be held.
Note: Rosanna indicated that this theme/depiction was only relevant to her
daughter Deanna.

**Theme 8: Part of holding you is being held by you – a kind of
daughtering**
Depiction: Part of holding you is *being held* by you – a kind of daughtering.
There is equality and real love in this type of holding. It is familiar to me as I
have always been the one to hold you, the one to Mother and now sometimes
you hold me, each of you in your own way.
Note: This was mainly relevant to daughters Elaina and Olivia, as Rosanna
wrote "very true of Elaina and Olivia, Deanna less so because she is using all
her energy to survive and not for Lillian at this stage because she needs to
'separate from mum'".

**Theme 9: I am grateful for the kind of holding that feels easier,
simpler, safer and free**
Depiction: I am grateful for the kind of holding that feels easy, simple and safe.
It makes me feel free when I hold you: free from guilt, free from attack. I feel
free to hold myself and others. With this kind of holding, I feel 'in the
moment'.

# 3 Just us

## Leni, Lucy and Alexander

### Leni, Lucy and Alexander

Leni and I met when we both were undergoing treatment for post-natal depression (PND). She had been admitted to a mother/baby unit with her youngest child, Alexander who was six months old at the time. When we commenced our sessions, Lucy was nine and Alexander was six years old.

We worked together over four longer sessions at Leni's request. Unlike Rosanna and Kitty, our sessions (until our final one) did not include explicit procedures to reduce data to come to meaning though we often found that a sense of understanding would emerge within session from representation making and exploration. It felt particularly important with Leni to allow for her words and imagery to speak for themselves and for the process of inquiry to follow her lead (this will be explored in more detail later in this chapter).

As our sessions progressed, Leni's understanding of how she held her children evolved from conceptualisations of responsibility and compartmentalisation of emotion and needs, to the many ways in which holding brought her a vital and unique sense of connection and love.

### Alexander: tick my boxes and a running commentary (Session 1)

> I remember holding him a lot, I was always trying to put him down, *always* trying to put him down into his rocker or onto the couch or in his bed or in his pram. I was always trying to free my hands up, because I had stuff to do, that was a big mitigating factor: I'd lots of things to do and if I held him ... which ultimately when I say I'd love to go back and have it all over again without the PND, I'd love to just be able to sit on the couch and relax and hold him.

Leni began with an inquiry into holding her son as an infant. She felt 'conflicted' about this period of time with him as she did not want to "paint (her) son in a negative light".

As with all participants, it was important to find a way to ease into the inquiry. For our first session together, both Leni and I held heat packs, found a space in the room to move and closed our eyes. The intention was to allow space for embodied experiencing to emerge. Leni immediately cradled her heatpack.

DOI: 10.4324/9781003104094-4

When we were finished, she noted that it was "just like you're holding a little baby, you stand there swaying ... that's bizarre, it happened so quickly".

Leni was silent as she constructed her first representation but once she felt it was done began telling me the stories shown within it (see below, note that there are two coloured lines in the upper right-hand side that were added later).

Leni explained that "it's always been in my head and I've probably never verbalised it to anybody ... I'm getting all teary ... [the hedge image showed] ... all my little compartments, my life, holding Alexander". The 'boxes' showed how she 'compartmentalised' her feelings, thoughts and tasks. She felt that both her PND but also her responses to her children as infants were shaped by her desire to "tick my boxes".

Removing the small cut-out pictures placed behind the hedgerow (see below), Leni described how the term 'hate' reflected her deep dislike of the feelings and thoughts she experienced during her PND. Of the two clowns and 'faker' images she said:

> I picked it because it had that really evil face on it and I thought "well, that was me", because I didn't want this little boy here, he was in the way, but then when I saw that [points to confused clown] I do remember feeling really confused as well about it all.

There were layers of experiencing that arose into awareness as she selected her imagery. Leni hadn't realised until now that:

*Figure 3.1* Leni, *Representation 1A*, Collage and pastel on paper, 420x295mm.

I was trying to show people, myself, that stuff wasn't right, and they were *laughing* at me, they thought I was being 'one of *those* mothers', no one took me seriously, I never did the right thing … there was fakery and the PND wasn't real, there wasn't really anything wrong.

Leni felt like a performer, a source of amusement and also a source of 'evil' reminiscent of literary bad clowns like Stephen King's Pennywise in *It*.

Leni had described how she was not an emotionally demonstrative person, other than with her children or partner. Making and exploring these images brought up intense feelings for her but she wanted to continue on with the inquiry.

During both of her children's infancy, Leni was aware of "how it [mothering] looks" to others. She had a "running commentary, running narrative" when she held her children (both then and now) that included how others might judge her. At the time of the PND she felt that she was "ruled by what other people think" and that contributed to her experiences of feeling fake (see Figure 3.3).

Fakery and multiple internal narratives were thematic throughout our sessions. Leni would at first describe how she felt or thought but then, looking at her representations, she would note that her initial descriptions were those *provided* for her, repeatedly, over years, by those who were close to her. She would then interrogate what *she* felt and thought about her relationships with her children, her sense of self and what it was like to hold them. Often these narratives and conceptualisations were quite different.

Figure 3.2 Leni, *Representation 1A Modified*, collage and pastel on paper, 420x295mm.

*Figure 3.3* Leni, *Representation 1A Close-Up of Images Removed from Hedges*, collage on paper, 110x80mm.

What Leni had at first described as hatred towards Alexander and herself when he was an infant, was actually not directed toward them, it was directed towards her chaotic environment. Her ex-husband defined her PND to her thus:

> *He* thought I hated Alexander … [I now] realise I didn't hate him, it was his behaviour … it wasn't even his behaviour, it was the uncontrollable, everything else going on *around* him.

Leni relocated her feelings of hatred to the uncontained nature of mothering during early infancy.

Holding her son while feeling "evil" and "fake", while everything felt "uncontrollable", that she didn't "deserve" the PND (her mother and ex-husbands opinions) and that she should "pull her socks up" meant there was little pleasure or respite to be found in those early holding moments.

Leni also believed that at around six or seven months she would "connect" with Alexander, as she had done with Lucy. Until that point, Leni felt as if she was "babysitting".

When we dove deeper into what the embodied feeling of holding Alexander at these times was like, Leni said:

Yeah, I don't want to, I can feel it, it's just a horrible, my stomach sinks, just goes through the floor. It's almost like a buzz … a horrible feeling.

At this point I decided to express a curiosity I had been feeling for a while. I suggested we imagine that the blue pastel I held was Leni and the "shitty brown" (as she'd described her choice of paper) pastel represented all of the other voices (her mother, ex-husband, former close friend).

ARIEL: … It's been pretty damaging.
LENI: Uh huh.
ARIEL: So, the people you love most in the world, i.e. your children, when they're at their …
LENI: I know where you're going!
ARIEL: Do you know where I'm going?
LENI: Yes!
ARIEL: You can't damage them.
LENI: I can't damage them!
ARIEL: The way you were damaged.
LENI: Oooh … Ariel that's a bit deep! We remained quiet for a little while.
ARIEL: I'm just putting into words what you've told me …
LENI: Well, because, I can take that a step further I think … because I can't put my shit on them if they're (independent) … if they're too dependent on me, I can put my shit on them … Because I was *very* dependent on my mum, she put her shit on me.
ARIEL: Yes, and that's caused you no end of suffering.
LENI: Of shit.
ARIEL: Of shit.

For Leni there was an explicit relationship between dependence and damage, and independence and safety. As infants, her children were utterly dependent, so she did her best to distance herself (though not consciously) in order to protect them from her own "shit". Once they were six to seven months old, Leni trusted that she would be able to keep them safe from her own pain; with a little bit of independence they were less likely to suffer from their mother's issues and concerns.

Both in this session and in following sessions, I noted that Leni often moved between different voices – speaking as herself, speaking as her mother, her ex-husband, her old friend and others. She also frequently shifted between speaking in the present moment and speaking as if she had returned to past events. At times it took a little clarification to determine whose point of view she was describing and whether that point of view represented how she felt *now* or how she imagined she felt *then*. In the above exchange, I had to be careful not to thrust my own voice into how she conceptualised and understood her experiencing.

Leni's flexibility with points of view and time provided rich information about the power of other's voices in how she understood maternal holding. It also represented Leni's desire to navigate these voices, including her own perceived voice from the past, in order to arrive at words and images that captured how she felt in the present.

After this exchange, Leni drew with the brown (other people) and blue (herself) pastels on her representation to record "the connection" between dependence and damage. She noted:

> I don't feel sad anymore, a bit pissed off mind you, but not sad anymore.

When she reflected on her parenting and how she held her children, Leni said: "It's definitely *my* voice now".

It was important for Leni to articulate that her PND was not due to her relationship with her son or in any way his fault. The dread and distress that arose for her when she recalled that period in her life was very familiar to me. My experience of PND involved far more anxiety than depression but like Leni, I knew it was not because of my son. My own fears, confusion and insecurity around repeating familial patterns with him contributed to the diagnosis.

While Leni needed to distance herself from her children for the first six months during their most intense dependence upon her, I found that I was able to reduce my anxiety and terror when I held my infant son. If he slept in my arms, I was at my most peaceful, keeping him close.

By the end of our session, an understanding emerged: while Leni held her son as an infant the impact of other's voices had confused her own determination to protect him (based on her own childhood experiences around dependence and pain). While the hedge still represented how Leni experienced holding her children – she was aware of the many tasks or opinions that flowed through her as she held her children – the boxes were no longer "dark cubicles" and *she* owned her "running commentary".

## Lucy: I *want* to cuddle (Session 2)

> [To Lucy] Holding you is changing from when you were little. It's becoming less about comforting and more about "I'm cuddling her ... because I love her, and I want to". It's not a necessity, it's not to pacify or put to sleep or burp, it's because I *want* to cuddle.

Like Rosanna, Leni populated her sessions with stories, each sparking off one another and the art making. In this session we explored stories that told of Leni's relationship with Lucy.

Having selected a soft toy Moo (see below) to represent Lucy in their relationship, it quickly became apparent that Leni's feelings for and attachment to Moo were perhaps stronger than Lucy's own. She noted:

> Moo's been around the world three times. He's gone to the UK and we've never lost him and so much of my life has been making sure that Moo has not got lost.

Leni held onto Moo so that Lucy would never lose that possibility of comfort, even if she no longer looked for it from Moo. For Leni, Moo had become "a part of her [Lucy] yep. Little Moo".

Talking about Moo served as an access point into Leni's experiences of holding Lucy. She described the physical qualities of "loving" Lucy:

> It's as though when I squeeze, like [she presses her hands together, bringing them to her chest and lowering her head toward them] you squeeze love.

She then went on to make a representation of her relationship with Lucy during holding (see below).

Exploring the representation, Leni kept returning to descriptions of how she understood her daughter. Lucy could be "haughty", "quite dismissive", "regal" as well as "kind", "soft", "serious" and "reserved". Leni very much recognised herself in Lucy; these behaviours and attitudes reflected a relational way of being that she was very familiar with.

When I asked how she might describe their relationship, if it were an entity of its own, Leni said:

> I think it would be a soft mooshy … little, piggy colour a … Pilsbury Doughboy, just that sort of feeling … not really a shape, not really a form,

*Figure 3.4* Leni, *Soft Toy Moo Representing Her Daughter Lucy*, digital photograph.

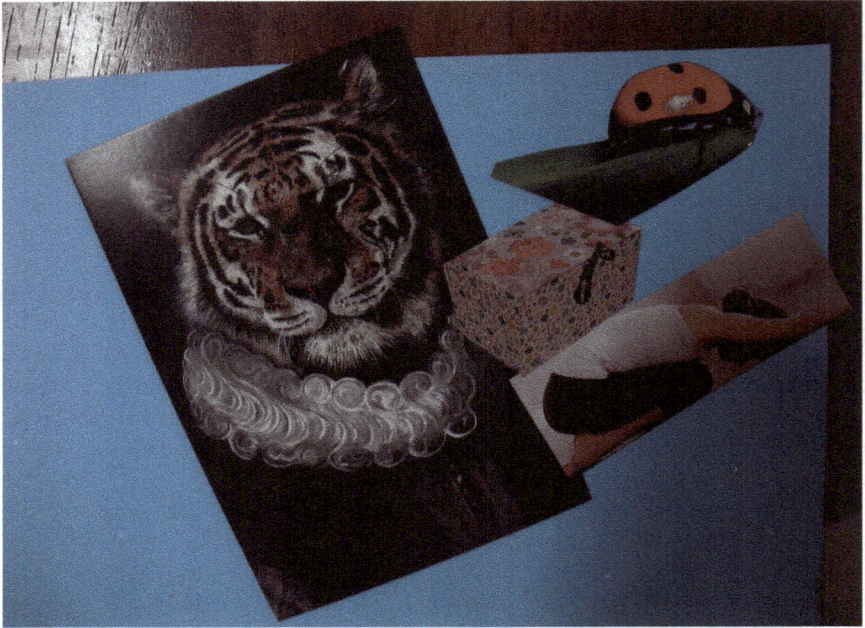

*Figure 3.5* Leni, *Representation 2A*, collage on paper, 420x295mm.

just a … [*moves hands around an invisible sphere type shape, quite close but in opposite directions as they move*].

Her gestures and words returned again to the experience of squeezing. When she held her daughter, Leni experienced their relationship as a moving, weighted sensation, two bodies deeply connected and complimentary, relationally intense, but fluid.

Leni then selected a postcard to represent the mother/daughter relationship. It showed two dancers in warm brown and golden shadows, untouching but very close and floating against a black backdrop. Their bodies were top and tail and they both looked towards the top of the postcard (unfortunately permission to include the postcard was not able to be obtained).

Leni felt that the postcard "was the closest [to her experience] … I loved the colours, they're nice and soft and warm".

When considering their relationship, the dynamism of the dancers emerged. It was important for Leni to be able to let her children be "pushed out of the way" by her occasionally and not be upset by this, she and her children could have their own "space" and still remain connected. Leni was not allowed that kind of space when she was younger and wanted to model this for her children. She felt that this desire for space was balanced by the sheer frequency and normalcy of their cuddles:

I think she [Lucy] knows there's nothing she could do to ever stop it, us being together, being mother and daughter, there'd be no estrangement, ever.

She added that "you can go in two directions but still be together" like a "yo-yo biscuit".

Leni felt there may be differences in how she held her children and how they experienced being held, noting that holding:

> Probably means a lot more to me than it does to them. It's just natural for them, maybe that's why it's a little bit forced for me, it's an effort, it's a thing I have to do … [and] I've got a lot of meaning behind mine.

The pleasing push and pull tensions described left me curious about how Leni experienced *herself* during the holding. She explained that: "I feel as if half [of myself] is not there" when she holds Lucy because there is such a strong sense of "onenesss" in the 'squeeze' of the holding. She clarified that she felt Lucy "is *mine*". This possession showed her children how loved and special they were to her, it meant the connection between mother and children would last "forever and ever". At different time's during holding, Leni's experiencing moved between deep connection, ownership and oneness.

I reflected on how the relationship appeared to have "a lot of leeway", with mother and child being able to move in different directions, have different focuses, yet in the *moment of holding* Leni felt an intense oneness, so intense that she appeared to vanish. Leni said: "Because I'm not cuddling myself, I'm not cuddling nothing, I'm cuddling her, I'm bringing her into me".

Something about the moment of holding Lucy broke down Leni's everyday embodied sense of self and other: on the one hand Lucy was absorbed into Leni, but on the other hand Leni herself was no longer present, they became, briefly, *one*.

When we explored this oneness further, Leni noted that the squeeze in the middle of holding led to a "release" and a sense of "calm", a kind of expansion of herself with her daughter. The word "oneness" captured an intensity and release that only occurred during holding.

Part of the boundary dissolution she experienced had to do with a sense of familiarity between herself and her daughter:

> I do feel very much she is an extension of me, bad parent thing [*said softly*]! But I think she mirrors a lot of what I do too, so I do feel we are very, very … much the same.

Leni clarified: "We're both individuals, we're not the same, but *part* of something".

I felt a strong difference between our first session and the present, and I brought this up with Leni. This time I noticed: "how much you get from it, more than just 'yep, I've ticked my box and I've shown them that I love them'". Leni strongly agreed: "I need it, I *need* it."

The relationship between need and maternal holding appeared significant. Leni made sure that holding was about meeting her children's needs for affection and comfort, that was an absolute priority, but she recognized her own needs in the relationship. Leni *needed* to tick her boxes and make sure that she'd met her children's needs, she *needed* to hold her children and she *needed* her daughter to never feel responsible for Leni's needs: Lucy "cuddles me because she wants to, because she loves me, she should cuddle *me* because it benefits *her*".

It was vital to Leni that her children did not feel Leni's needs were a "burden" upon them. She was aware of the power inherent in her relationship with her children and wanted them to know that she would do anything for them.

Delving further into the changes in boundaries before, during and after holding Leni explained:

> LENI: There was (me) maybe before the cuddle and how I feel after but at the time (of the cuddle) it's *us*.
> ARIEL: I wondered about that 'usness' …
> LENI: But even, we went out to get the Dyson (her new vacuum cleaner) yesterday and we're walking along and I had one – both of them, their arms around my back, I had my arms around their shoulders and we're just walking down the street and it was like 'yep, our little family', that's … I remember thinking that "this is just lovely, this is just *us*, this is just *our* little group, all having a cuddle".

This valued experience of "just us" was reinforced through our inquiry as Leni often returned to and emphasised the expression. For Leni, the word "cuddle" rather than holding, captured this 'usness' during the hold and when touching and being touched by her children. Before and after the cuddle she may have her running commentary but for a moment, during the cuddle, she felt the simplicity of being "just us". Importantly, holding and affection as part of this 'usness' was "not to be shared about with everybody else" it was special and unique to them.

The idea and sensation of 'us' intrigued me. It wasn't until later when I began working with the three women's data (as well as my own) that I started to formulate a clearer conceptualisation of 'usness' as an experience of expansion into a felt self-in-relationship or intersubjectivity. At this point, what captured me most was Leni's use of the yo-yo biscuit to describe the deep connection of the mother/child relationship. Imagining a precise pressing together of the biscuit, Leni's "squishing the cream in the middle", conveyed a deeply satisfying sense of intimate connection. Each biscuit remained distinct but in that moment of holding, their relationship to one another was tangibly brought into awareness; briefly, the *relationship* became each other's identity.

## Alexander and Lucy: giving and receiving (Session 3)

> Everything's fast (during holding) but then you're enveloped in it as well, so everything just seemed to have an opposite, there are so many, there's a flipside to everything.

This session began with an intention to explore experiences of time while holding her children. As with Rosanna, there was something about the differences and similarities Leni perceived in each child and herself, conveyed by stories around personality and needs navigation, that captured what holding was like.

Sitting quietly for a little while, Leni re-engaged with memories of holding Lucy. She then cut images out of magazines. Spending about ten minutes selecting and arranging images on the page, Leni appeared purposeful and focused (see collage below).

Leni's first impressions were of the many contradictory feelings and impulses she had experienced while holding Alexander as an infant and holding him now. Time manifested as a 'then and now' felt quality.

Differences in then and now were particularly salient with Lucy who had started to initiate cuddles (identified in the collage as 'a very different perspective'). This new behaviour "freaked" Leni out, as she described:

> That *time* element has come into it because it's "oh, how long am I to do this for?" How long does she need it for? Should I stop this hug now?'…

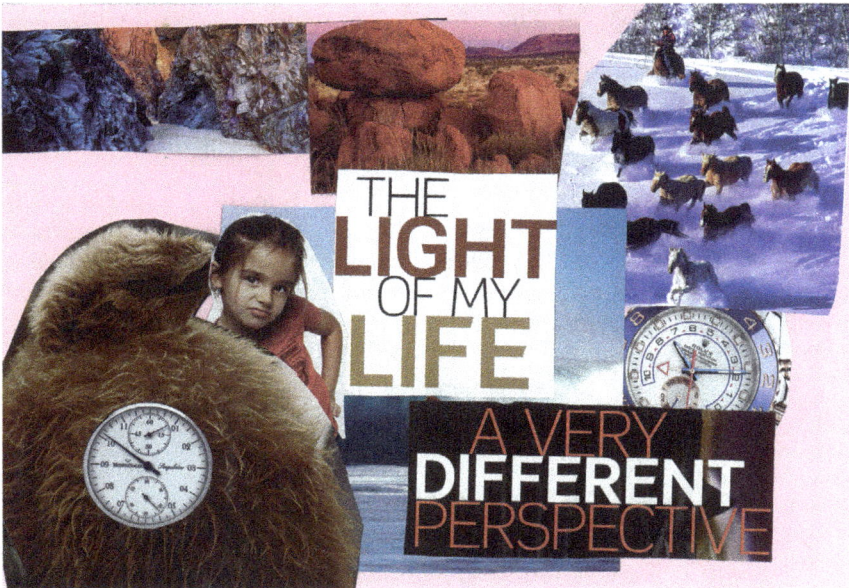

*Figure 3.6* Leni, *Representation 3A*, collage, 420x295mm.

Then again, there is half of my head going "this is just nice, this is just ... we're giving each other a hug, lovely".

Echoing Leni's experiences during her children's infancy, a relationship appeared between time and anxiety (note the two watches in her collage). She felt tensions around time duration and needs navigation. She noted that holding was a "job I have to do, but it's not a chore" and that "it's not all ticking *their* boxes, *I* need it too". Leni's task orientation in the present was no longer accompanied by distress and pain but it did create an acute experience of time.

Unlike her children's infancy, holding now included moments of "calm" shown by the "movement" in her representation: hour hands circling a clock face, waves ebbing and flowing. Leni reflected on how holding her children had changed now that they were maturing – it was becoming "calmer" and "easier". Again, there was a sense of a deeply satisfying 'squeeze and release' to her experience of holding. The power of that squeeze, no matter how brief, was conveyed by the galloping horses.

Leni was aware of wanting to appreciate these moments of holding her children because they were finite:

> It will get to the point of, as they get older, they pull away naturally as teenagers but you can still have a cuddle with them, but when they get into relationships it then becomes not right for you to have cuddles with them? ... that wall is then put up because they have a partner.... I still shouldn't be getting cuddles from them for whatever reason.... I shouldn't be there to comfort them like that, on that emotional level. I don't want it to happen, but I would find it very strange if I were to be with someone who was still giving their mum a lot of cuddles.

Once her children were in a relationship, Leni believed that their partner would be their "number one" and that physical contact would be shared between them: "It's as though I'm passing the baton to their partner". She had fulfilled her task as a parent in terms of physical affection, she had given her children what they needed. Leni felt that once this had happened, her need for holding would be fulfilled by opportunities to hold her potential grandchildren; maternal holding had a time limit that would end with her children's maturity and/or new relationship.

From the perspective of her children's needs, I wondered if a relationship with a partner and a relationship with the parent were different and therefore it might not be possible for one to replace the other? Leni explained:

> There's that history of it [maternal affection] already being there and you would hope, because then they become adults and they themselves become parents, that they don't need that parent? As much? My kids won't need me as much for emotional security because they've had a good basis and they will have a partner that should hopefully give them that.

I asked Leni if "hugging and holding is associated with need" and she confirmed this: "I need to hug them, and they need to have hugs from me". However, as adults, Leni's holding "would probably end up turning it into hello, goodbye hugs and maybe just tactile, maybe more just touching, I can't see myself sitting on the couch as I do now, giving them a cuddle. There will be a different type of contact." This helped clarify what she meant by the cessation of holding. Affection would remain but it would be different. Primacy was placed on meeting her children's needs rather than her own.

Highlighting what was different for Lucy and Leni in cuddling, compared to her own experience, had to do with responsibility and needs navigation. As Lucy's mother she had a "*responsibility* to do this" while Lucy, as the child, had no responsibility toward Leni during holding.

Through cuddling Leni felt that her children "must know that they are wanted, and adored by me, if no one else". While Leni experienced cuddling as a "duty" and "responsibility" which involved a particular experience of time and while she made conscious decisions around how to hold her children, she did her best to make sure that *they* were never aware of that.

This narrative around holding and need left me wondering about Leni's position, if any, in her representation. When I asked her where she would place herself in her collage, she indicated that she was the "watch ... [she] goes in the background, I suppose that would be me thinking about the time, being the time". Leni was "tucked away". The watch also reflected how Leni felt she had to "click [her] warmth on" when she cuddled her children. She had to "go into cuddle mode" because, while she believed she was very tactile, cuddling still wasn't natural for her – it was a deliberate choice to give warmth and love to her children.

During the cuddle Leni wanted her children to experience time as "endless". She recognised that what her children experienced and valued in their cuddles and in their shared history was different to her own experiences and values: "Because they don't have the baggage, it doesn't mean the same thing as it means to us [Leni and I], they still love it and are excited by it but not to our level". Leni hoped and believed that when her children were cuddled by her, they would "get ... more of the experience that I *wish* I had".

A sense of shared history was very important in the relationship between maternal holding and need. Providing her children with frequent and normalized holding over time would give them as adults a sense that their needs around maternal holding were fulfilled. This would go a long way toward mitigating her own ongoing need to hold her children.

As with Rosanna, Leni experienced difference in her children's personalities as she held them. Cuddling Alexander was much simpler than cuddling Lucy because he frequently approaches her for cuddles, and she is able to discern his "emotions a lot better". With Lucy, the cuddles are faster and there is a "coolness" to the cuddles.

With the red and blue tones in her representation, Leni showed us both the warmth and coolness she felt that *she* brought to the holding. She noted the warmth of their mother/child cuddles (the blue and red rocks on the left and middle top of the representation) but also the "clinical and cold" (later altered to "cool") quality of the cuddles denoting Leni's need to 'tick' her boxes (the cooler blues in the snow imagery).

Leni enjoyed the immediate sense of ticking her boxes: "I'm in the middle of doing something, 'you need a hug?', right (hug done), what now?" However, sometimes, in the middle of holding, a wave (at the bottom of the representation) "sort of envelops you as well", a sense of calmness and timelessness prevails: "amongst all of that there will be just *being* as well" and "it's lovely and nice" for a fleeting moment "but the brain doesn't stop". These experiences of time and timelessness, warmth and "natural coolness" captured the felt differences in time, emotion, relationship and thoughts involved in her holding experiences:

> There seemed to be an opposite to everything I thought of … nice and fluffy and soft and then attitude, warm and cold … everything's fast but then you're enveloped in it as well.

Cuddling her children involved having ongoing internal dialogues around how Leni felt about them in the moment and what choices she needed to make for their benefit:

> If they come for a hug and you think "I could fucking kill you!" [*said very softly as if under her breath*] so even with the attitude, and all the crap, you still give them the hug.

As the session progressed, we returned to exploring how Lucy's cuddling had changed, causing Leni to feel more aware of time and generally anxious about attending to her daughter's needs. Leni considered that perhaps Lucy was now simply exhibiting the behaviours that Leni herself had modelled.

Looking at her representation, Leni acknowledged that she had taught her children that cuddles were a frequent and "quick check-in" and now Lucy was initiating those kinds of cuddles. Lucy appeared to enjoy and want these cuddles but not from a place of need. The change for Leni was that the locus of control had shifted from resting entirely with her to moving between Leni and Lucy; as Lucy matured so did their relationship. Leni was compelled to first examine any possible want or need but was then prepared to accept that Lucy's "daily hug" might be an expression of love unaccompanied by the contradictions, concerns and anxieties that ran alongside Leni's expressions of affection.

In her representation, the centrally placed 'light of my life' showed how important Leni's children were to her. Needs navigation played a central role in holding and thus her awareness of time would also likely continue, particularly in her comparisons around what she experienced as a child and what she wanted for her children:

> Even the way I raise the kids, completely, everything is thought about and a reaction to how it was with me growing up, without a doubt. 100%. Everything, there's a choice made, there's a decision made.

At the end of the session, when I asked Leni what she might change, if anything, about the representation, she noted that she would have a bit more of the wave and a bit less of the clock face. This reflected her belief that the time left for this kind of enveloping holding was reducing as her children matured but also that she wanted very much to extend *her* experience of that timeless, relaxed wave of affection while she could. Leni was "trying to ignore it" but felt that the loss of physical holding was inevitable and necessary.

In this session we touched on how Leni experienced changes in the mother/child relationship and on what she gave but also received during holding. Differences between mother and child needs were explicitly described in Leni's anticipated loss of physical holding once her child matured. Both Leni and Rosanna recognised that this was painful and that it had something to do with a partner assuming the role of 'holder'. They both also recognised that other kinds of holding (emotional, psychological) based on a shared history of holding, would expand and change as their children matured.

While I did not examine these ideas further at the time, I was aware of the need to explore cultural and familial assumptions around physical affection between parents and children as those children mature, particularly with the presence of the term "should". This session also drew my attention to the felt differences in mother and child needs experienced within relationship. Leni's imagery of the dancers appeared significant to me, the energy of pushing and pulling together and away. While physical distance may grow between mother and child it did not mean that they couldn't return to intimate affection (embodied, emotional or psychological); I felt that there was something in our work so far around how the mother/child relationship remained and always held a space for them to be together however different that holding may look.

## Alexander and Lucy: just us (Session 4)

> This is *just us*, and not *just* as a negative.

In between sessions, I created some preliminary findings for Leni. Each included a sentence followed by a paragraph that I felt spoke to distinct qualities of holding for Leni thus far. I endeavoured to use her own words as often as possible. I felt it would be good to have something for each of us to consider and launch from in this, our final session. Additionally, given Leni's experiences in the past with dominant voices re-storying her experiences, I wanted to offer her as much input as possible into our findings. She generously responded to these offerings before our session.

I laid out all of Leni's prior representations, printouts of all key words/phrases I had selected from our previous sessions, and the findings I had emailed her (including her comments on each). A curiosity emerged around the tensions Leni experienced with allowing and encouraging independence in her children as they matured. On the one hand, Leni wanted to protect her children from the pain that too much dependence might bring (explored in our first session).

Consequently, Leni encouraged her children's ability to cope with being "pushed out of the way". On the other hand, Leni needed and wanted her children's affection. She recognized that by giving her children independence and by enabling them to accept that they all need space sometimes, her children were confident enough to 'reject' her if she offered them a cuddle: "it's reaping dividends now … it's the right way … yeah, but it's hard". This was explored in our third session, as Leni described Lucy's new initiation of cuddles.

With these stories around dependence and independence, Leni had to remind herself that, for example, when Lucy didn't want cuddles "it doesn't mean the same to her as it does to me". Leni recognised that Lucy's experiences around holding, affection, dependence and independence were likely quite different to her own. This spoke to differences in maternal and child needs within the relationship, in how Leni interpreted these needs and in how they were navigated by both mother and child.

I was drawn to the appearance of Leni's needs during holding in our third session, particularly her experience and desire for envelopment. We clarified that this "just being" quality of cuddling her children happened in the *middle* of holding: "my whole, my brain just stops and I'm just there with them".

This kind of 'being' was in stark contrast to her task-oriented internal commentary. These still moments were not present in all cuddles but did occur during optimal holding. These cherished waves of being were associated with Leni's sense of 'oneness' while holding her children.

We explored how 'oneness' was a *shifting* quality – her experiences moved between oneness, togetherness/connection, an extended sense of self with child, and possession during holding. Leni noted that holding included: "a little bit of touching on everything because I have four circles of each, and just a little bit touches". Like the clock face movement Leni described for Representation 3A (Figure 3.7), she experienced shifts in relational boundaries with her children; these manifested as quite different experiences of self and other within one quick instance of holding.

Leni noted that she 'earned' cuddles. She elaborated: "when I get a cuddle from them … I have earned it, it's like a praise, it's like a thank you … I did it right, it worked". I asked: "You met their needs?" and she responded "Yes". Holding required effort and was a "duty", it was Leni's work and responsibility but when she got it "right", she'd earned the gift of the cuddle that her children gave her, she'd earned the right to 'us'.

A new understanding about Leni's holding experiences emerged in this session. She told a story of her relationship with her father. She couldn't recall many memories from before her father left (when she was eight years old) but there was just a general sense of loveliness: "it was lovely, his family about, and everything was there, and then it went pear-shaped" [when her mother and father divorced].

Leni remembered: "having cuddles with my dad and sitting on his knee and fighting [with her brothers] to sit beside him". She felt "very close to him … and he *was* protective, he *was* our protector". Unlike her mother, her ex-husband and her friend, Leni always felt that her dad was "on [her] side". With her

*Figure 3.7* Ariel Moy, *Representation 4A Detail #1*, digital photograph.

dad, she didn't have to earn cuddles: "Nope, definitely not, I was daddy's girl". She was her father's possession, just as Leni's children were *hers* and this was deeply pleasurable for Leni. This meant that she did not have to work for cuddles from her father, she simply had a right to them. That was the kind of holding she wanted for her children.

Looking at all of the representations laid out on the ground (Figures 3.7–3.10) I asked Leni for her first impressions: "I find it interesting how we first started with my compartmentalizing everything, how it's loosened up a bit". The first representation felt "*very* stark" for her.

I wondered if Leni would like to do anything with the representations and she said she wanted "take a little picture of them all in a line". This reflected how much her understanding, but also her experiences of maternal holding had developed over the sessions; the changes were "huge". The images showed a transition from experiences stark and fixed to a recognition of the presence of mother and child's changing needs during holding and the joys to be found in meeting them.

Reflecting on the third representation, Leni noted that she didn't like to label her children though she tended to label others. She had spoken of the differences in her children's personalities but went on to consider: "there's so many different facets [to her children]. There's usually a reason for them doing something" and that reason could be more contextual or relational than a function of a definite personality type or label.

While Leni held her children, she had a strong sense of who they were in their *relationship* with her but that was not fixed in stone, even when she relayed qualities like "aloof" for Lucy, she later indicated that could depend on the context or relationship Lucy was in at the time. Leni also recognised that there were different qualities that *she* felt she shared with Lucy and Alexander and so sometimes descriptions of qualities she ascribed to her children might also be qualities of her own or the ways she and her children interacted with one another.

Leni talked about the labels and stories her own mother had ascribed to her: that Leni was a "big girl" or that she was "good at languages" and how these were problematic. When Leni didn't appear to enjoy or be good at languages, for example, she then became "confused, I didn't know what I was good at". Leni now believed that her mother had told her she was good at languages because "*she* wanted to speak languages and *she* wanted to travel". Leni was aware of the power inherent in the mother/child relationship and wanted to navigate her understanding of maternal and child needs as well as appraisal of fixed personality traits sensitively.

Unlike her mother, Leni had begun openly considering contradictions and allowing an ongoing, changeable commentary to occupy her mind:

> [It's] okay to actually have ten different thoughts going on in your head. Because I have changed my mind: "I'm going to buy a house, I'm not going to buy a house, I'm going to do this", that's the sense of failure, with my mum, if you do that, you're "airy fairy" you don't know what you're doing.

Additionally, Leni's frequent movements during holding between a stage of "just being" and one of "ticking her boxes", between fast and slow, warmth and coolness (shown in Representation 3A) were "okay". Leni felt that she was allowed to move between seemingly contradictory states without diminishing her love for her children and her responsibilities toward them.

I invited Leni to further explore or consolidate her understanding of holding by selecting postcards that spoke to her different representations. She placed a number of postcards around different parts of each. These provided an, at first, visual and non-conceptual commentary on each representation as she understood it now (see Figures 3.7–3.10).

Talking about the representation/postcard relationships, Leni described how she felt she had "lost (her) identity" (referring to the 'Who' postcard in Figure 3.7) at the time of her PND. She did not receive support from others, she could not speak about her experiences. She had felt "shut up" throughout her life and loves that Lucy appears more "bolshy"; "she knows who she is" (in Representation 3A).

The 'you're beautiful' postcard placed over Lucy's soft toy Moo (Figure 3.8) was about "me thinking it about them (her children)". Leni noted that the character traits she'd attributed to her children were more a recognition of what she experienced of her children within their relationship. For example, Leni could imagine her son saying: 'you're beautiful' to her because he often gave her lots of positive 'feedback' (she also noted that that's "usually because he gets a sweetie").

In Figure 3.9, the 'Love and Music Last Forever' postcard was chosen for its shape and colour. It showed how Leni experienced her relationship with her children as she held them. There was a "fluidity" while cuddling them; during optimal holding moments she felt "calm, peaceful, just nice". This new postcard was complimentary to the two dancer's postcard she had selected in Session 2A.

Returning to themes of independence and dependence, Leni explained that she no longer needed to "save" her children from "being fucked up by their father", "by my shit" or by "their grandmother". Now that the children were older, Leni felt "they are *them* now rather than my little packages that I've got to save". Her children had established who they were in their own lives as well

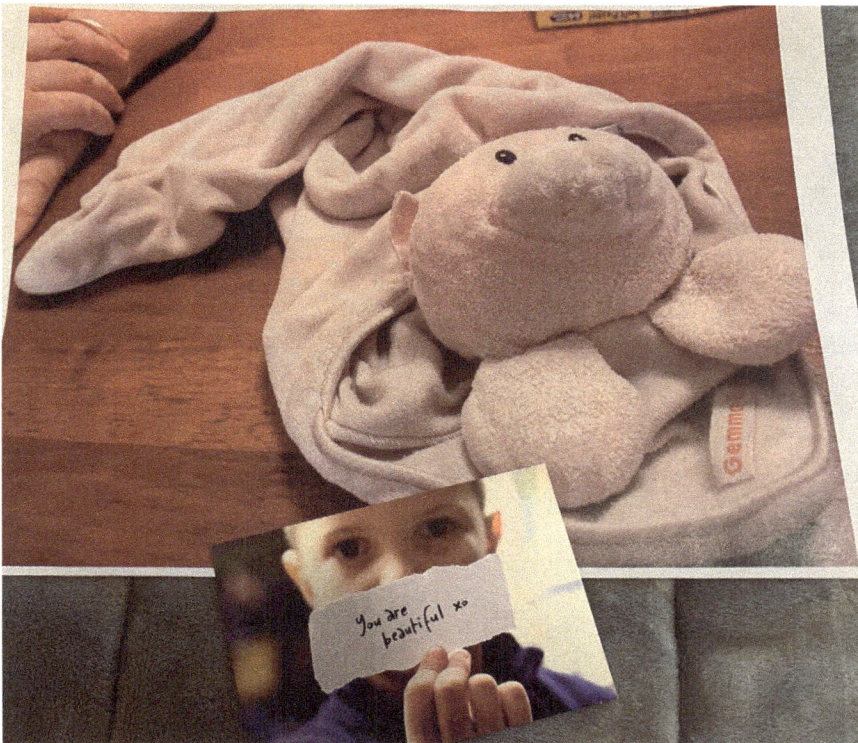

*Figure 3.8* Ariel Moy, *Representation 4A Detail #2*, digital photograph.

*Figure 3.9* Ariel Moy, *Representation 4A Detail #3*, digital photograph.

as in relationship with her. Complimentary with this was her understanding of how she experienced a changed sense of self in relationship with her children. Placing the Wallace and Gromit postcard on her 'light of my life' representation (see Figure 3.10) she said:

> See, I think that's *me*, that's *us*, that *is our life*, that's what *we're* like. We have fun, we have jokes, we have a laugh, a carry on, I adore my children, they know that, they adore me. That *is us*, that funny gnome face and Alexander and his Wallace and Gromit smile, that is *us*.

I clarified that this was an experience she felt when she was cuddling her children and Leni confirmed it.

Over the rest of the session, Leni repeatedly referred to an experience of "*just us*" explaining:

> Just. Us. Just. Us. [*said softly, with satisfaction, emphasizing the full stops*]. And there's nothing wrong with us, and just accept *us* because we accept each other, it's *just* the way we are.

*Figure 3.10* Ariel Moy, *Representation 4A Detail #4,* digital photograph.

This 'usness' was incredibly valuable to Leni and was present across many of her representations. There was a distinctly contained and defended quality to this mother/child 'us' that intrigued me. Who mother and children were when they were together, particularly in moments of affection like holding, was inviolate, unassailable. This was an understanding that responded to those troubling voices and judgements by stating that what mattered was who mother and children were for one another in the moment of holding and affection. Further, Leni carried this understanding with her throughout her everyday life, when she wasn't holding her children or around them. Moments of optimal holding and touch simply brought the felt qualities of this experience of 'usness' into awareness.

At the end of the session, I asked Leni "Is there anything you feel you … understand now, that you might not have known before?" and she responded:

> It definitely made me think … that my children cannot mind read and they do not have my shit. It really reinforced that they are oblivious in a good way, and they're perfectly happy, and my shit is getting sorted, and it's not been transferred onto them.
>
> It was also good thinking about the cuddles; going through the process of what I do when I'm cuddling and why I do it. Just to see that thought process and go "oh yeah, I *do* do that", makes it clearer and now I can see myself doing it and going "yep, that's fine, that's just how you're sorting it

in your head. That's fine, you're having a quick thought" because with Lucy, if I hadn't thought about Lucy asking for cuddles, I would still be thinking "oh my god, what's wrong?" Whereas now I'm going "well, that's my shit, there is nothing wrong with her, just give her a cuddle". Whereas I wouldn't have been able to do that before the sessions, I would still be going "why is my daughter like that?" Definitely a *big* learning curve. From such an innocuous little word – cuddle [*said very softly*]. "I just give them a cuddle, I just do it", but no.

In the end, Leni felt that cuddling was something that:

> Works ... because you know what I'm like (generally not very affectionate with others), and I wasn't cuddled, and many other things, but the main thing was I wasn't given the physical affection like that, whereas my kids are, and they are so different to (me), so different to what I grew up with or what I was.

The physical affection that Leni gave her children also changed how she experienced herself in moments of holding. Who she was as a child, and who she had been prior to her children, was not the same as who she was when she held her children. Moments of holding appeared to capture a cherished and different experience of self and 'us' or self in relationship.

## After our sessions

I wanted to offer Leni a visual response to the work we'd shared together and the new approximations to meaning around maternal holding we had generated. I had developed the findings we had shared in Session 4 after our sessions were complete to take into account her feedback as well as new insights arising in session.

The qualities I wanted to share with Leni focused on the dynamic relationships between maternal and child's needs experienced and navigated as she held her children. It felt particularly important that I represent the 'usness' so valued and thematic through our work together. I sensed a fierceness and strength to this 'usness'.

I thought about the colours red and blue for the warm and cool qualities of her experiences during maternal holding; the contradictory experiences of an enveloping wave and ticking boxes that were nevertheless acceptable to Leni by our final session. I wanted to represent the "backbone" of the relationship Leni had provided for her children so that their bond would never break (see Figure 3.11).

When Leni received the ISR she did not say much. I felt as if she was uncomfortable with the polar bear. She said that she agreed with the findings I had provided but did not offer any further commentary at the time.

*Figure 3.11* Ariel Moy, *An ISR for Leni* (after our sessions were complete), felt tip pen on paper, 295x210mm.

After a few months, Leni looked at my ISR again and re-read the findings we had shared. She wrote to me:

> Re-reading it brought back a lot of memories – some good, some not. I agree with what you have written but want to deny it too!! I still feel the same a bit, but now I get cuddles from [her new partner] and I demand and ask them of him, but not of the kids. But [I am] still very aware that they need their fair share too. They are cuddlers too. Lucy cuddles her school friends and they both cuddle [her new partner] freely. The polar bear makes more sense to me now. I like the [coolness] of the polar bear but also the protectiveness it is showing. Weird thinking about it all again!!

Leni's response was a welcome reminder that patterns of being not only change over time but memories of these can also be upsetting and hard to return to. Leni's family had taught her (though she had questioned their values) that the past was in the past and best left there. It took time and space for Leni to feel okay with acknowledging how she had experienced and understood maternal holding particularly when her children were infants. So much had changed for her since some of those early experiences and since we had finished our sessions. It was important to reiterate to both of us that patterns are not fixed, that what we worked on together and the findings I developed were a part of Leni's knowing *at the time of our sessions*. These findings contributed to how Leni understood maternal holding now, but they did not limit or define it.

As Leni noted in her final session: "It's very transitional, isn't it? It's very … in the middle of something, going from one place to another" and that that was okay. She understood that their relationship was built on an unwavering foundation of love.

## Leni's themes around maternal holding

As described in Chapters 1 and 2, I selected themes and depictions to describe our findings for Leni.

### Theme 1: Ticking boxes

Depiction: My mind doesn't stop – have I given my children what they need? I make sure I listen to my own voice and not the judgments of others. A cuddle is my way of checking in with my children and myself and making sure we're okay. I make conscious choices about when, why and for how long I cuddle them.

### Theme 2: Cuddles are normal

Depiction: I choose to cuddle my children a lot so that they know that giving and receiving affection is normal and makes us all feel good.

### Theme 3: Cuddles are a thank you

Depiction: Cuddles are a thank you, I have given my children what they needed. I will be there for my children, always. I need their cuddles and affection, but I will never ask it of them. Fulfilling my needs is not their responsibility; cuddling is first and foremost about them.

### Theme 4: Each cuddle is unique

Depiction: Cuddling each of my children at any one time is unique, their personalities are different to one another but their concerns at the time are also different and so are their cuddles.

### Theme 5: We are just us

Depiction: We will always be Us: together, connected, a part of something lovely. Just us.

### Theme 6: Parts 1, 2, 3 Each cuddle builds an invisible thread connecting us

### Theme 6.1: Past: in the way

Depiction: As a child, she and her brothers were in the way. Dependence was painful, it meant rejection. She was punished for her independence. There was no balance between dependence and independence and now the relationship with her mother is severed. She was overwhelmed by her children's dependence in their infancy. Once they reached six months it was safer to hold them and be close to them.

### Theme 6.2: Present: squeeze love

Depiction: Cuddling her children now is dynamic: there is a balance between dependence and independence. During the cuddle she squeezes love, the comfort and oneness of an enveloping hug leads to a calming release. Her children will always be hers and the centre of her world. But she can also push them away, she can have some space for herself. They know they are always loved.

**Theme 6.3: Future: invisible thread**

Depiction: She knows that as the children mature, they will naturally pull away. She is getting as many cuddles as she can right now and making a history of closeness for them all. Though they may cuddle less, they will always be close.

# 4   Interconnectedness

## Kitty and Harley

### Kitty and Harley

Kitty and I shared seven sessions together, each taking place at Kitty's home. Sessions were structured so that one session would involve an exploration of a particular holding experience followed by a second session that would inquire into a quality of that experience in more depth and then reduce the data to come to some sense of meaning.

Kitty was unfamiliar with an arts-based approach to inquiry but was enthusiastic to learn more. Surprisingly, she found herself returning to scientific and biblical imagery to describe deeply felt experiences of love. Kitty does not consider herself to be religious and her background educationally and vocationally is in the areas of social and environmental issues.

### Harley as a baby: "my heart is full" (Sessions 1A and 1B)

> So, this is us bending into each other, my body bending around and … the waves of us spreading out … in terms of the emotions and thoughts … it's very peaceful and calm.

Our first two sessions explored Kitty's experiences of holding her daughter as an infant. Kitty wanted to explore the embodied qualities of holding after noticing precious photos on her wall that showed her holding her daughter at a distance.

As with the other participants, I offered an exercise to warm into the inquiry. With Kitty, this went on for quite some time (twenty minutes) as she'd been apprehensive about entering back into memories of something so intimate. Kitty noted afterward: "It was bizarre, I never expected that to happen … some of the stuff I'd sort of forgotten too".

Kitty was now noticeably relaxed and articulate about her recollections of holding Harley. She immediately described how she felt as a new mother, as if her "breath's been taken away". She remembered her sense of "responsibility" and an "overwhelmingness" that accompanied holding. She felt a sense of being "separate from the world, it's just she and I". The recollections had

DOI: 10.4324/9781003104094-5

intense embodied qualities to them, she was "flooded with emotion" and felt as if she could "almost smell" Harley.

Two thematic qualities of holding emerged from the warm in and these were inquired into over these two sessions:

- The physical qualities of holding Harley as an infant;
- Kitty's capacity for motherhood.

Kitty relayed stories as she made her representation.

Giving birth to Harley and holding her had a profound impact. She described how these experiences were "the first time that I knew what love was, or what it could be". These emotions were "big" and not common for Kitty prior to Harley's birth. They came into awareness when Kitty had "the time and space" to simply be with Harley. She spoke to Harley as if she were present: "I can't *believe* how much I love you" and "I can't believe you're mine".

Kitty told a story about bringing Harley home from hospital and holding her over the next few days. She focused in on a moment when they lay together on the bed, Kitty was "holding her against my body" and it was "probably the first time that Harley slept". Unfortunately, the Health Nurse came to visit and woke them up but this moment of "peace and calm" was "the first time I realised about having ... what the holding was going to mean".

Continuing to make little changes to her representation, Kitty explained how the white/blue middle shape and the pinkish/white oval at the centre of the representation showed "us bending into each other" surrounded by "the waves of us spreading out" (see Figure 4.1).

Kitty was "really absent of thought" as she made her representation. She wanted to show holding "more as a feeling and being".

Kitty purposefully "blurred" the lines on her drawing to show how she and Harley were "really together, there's no real separation". In that particular moment of holding, when Harley slept, Kitty felt "very fluid ... which was not how I felt most of the time when she came home". This kind of holding felt "more instinctive than what everyone else was doing" and it "worked".

As Kitty drew, she noted that she was "very, very happy with this part here" (the blended part between the pink oval and the white/blue curve). I asked her if that was the part that "connects you and Harley" and she confirmed that it was.

At first, holding Harley as an infant "was more complex and not as clean" as it is today. In the drawing, the intensity of their early connection was "contained" by the imagery and the boundaries of the black page. However, a spaciousness inside the central curve captured a glimpse of their present day holding, forecasting "more room, like what I needed to do, like for what was to come". Kitty described how that space showed her "capacity for motherhood".

Finishing her representation, I held the drawing up before Kitty and she exclaimed:

*Figure 4.1* Kitty, *Representation 1A*, soft pastel on paper, 420x295mm.

Does that look like a boat on a river or what!? Like Moses or something.…
Oh my god! How incredible. It's probably the best piece of art … I've ever
done, I'm going to cry I'm so happy! I love it! Like how beautiful is that?

She then added: "And there's my little baby, going to float away. Oh, how
incredible!"

The surprise and intensity of her response encouraged us to stay with the
movement of the 'boat and baby' and so I asked Kitty where Harley might
float to. She said Harley would float up and right and I wondered if that would
go "against gravity". Kitty confirmed that it would and added that it was
"good … she's not going to float away from me" because Kitty's curve would
travel with her and the pressures of gravity would keep them together.

Kitty had feared that she might not "be enough" for Harley because "I'm
always feeling that there's a lack, lack, lack". Looking at her drawing revealed
that "it's not the case, or it doesn't have to be". With Harley floating up in the
same direction as Kitty, she felt that "I'm big enough, or I will be when it
comes (to it)" to give Harley the mothering she needs.

Recently, Kitty had felt like she was "drowning", but in her drawing the
water and the boat showed the mother/child connection and her capacity to be
there for Harley. She acknowledged that "my heart certainly grew enormously
once I had her … there was like an endless space" within their relationship for
*each* to change. She said:

I'm actually really surprised at how powerful this has been and how interesting because I've been to lots of therapists ... or counsellors, and very rarely had an "oh wow" moment, so that's been really interesting, using this medium to have that happen.

Holding provided opportunities for Kitty to "pause right now and just be in this space, in this moment". I particularly resonated with the idea of holding providing a 'pause' for the relationship. I had noticed this quality in the longer moments of holding my son when he was an infant, a toddler and when he came home exhausted from kinder and would curl into my arms.

Kitty was shocked by the Biblical imagery that arose "because I'm not religious at all ... it was *never* in my mind". The significance of these intimate experiences evoked a different way of knowing and telling for her.

In our second session, Kitty noted that experiences of light and warmth while holding Harley as an infant were about how she "protected" Harley, but their holding also "radiated" from them "blurring ... the space between us". In some moments, the space between mother and child reduced to nothing, in others, there was a deeply satisfying sense of "fit" as they folded into one another's bodies. Kitty described it as "we are one becoming we are connected".

Qualities of "omnipotence", "bigness" and "vastness" spoke to the enormity of emotions and the "unreal feeling" she experienced during those early days of holding. Kitty felt that her "heart (was) full", as she leaned into "feeling love". She wished to explore these qualities further because the "emotion stuff" felt "richest" and was "going to be hard for (her) ... to represent".

Again, as Kitty drew, she spoke about her process as well as holding experiences (see Figure 4.2).

She explained:

> When I think about this stuff, it makes me very teary, but it makes me stand up tall, like when I talk about it, I always bring my chest back ... and sort of like push my heart forward.

In the past, Kitty had experienced emotion as more conceptual but with the birth of Harley "for the first time, I felt emotion *in my heart*". In a sense: "Harley became my heart".

Kitty was less satisfied with this representation as she felt her experiencing might be "too big to be able to put into a drawing". She then changed some of the symbols (a heart, wings and an infinity sign) into colour filled ovals as these appeared to capture the "bigness ... of motherhood" without limiting it to preconceived ideas embedded within symbols. She noted that she was "much happier with that now! That makes sense of a few things".

A "fluidity" existed between mother and daughter during holding touching on the "big universality of the foreverness of it". Kitty wondered if "this difficulty with me too is knowing who I am in all of this?" The experience of

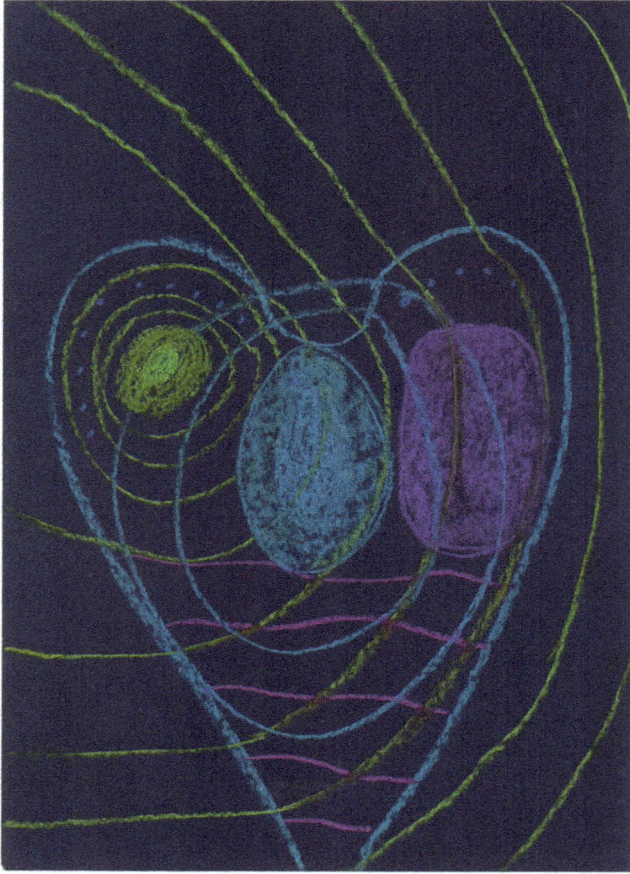

*Figure 4.2* Kitty, *Representation 1B*, pastel on paper, 295x420mm.

"big" and "real" emotions and of movement between states of connection, blurriness and oneness were hard to articulate and marry with our everyday notions of self and other. Though her experience of holding Harley in the present were less "intense" than when she was an infant, there were moments in holding that still defied language and were better described in image.

## Kitty and Harley: reciprocity and interconnection (Session 2A and 2B)

> It's amazing how many times … I can be furious at her but then I'll go in, and see she's upset, and I'll say: "do you want a hug?" and then I'm not so furious anymore, so that sort of circuit breaker thing.

With a focus on relationship over the next two sessions, I asked Kitty to bring three objects or images that would represent herself, Harley and their relationship during holding. She selected three photographs that captured a time in their lives when the holding changed; it became "less about holding her – but holding together" when at around six months of age, Harley began to "cuddle back". These photographs served as access points into our inquiry.

## Kitty's experiencing

We began with Kitty imagining herself back into these earlier moments of holding. I asked her to speak at first from her own point of view, as this was the most easily accessible. She conveyed that holding Harley felt like less of a "burden" at this stage, she felt more "comfortable" with her daughter. She noted that as there were never many others around to help with Harley: "It just became very natural that she was with me, *I* was holding her" most of the time.

The photograph Kitty had chosen showed how she had "blocked" out her nanna (who's house they were in at the time); a very rare thing for her to do. Kitty said: "Her [nanna's] needs are on the outside, and this is *us*". In this moment of optimal holding "time and space and the environment [were] sort of irrelevant".

Kitty's sense of 'us' was particularly related to "the touch, like the skin to skin ... touching". She still experiences moments like these: "of just she and I" even though Harley is no longer a baby.

## Harley's experiencing

We then inquired into what it might be like for Kitty to speak as her daughter in the moment of holding and being held. Kitty picked up a photo of Harley showing "absolute joy and happiness and she's giving me a hug ... after a breastfeed". Kitty found it much easier to speak *about* the holding rather than *as* her daughter.

She wondered if Harley might sometimes feel "overwhelmed" by her affection. When she held Harley to "contain her or calm" she imagined her daughter might feel holding was a form of "restraint". She related how Harley sometimes says: "Mama, I've run out of kisses, I have to go to the shop, I don't have any kisses left" which is her way of saying, "stop, enough already"!

However:

> On the whole, she feels lifted up, like her spirit and her soul feel lifted when she's held, both physically and metaphorically, because she'll even now ask me "pick me up mum, pick me up".

When trying to speak as her daughter, Kitty said: "I think I'm going to cry". She experienced intense emotions and was afraid of "losing control". She breathed deeply and then, as Harley, she said:

I love you mamma ... when you hold me like this [*in the photo*] I feel ... very safe [*Kitty's voice quivers*], I feel so wanted ... and I feel I can do anything ... .I trust you and you will always be there ... I can feel your love going into my heart.

The experience of 'heart' was strongly felt and served conceptually as a way of emphasising the centrality and embodiment of holding for both Kitty and, as she imagined, for Harley.

### The experiencing of the mother/child relationship

Kitty considered that their relationship was probably "more about Harley's needs than mine ... but having said that, this is the happiest I've ever been in terms of my life and how I'm living it ... there's stuff in there for me too". While "the general relationship is more balanced towards Harley ... in the *holding* part, I think it's a much more equal". Kitty felt that holding and touch provided the rewards and balance that perhaps were not always present in their relationship overall.

While the holding could be "draining" on her, Kitty felt that "when I *do* hold, I usually feel better about whatever the situation is or whatever is going on. So, it does actually ... change things emotionally and physically". In this sense, there appeared to be a constant flow between Kitty's needs being momentarily tabled, her needs being met, Harley's needs being met, and *both* of their needs being met: "The relationship would say that ... it evens itself out, and there's a lot more positives, a lot of strength in it".

When Kitty spoke *as* the relationship she said: "Keep doing what you're doing, do it as much as you can, as often as you can, get it while you can [*she laughs*] ... [and to Harley] keep giving and keep asking". She also felt that if the relationship wanted anything, it was for them to "slow things down a bit, to have more of that (holding) time".

Having explored experiencing from three different perspectives, Kitty said that she wanted to explore qualities of "lifting up" and "twining" as she held Kitty in the present day. As with her other sessions, she described the experience she was re-engaging with and her artmaking process as she went along.

The representation showed Kitty as the long white line lying on a couch with her arm around her daughter's white line and their cat's white lines twined at their feet. She used the magenta pastel to draw "their [heart] beat flowing out but also getting smaller and calmer". She used a pale blue pastel to draw the "expansion of my breathing ... filling in and calming and across the both of us". She felt that this kind of holding fills "the heart with the connection" and wanted to emphasise the white lines so that the embodied experiencing of mother and child was the most salient quality on the page.

During optimal moments like these, Kitty experienced time as "very fluid" and "distorted". Kitty drew the top right "window" to convey this. "The outside", "the physical world" and "time" sat in this window. She explained that she wanted to convey how holding like this was "not a complicated time";

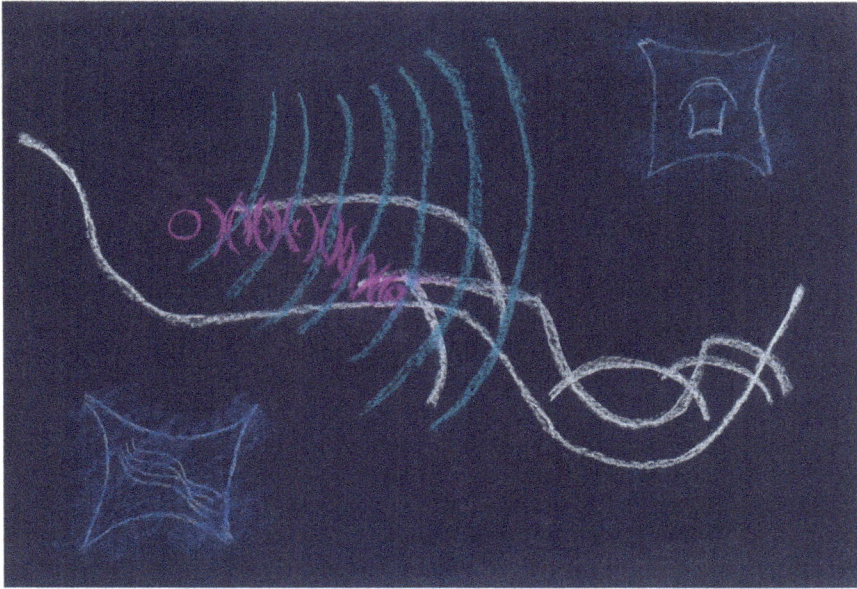

*Figure 4.3* Kitty, *Representation 2A*, soft pastel on paper, 420x295mm.

it was "cosy, warm, comforting ... and about being in a moment". Another window in the bottom left corner conveyed the "musicality to this breathing and rhythm". Their touch was "connected ... reciprocal" in these moments. Other voices, space and time were less relevant.

Kitty noted that her representation didn't show either her daughter or herself with 'heads':

> It's just really a moment of being [and it] doesn't have the shape and structure that it would ... in [a] practical head space type of day or moment.

Her drawing conveyed "a growth in me and expansion, a filling out in me". The twining of the figures in the representation was conveyed as dynamically and clearly as possible, including the breathing in synch, the shared heartbeats and the reciprocal touch, in order to capture this valuable sense of expansion Kitty experienced.

I asked whether there was anything new understanding she had arrived at as our session was ending and she said:

> The relationship actually gives to me, in terms of the holding, that I'm actually getting quite a lot back from this, the holding and the closeness and everything ... for my physical and mental health, it's calming me, and grounding me, and ... it's also filling me.

Kitty felt "lucky" that her daughter was "so reciprocal and so affectionate and that's she's got such a benefit from this". She noted also that making the representation was "quite empowering" but she felt "exhausted ... it's actually really hard for me to be this honest".

*****

A sense of embodied reciprocity became the focus of our follow-up session. Kitty felt that their optimal holding was "building resilience" in Harley *and* their relationship. It showed both mother and child that they were "always loved and ... wanted", a considerable difference from Kitty's own childhood experiences.

Working side by side we both reduced the previous session's key elements down to meaningful groups and words. What intrigued Kitty the most in this re-engagement with and development of her previous session's work was the sense of "interconnectedness and the reciprocal nature of it ... like a biofeedback or something!" She then collected art materials and spoke about her process as she made her representation (see Figure 4.4).

Kitty saw an "infinity" symbol, representing "no end". It was important that the image showed movement "an ebbing and flowing, in and out" between mother and child. The right-hand loop showed Harley and the left-hand loop showed Kitty. They met in the centre of the representation where the loops crossed over and this showed how the "heart" was the locus of where Kitty felt

*Figure 4.4* Kitty, *Representation 2B 'The Interconnectedness of Reciprocity'*, soft pastel on paper, 420x295mm.

their "connection". The different colours showed the different emotional intensities experienced during holding.

Having finished the drawing, Kitty noted that representing her feelings on paper "put the connections in my head much stronger than just what I could sort of see (in my mind)". A period of time in between sessions to simmer on new insights about holding appeared to enable access to the harder to capture and 'esoteric' qualities of holding for Kitty.

Kitty described how "the energy will move out of this picture into and out of those loops (showing) expansion and growth". Beyond the moment of holding and the boundaries of the page, the energy generated between them would move into their everyday relationship. The black space around the drawing also showed "stopping time and being in space. So, it's almost like a void". During holding, she and Harley got to be "in this time, in this moment".

Kitty felt real "joy … in getting that out of my head and onto paper! And to be able to just talk about that and see what that was, was great!"

I asked Kitty if she could think of a sentence or title for her representation. She named it *The Interconnectedness of Reciprocity*. Describing it to her daughter she would tell her how they "give each other energy and we take from each other and … we're always connected".

Focusing on relationship had brought to our awareness a very particular quality of the mother/child bond valuable and central to Kitty's experiencing, and how she imagined Harley's experiencing. With a balance of give and take, of needs negotiated and met between mother and daughter, their experiencing flowed. Optimal moments of holding required time of both mother and child but also gave them time in which their experiencing slowed down to a stop, a perfect moment of being together.

## The heart of us: a new kind of relationship and ways of holding (Sessions 3A and 3B)

> I still very much feel Harley is a part of me … physically, as well as emotionally. She … knows she's an entity in (her own right) but I still feel very connected to her? Like that she's very much still a part of my body and part of who I am, I still feel that very much.

As with Rosanna and Leni, I offered Kitty the option of attending to her experiences of time while holding her child in our fifth and sixth sessions. Kitty had already described how during optimal holding, time felt fluid and muted. She also experienced time as something that mother and child gave to one another. This was an important request made by the relationship for Kitty and Harley: attend to this moment of holding while you can.

Our warm-in oriented Kitty toward lived time. As we sat together I steadily counted the years backward from Kitty's birthday to the day on the year she was born. This warm-in brought up a range of memories and thoughts for Kitty. She noted that with Harley having started school, she had reflected a lot on how different Harley's family experiences were to her own. Considering her past, Kitty felt "desolate and sort of empty".

I wondered if Kitty felt that her past impacted how she held Harley. Kitty explained that she felt a "lot of pressure to hold" Harley as a newborn and that this was "suffocating". At times when she was overwhelmed, she chose not to hold her "for fear of hurting her". At the same time, if Harley was distressed, Kitty would need and want to hold her. "I think that I did make a bit of a decision.... I knew in my head that *I* needed to hold her and touch her if *she* was going to be able to do that to herself?" Kitty wanted to develop in Harley the capacity to receive and give affection, something she hadn't felt capable of until her daughter's birth.

When she was a child, Kitty was "*definitely* smothered ... there was no room to breathe or be in myself or take up space". She did "feel ... that weight on me now, the weight of the past" in her everyday life, though significantly, she did not feel that when she held Harley. This is perhaps one reason why her experiences with her family of origin rarely manifested in our sessions together.

Holding her infant daughter included a desire to normalise affection (given Kitty's personal past) but it also included a "natural" impulse "that was in me". She described how the "past is not really influencing the holding" because her "relationship with Harley" was "new".

Rather than bringing her past into the present, Kitty felt more like she was "re-doing" or "re-experiencing" a new childhood of her own in the present. These were "positive experiences" of holding and in a way, being held, unlike her own painful experiences. Kitty felt any influence of her past on their mother/child relationship had to do with how: "*I* could have been, if I wasn't there" (in her family of origin). She still resented her parents and felt "sad" about what happened to her but tried not to bring that sadness or resentment into her relationship with Harley.

I was very aware of my own assumptions around the impact of the past on the present. Having explored attachment literature and worked therapeutically around my own past, and the way it shaped my present with my son, I was intrigued to hear that Kitty felt her past had little to do with holding Harley. I was deeply curious to see how this newness was expressed and understood.

As Kitty drew, she noted that "with the holding ... it's almost like its *own* entity or its *own* thing that hasn't come from anything else". This 'newness' had just "happened": as a natural emergence rather than a deliberate decision on her part.

Kitty described her representation as a "vortex":

> You know how you have a vortex in Dr Who? And the vortex goes in that way [deeper into the centre of the shape] but I'm feeling my experience is coming *out* that way, so it's going from the small to the big?

Holding Harley was "*more* than my past, and it's not *tainted* by my past". The central point of the vortex showed her holding Harley as an infant because their relationship began with Harley's birth and not with Kitty's own past.

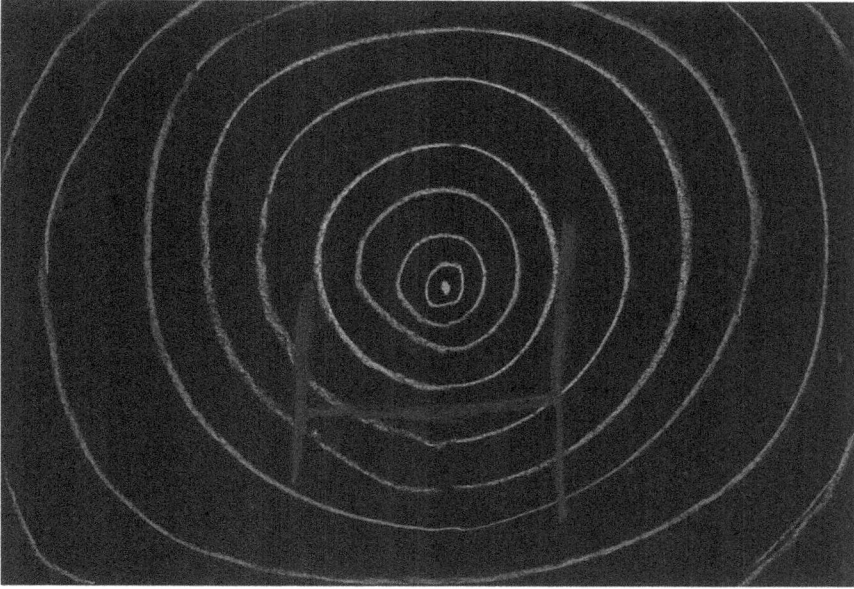

*Figure 4.5* Kitty, *Representation 3A*, soft pastel on paper, 420x295mm.

While a vortex denotes energies pulled into an empty centre, Kitty's relational vortex represented the energy of their love radiating out into the future.

She placed darker green figures in the representation to show Harley and herself holding hands and "striding" together outward "into the future". Their future was also "expanding and getting bigger, as our – her world – is growing".

Holding Kitty now felt less "intense" and frequent than holding as an infant with less all-enveloping holding. She was aware that holding would change over time, the level of affection "might stop eventually". She felt that this might occur partly because Harley might become less affectionate with her as she matured, but also because "I won't need to hold her". Kitty said that she felt sad about time moving them apart "physically" though "hopefully emotionally, that won't happen".

Kitty wondered about other cultures that celebrated a child's connection to their mother. She considered that in our Western culture we're told that we "have to let go" but she questioned what it was exactly that you had to let go of and why. I too wondered about this. It felt like 'common knowledge' that children were supposed to separate from their mothers, a growing separation equated with independence and health. But all participants, and on reflection, I too, had struggled with painful feelings that arose with the idea of less holding, less touch and less connection as our children matured. I had no answers for this, only an awareness that this sadness and sense of loss was a part of mothering for the four of us.

She explained that new phases in Harley's life kept arriving and "I'm never ready for them, I'm always the one catching up". But Kitty could see in her drawing that their relationship was "strong"; the two of them were like "goalposts on a field … standing tall". Kitty stated that: "I won't ever lose her in time or space". This strength was experienced and reinforced by the moment during maternal holding where it was just "her and I, *no one else*". The holding they had already shared contributed to how the relationship was "structured and set"; they faced the future together no matter how their holding transformed over time.

Kitty's familial past did influence their holding when she wasn't coping with Harley's behaviour. When angry or highly stressed with Harley, she sometimes felt that her responses (emotional and physical) might be "aggressive". However, she did not feel that this reflected her usual experience of holding her daughter as the very act of holding would usually transform her emotions, calming them both. Holding Harley was not only good for her daughter but "good for me". Kitty felt it was "enriching and I feel loved and held". In times of stress or difficulty with Harley, offering to hold her daughter gave Kitty the chance to "calm down or remember why I like her".

I made an ISR (Figure 4.6) at the same time as Kitty drew. I recalled her initial description of the vortex "radiating out" and how the movement of energy within and from the relationship had been a difficult quality to convey verbally and artistically. I described how my drawing represented a sense of

*Figure 4.6* Ariel Moy, *An ISR for Kitty's Session 3A*, soft pastel on paper, 420x295mm.

growth and expansion when Kitty talked about "radiation". Kitty said she saw "fire and birds and flowers" and noted that "even when the petals fall and die, they go back to the ground": while her relationship with Harley might change, those qualities of holding they shared did not disappear, they transformed, growing mother and child each time.

Kitty considered that perhaps her past was not part a part of holding Harley because *Harley's* experiences of family were so different to her own and this fed back into their relationship. Kitty did not have that kind of relationship with her parents; she didn't have any holding experiences that she could recall: "Closeness … is something outside of the norm for us [her family of origin]". She described how:

> The last time I remember being touched by my parents, and really, the last time I remember, was a slap, across the face, from my mother. But I don't remember any other touching from her at all.

Kitty's holding experiences with Harley were green and new because mother and child co-created a ground upon which their relationship could grow and evolve; their shared history fed back into their relationship to keep them connected into the future. This was a powerful way of understanding how the past mingled with the present. It was not that the past had no impact, it was that any impact it had was always reshaped by the relationship – by the presence of her child co-creating experiences with her mother. This resulted in something more than a replication of Kitty's experiences with her mother, something defined by the contributions of both mother and child. This showed a recognition of the power of the child in a mother's experiencing.

*****

Due to life circumstances it was a number of months before we returned to Kitty's vortex drawing. It felt important to attend to our previous session's work before we went on to exploring this further. I was aware that by doing this we might get overly focused on conceptual knowing, at the expense of experiential and artistic knowing. Therefore, before the session, I sent her a full transcription as well as a list of key words and our representations in order to re-familiarize her with her feelings and thoughts around holding from our previous session.

Kitty noted how her representation was "a personal rendering of something to me, this is *very* powerful and has so much in it". At first, she had seen the darker green figures as a bed in her drawing. This reflected positive times of sleeping beside Harley and holding her, there was a structuring and supportive quality to the image mirroring Kitty's prior description of their relationship as a support to each of them. However, she noted that "intimate holding and touching … it's *really* changing", holding experiences had diminished and this was a concern for her going into this session.

Her current experience of time with Harley was about the *lack* of it. Harley was living more of her life, and affection, out in the world with school friends. Kitty felt as if there was "me being here (at home) and her moving out into the world but coming back to me again" at the end of the school day.

Over the recent school holidays, Kitty had hoped to "build up" their intimacy again with quiet times together and holding. Unfortunately, this didn't happen because they were very busy with play dates and her partner was also home a lot. Their intimacy had been "diminishing" anyway with Harley at school, but it had continued to do so over the break.

Historically, their relational experiences had been "intense"; it had been "*us and our time*" but now they shared significantly less time together. With the inclusion of friends and family, Harley's "needs" were being met by others, but some of Kitty's intimacy needs, previously fulfilled with her daughter, were not being met.

The consequences of feeling less connected to Harley had an impact on their relationship. Kitty felt less "patient or as soft as I have been" in the past. Holding and intimacy used to provide a "buffer" to times when Harley was "feral" or "unpleasant", enabling her to cope with her daughter's difficult words or behaviour. But now, being with Harley had become less "enjoyable" at times because Kitty wasn't receiving *or* giving the kind of intimacy she had in the past, instead, their interactions were less about intimacy and more about managing behaviours.

> I haven't really thought about or experienced the feeling of it [the diminishment of intimacy] because I keep thinking ... you know ... we'll *rebuild* or get there again, or I just have to wait until the holidays or whatever, and when she's not as tired.

On reflection, Kitty could see that it was only the last few weeks that the significant diminishment in holding had happened and that Harley had been angrier and harder to manage during that time as well. Kitty also recognised that her longing to hold and be with Harley contributed to the tensions between them: a "lot of my time ... [is spent] just waiting for school to finish, so I can go and get her".

Unlike her previous representations which captured optimal moments of maternal holding, Kitty wanted to represent the compelling "separation occurring" between her and Harley. She understood that Harley might not be experiencing a loss of intimacy in the way that she was. She wondered if this was a need that arose from her alone and perhaps wasn't present in the relationship.

Selecting a blue piece of paper, Kitty returned to the imagery of the heart to "see where it goes". Within the heart, she felt that the "radiating ... light" from their relationship still existed. It occurred "at night, before sleep ... and then in the mornings". She recognised that holding now occurred "a lot around sleeping or in the bed or just out of bed and that ... sort of dream world before being fully asleep or fully awake".

Kitty's feelings and ideas changed as she filled in the heart (see Figure 4.7). She explained that by drawing it, she could see "what I have ... what is sort of coming to me rather than what I've lost, or feel like I've lost, when I think about [holding]". At these times there was a "refilling [of] our hearts, or my heart, through my touch of her". She could see in the drawing that the holding and intimacy *were* still present; she could still receive Harley's love; it was just that the frequency and intensity of it had reduced and changed.

Positioning the heart "off centre" acknowledged that right now, holding and touching Harley was "not everything that it was or everything that I need".

Kitty then filled in the upper part of the page with a pale pastel blue (including the upper part of the heart), representing herself, and then a darker blue on the bottom right-hand part of the page and the heart, representing Harley. She described the differences in the quality of feeling in the previous representation (Figure 4.6): where the energy of holding Harley had radiated out in circles, in this representation that energy was "emanating out" but in a "calmer" way.

An idea emerged for Kitty, represented by the two different shades of blue, that perhaps she and Harley "*need* to differentiate more". She understood that she was disappointed with the holiday because they hadn't returned to the kind of intimacy that she wanted. While this was painful, it was also transitional, represented by the "blue" as "water" that was "life giving and affirming". She thought perhaps she might find a "different way of seeing that holding".

*Figure 4.7* Kitty, *Representation 3B*, soft pastel on paper, 420x295mm.

With their opportunities for holding centred around going to sleep and waking up, Kitty could see in her drawing the ways that holding now felt "mystical". It was "very quiet, the mind is quiet, the body is quiet ... almost like in between worlds ... bigger than our physical experience". The experience and the "importance of it" were emotionally "filling" for Kitty. She *was* receiving the intimacy she craved, it just manifested differently and required she pay attention to it.

This resonated with my own experience. While acknowledging the loss and sadness that accompany the changing mother/child relationship, there is the possibility of also attending to the ways in which those changes give something new to the relationship. At the time, I did not share this with Kitty, but I recalled a friend telling me that people are always so aware of what they'll lose when they choose to have children, yet it's harder to know what one might gain. I now understand my future with my son is a series of forays into 'undiscovered countries' that I'll never be fully prepared for, and I will inevitably feel the loss of things I have cherished, but it need not be a loss of the relationship, nor the possibilities inherent within it.

I held up the representation for us to look at. Kitty felt there was too much black and filled up the entire page with pastel shading (light and dark blues). She then noted that "it's like a shore and waves meeting at the shore, like coming into there [the heart] again". She likened the darker blue area (representing Harley) to the "drop off zone", a place she'd swum with Harley where the "continental shelf ... just drops off"; an incredibly deep, cold and "scary" part of the ocean. Kitty felt "frightened" by the drop off zone and "uncomfortable". She then made the connection between this and forming an attachment with a child: parents "have that intimacy and then they're [the children] their own person, and they're going to go their own way, and that's scary".

Loving her daughter and holding her included the fear of losing her and having to accept that the relationship would continually change. However, bringing these ideas into awareness led Kitty to feel "*much* happier with" her drawing and what it told her about holding: "I think maybe what's in my mind, is that what we have can be *enough*, I can make it be enough" for now and in the future, by paying attention to what she received during holding as well as what she gave.

At the end of our session, Kitty explained the power of the heart as a symbol and an experience while holding Harley:

> This just used to blow me away, this little heart beating in this little body ... and I think when you're not religious, and you can't talk about souls, and this sort of stuff, it's almost, this is our ... *repository* for all of that sort of stuff, the heart.

Kitty had found a way of attaching what she received from holding to a valuable image and a physical experience that she could return to at any time. This image and associated sensations, emotions and thoughts reminded her of what she cherished about holding Harley and of the different kinds of holding possible for them.

On reflection, I noted that an image of mother and child curled into one another stored my memories, sensations, emotions and ideas about holding my son. I have returned to this image/sensation when I've felt distant from him and anxious about our changing relationship. The image captures and reinforces our shared history but I'm aware that different images will layer over this as our relationship evolves.

## Mother and child: "in this universe and of this universe and having something that's big enough to fill it" (Session 4)

> That's what we are.… Heat energy, lots of energy, powerful, strong energy.

In our final session together, I spread out all of Kitty's representations and my ISRs on the floor. I also brought along our key words lists and transcriptions from prior sessions to give us both the opportunity to reflect upon what we had explored and come to know so far. We acknowledged that how Kitty saw the representations now would not be exactly as she saw them at the time of making, as she had explored her experiences further and lived more experiences since then.

Kitty moved between drawings, pausing with each, sometimes closing her eyes and standing still as I read out key words from the relevant session. She spoke at different points, articulating what she recalled of each session and representation; what was consonant and what was dissonant for her now. This included reflections on what she felt she knew at the time of our sessions, and what she knew now.

Of representation 2B (Figure 4.4) Kitty felt that the loops looked like "kissing … the smaller head (left hand side) coming and kissing here (the right-hand side loop). At this point, Kitty felt that she was "developing an image in my head … of drawing and bringing this all together". I offered to stop reading key words if she wanted to make her representation, but she asked for me to continue so she could hear them for all of the sessions we had shared.

Re-engaging with her representations and making sense of them arose in a story-like way for Kitty. She felt that some of the representations spoke to the moment in time that she made them (even if the representations were about previous times) while others felt more "universal" or related to her overall understanding of holding Harley.

> What I'm hearing in my head, I've got so much going through my head at the moment, it's incredible!… I'm seeing angels and … biblical things … but I'm also seeing a universal … like a science thing … space and time and light … infinity … movement and heat … the stories explaining the universality of human experience.

Kitty felt that her overall experience of holding Harley attended to the "day-to-day physical experience" of it. She could see "stars and galaxies and being pin-points in that? The *feelingness* that we're out, in, amongst that". These qualities included a sense of the two of them together "moving forever, [with] no boundaries".

She was surprised that "the feelings I *did* have about things are still all very much alive, it's still very much how I feel". The more "negative" feelings she had explored during some sessions appeared very specific to that time and place for her now. They were not indicative of how she experienced holding Harley in general but were rather chapters in their story that gave it texture and reflected how their relationship adjusted to changes in holding.

As Kitty began her drawing, she noted that looking at all of her work felt "spectacular" and this feeling carried over into what she wished to express about her holding experiences.

She drew white pinpoints across her paper and described them as "all my stars in the starry, starry sky ... my version of the universe" (Figure 4.8). In the centre of the page were "two separate stars but together ... bursting out" with "a sunburst of light, energy and heat and life".

It was important that everything in the universe she was representing appeared and felt "interconnected" in the "vastness". The universe was around Harley and Kitty but was also *of* Harley and Kitty. This conveyed that holding is "just as big as the universe, in terms of what it means for me".

Different stars, movement and colours in the universe showed "the different forms of what's been happening for us" over the years. The overall meaning of

*Figure 4.8* Kitty, *Representation 4A Starry Night*, soft pastel on paper, 420x295mm.

her holding experiences was comprised of the many different kinds of holding she and Harley had shared, including some of the less positive moments.

The representation was quickly made. Some images had arisen in Kitty's mind when we'd first moved amongst her drawings from previous sessions but what emerged was less thought out. She described how: "I didn't really have that image (Figure 4.8) in my head … what's come out was not … fully formed, I sort of had a *feeling* of what I wanted of it". She took that feeling, began with the white stars and then just went with what her body in interaction with the materials felt compelled to do in the moment.

Kitty passionately described the possibilities of their growing universe and its movement. She decided to make the central markings bolder and larger, this reflected the "big bang" like quality at the "start of all this", the beginning of their holding experiences and relationship that continued to flow out into their other holding experiences. She then called the representation *Starry Night*.

Making *Starry Night* left her feeling "quite calm" but also "invigorated". When she was "listening to the words and things [at the beginning of our session] I was feeling quite emotional … and reminded of how blessed I am" with their love. Making the representation brought a feeling of "clarity" to all those big emotions.

Having Harley had given Kitty an understanding and experience of "what love was … and now I can see why there's poetry, and why there's art and why there's Bible stories". She could see in her representation how her experience of holding Harley was "*amazingly* so much more than this little place that we hold them" or just the simple act of physically holding Harley: "I can *feel* that connectedness … maybe it's a nature, being … *in* this universe and *of* this universe and having something that's big enough to fill it".

We walked over to all of her previous representations. I held *Starry Night* up so that she could look at them together. She was struck by the stories and imagery of science and religion that arose for her throughout our sessions. These approaches reflected the "biblical world of explaining scientific wonder and cause" for Kitty; a way of grappling with and making meaning of maternal holding. Experiences and imagery of "powerful explosions, colour and movement and joy, expectation, anticipation, all that stuff when you go to see fireworks" and the "noise, smell" showed the power of holding.

If Kitty were to describe *Starry Night* to Harley, she would say how the "energy" of their universe was "ours and belongs to us and we can use it". The experience and meaning of maternal holding for Kitty gave back to their relationship. "Deep down" the love and connection felt within holding experiences was "so big, that it will always be what it is".

Reflecting on our session work, Kitty said:

> It's been very moving and very touching to see it all like this, and to explore it all, *incredibly* moving, and it's given me an insight that … wasn't there for me before? So … we all know the importance of touch and everything but to see … the actual profound impact it has, and the

profound importance it has in *my* relationship with Harley, and the blessing of it. Because I hadn't really thought much about it before.

That maternal holding had brought into Kitty's awareness a relational universe of mother and child was profoundly moving. Particularly so, given her difficult background. From our sessions, I gained a tangible sense of what relationship felt like during maternal holding for her and recognised many of those sensations and emotions in my own holding of my son.

Kitty noted of our inquiry:

> I think about it (holding) a lot more. Even this morning, I was thinking about it when she came into our bed, and I was holding her, and I thought: "you haven't done this for such a long time" but to feel it, and remember it, and the importance of it.

From working with participants, I too paid more attention to holding. From my sessions with Kitty, the last participant I worked with, I began to see the softest of outlines of what might emerge as significant for all four us about our holding experiences. I wondered what words and imagery might represent these rich, intense and meaningful experiences.

## After our sessions

I sent a number of themes and depictions to Kitty to see how she felt about them. Once I had received her feedback and settled on the below individual findings, I created an ISR for her.

I considered how Kitty saw herself and her daughter as one from a distance but on closer inspection, as two clear identities. Kitty's sense of fitting with Harley, her physical experiencing and the energy she received from optimal holding moments were important elements and I wanted to respond to these. I also considered how Kitty felt that she and Harley were a part of the universe but also that their relationship *was* the universe entire. I wanted to convey the "bigness of love", the movement, nourishment and fullness that came with holding in this universe of mother and child.

Kitty responded to my ISR with the words: "extraordinary, absolutely stunning, am blown away". I asked her if she would like to make a visual representation of either her reflections on our explorations of holding together, or on what it feels like to hold Harley now, but she felt happy with what the inquiry represented and did not feel the need to add to it for now.

## Kitty's themes around maternal holding

As described in Chapters 1 and 2, I selected themes and depictions to describe our findings for Kitty.

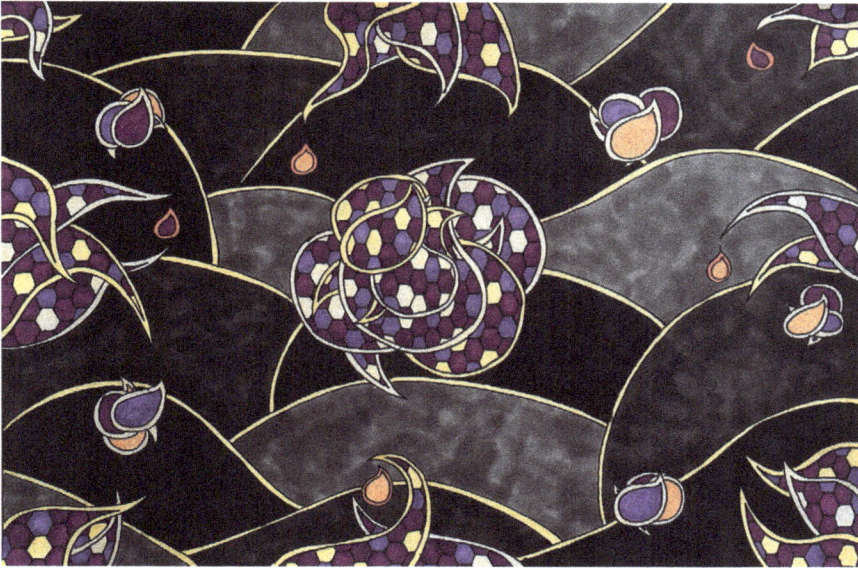

*Figure 4.9* Ariel Moy, *An ISR for Kitty (after our sessions were complete)*, felt tip pen on paper, 295x210mm.

**Theme 1: Science and religion are ways of describing the immensity and timelessness of the love I feel when I hold you. I can't believe how much I love you**

Depiction: The love I feel for you as I hold you, and the love we share, is immense and infinite. You fill my heart. Holding you, I am the universal mother, we are bigger than our physical experience, we are galaxies and our love is the Big Bang.

**Theme 2: I hold you and our heartbeats touch**

Depiction: I feel your humanity, the wonder of your body and the weight of you. Together we radiate warmth and our hearts beat in rhythm becoming calmer as I hold you.

**Theme 3: When I hold you, it's just you and I. We pause in the dreamlike dawn between worlds: this is our moment**

Depiction: When I hold you everything around us is quiet. It is just you and I in the world, in our world, and we are the centre of it. The strength of us and the intensity of us removes time and space. We are calm, we have paused, we are without thought. This is our moment.

**Theme 4: We are one**

Depiction: There is no real separation between us, you have become my heart. We are one and perfect, one heart, one structure. You are part of my body and who I am. From afar we look like one star in the universe, the universe of us.

**Theme 5: We are forever connected. Our energy flows between us and makes us strong**

Depiction: Energy ebbs and flows between us; we will fit together and always will. I will never lose you in time or space, we are two stars twining, touching, overlapping and permeating through one another. Our bond is so strong. Physically, emotionally, spiritually we will be forever connected.

**Theme 6: Our love flows through us and into our world. I know what love is now**

Depiction: We are surrounded in warmth and light, it protects us. We expand and grow, waves of us spread out, emanating into our universe. We are heat and light and movement. Holding you, I came to know what love is. We are the energy of love.

**Theme 7: We grow together: I am and will be big enough for her as our relationship changes**

Depiction: I realize I have the capacity within me to move with her, to grow with her and to expand. I am and will be big enough for her. There is so much space around us, we are out amongst the stars and we are the stars and the space. It can be bittersweet watching her change, having to change with her. Our touch diminishes as she grows older, but we move infinitely together, flow together, through each other and away but never apart.

**Theme 8: I am afraid that time will move us apart. I wish I could hold her more. I'll get in as many kisses as I can, while I can**

Depiction: I wonder sometimes if I am enough, if she will flow away from me, if time will move us apart. I wish I could hold her more. I try to get as many kisses as I can. As I hold her now, I tell myself to feel it and remember it and the importance of it, I refill my heart with her.

**Theme 9: As I hold my daughter, I too am held. We are in this together**

Depiction: When I hold her, I can feel her love going into my heart. We hold one another more equally now. I get as much from holding her as she does from me. I feel enriched, I feel loved. There is great joy in holding or being held by Harley.

**Theme 10: Holding you I feel such joy; our warm light protects and enriches me**

Depiction: Warm soft light surrounds us when I hold you. I feel such happiness holding you, such joy. I am blessed and enriched. Our life and heat glows around us: our love is protected.

**Theme 11: I wanted to normalize touch. She is very loving**

Depiction: My daughter is very loving and very affectionate with her friends. I made a conscious decision to hold her, I knew that she would need that, but it was also very natural, I always respond to her with touch and holding. I wanted to foster that physical intimacy within her; I wanted to normalise touch.

**Theme 12: Sometimes my reserves are low: I need more intimacy with Harley so that I can give that intimacy in return. At times like these, when she wants to be held, I do not want to hold her**

Depiction: There are times when my daughter needs comfort and I don't really want to comfort her, I don't want to hold her. In highly stressful times my past comes back to me and holding can be too draining. I might move away; I might push her away. I don't have the reserves in these moments.

**Theme 13: Holding you can be a circuit breaker. Tensions change to calm; we relax into one another**

Depiction: If we are having problems, if my thoughts or feelings towards you are troubled, holding you can resolve the issue. We influence one another, we calm one another down and we can find a new perspective on a problem when we hold one another. These are our shining moments – holding you is a circuit breaker.

**Theme 14: Holding you is a new experience**

Depiction: When my daughter was born, I could not believe how much I loved her. I now know what love is: holding her has awakened real feeling in me. Holding my daughter has nothing to do with my past, it is its own entity, it is entirely new.

# 5   Inquiry findings

## Introduction

In the previous chapters I provided session stories for each participant. As described in Chapter 1, individual themes were generated for each mother once all sessions were complete. From these individual themes, I then elected to explore shared qualities of participants' knowing.

Certain qualities within each mother's individual themes were consonant with one another and formed the building blocks of this inquiry's findings. However, these general findings did not necessarily encompass every aspect of each participant's individual themes: Some individual themes did not contribute to any of the three across-participant findings which is why I have included them in the previous three chapters.

As described in Chapter 1, data was comprised of:

- All key words/phrases taken from transcriptions and participant's own work: these were sourced from our work with representations but also our content in process
- Each mother's representations
- My ISRs (intersubjective responses)
- Individual mother's themes

I elected to explore potential relationships between co-generated materials multimodally inviting all forms of knowing into the endeavour. After placing all of the material on the floor (including print outs of all key words), I walked amongst and moved information around. I attended to sensations, emotions and imagery that arose, alerting me to potential connections between data.

By this point, I had established intimate relationships with the material, both with participants and alone, and there were explicit and tacit assumptions I had made about it as well as the generation of individual themes. However, I wished to give myself the opportunity to look at the materials 'as if for the first time', a process of placing all data on an even, equal plane and attending to experiential knowing. I recognized that my relationships with the data were present, but I hoped to gently put those already conceptualized understandings

DOI: 10.4324/9781003104094-6

in the background, in order to shine light on possible *new* or less well-known connections between materials.

At different stages in clustering (a data reduction procedure) and exploring findings, I focused on artistic and experiential knowing, paying attention to any unifying images or sensations that arose. To aid this process, I would engage in physical movements that captured qualities of connection between data. At other times, I would represent these sensed connections in a creative piece of my own (for example, an installation or a drawing). Often, I would place resonant images (for example, from postcards) near or upon groupings to see what they might tell me about them. I attempted to employ the various ways of knowing in this approach to investigating what connections between data were meaningful as this would alert me to different qualities of connection.

It was also important to check the context of each key element (that is, for which participant and in which session did they arise) against my own inter-pretation of that element's meaning. For example, the term "sun" immediately indicated warmth to me but in Rosanna's first session where the word origi-nated from, her "sun" referred to the power, intensity and energy of her youngest daughter Deanna, and how that energy pulsed and pushed Rosanna away. In this instance "sun" was not about warmth. Later, "sunniness" referred to Rosanna's eldest daughter Elaina and *did* mean warmth and invitation. It was vital that what the word meant for the participant contributed to what cluster it formed and/or contributed to in my work towards inquiry findings.

Constant checking between the key elements lists and transcriptions helped to clarify the presence of my own associations with certain words and the meanings they held for the participants.

I maintained the integrity of the location of the key elements, that is, the sessions from which they originated, by allocating specific colours to each ses-sion and participant. This colour coding enabled me to quickly recognize which sessions key elements originated from. This was valuable because as described above, the key element "sun" for Rosanna, for example, represented certain qualities in Session 1A but quite different qualities in Session 3B.

When I began forming data into findings, I moved back and forth between experiential, artistic and conceptual knowing to further make sense of them. I also engaged regularly with my supervisors who offered creative ways of working with the data and findings, for example with body sculptures: We would focus in on qualities of the finding and attempt to embody these, taking photographs of the embodied shapes and movements that felt consonant.

Three very large groups emerged, and these comprised my findings. Each of these groups consisted of smaller sub-groups that spoke directly but in slightly different ways to the particular finding.

I gave each of these findings a title:

- Holding is purposeful
- Expansion into the mother/child 'us'
- Stories of us

This inquiry's findings reflected qualities that appeared valuable and significant to participants' experiences of maternal holding in general. These findings tended to represent optimal maternal holding experiences more often than difficult or painful experiences. Fear of rejection, lack of holding, distress around identifying and meeting needs, fear around losing intimacy, aggressive holding and holding as restraint were all experiences raised by different participants, but as we worked together, it appeared that what was valuable to them, predominant and intriguing about their knowing and what was ultimately explored and expressed were positive qualities. These included the moments that provided these mothers with warmth, connection, purpose, belonging, strength, reinforcement, insight, integrity, oneness and love.

### Holding is purposeful

This finding described the value participants placed on maternal responsibility. This most frequently manifested in their experiences of identifying, navigating and adapting to changing needs in the mother/child relationship. Mothers deliberately, as well as spontaneously, became aware of and responded to the physical, psychological and emotional qualities of their relationship during holding. Both in the moment of holding and on reflection, mothers considered the location of needs, attempting to figure out what needs were theirs, and what needs were originating from their children. They also wished to normalise affection and thus modelled this for their children during holding.

The sense of need and the intention to attend to needs appeared in many of the mothers' explorations and representations stated in words (their own) and imagery around: responsibility, work, capacity, supporting, reasons for holding, duty, the growing of roots and wings, a constant consideration of need, earning, privilege, power, praise, craving, goal posts, clocks, choices made, fault, developing needs, adapting, guilt, burden of needs, effort and the feeling that without their children they could not live.

Children's needs were identified as the focus of maternal holding by all participants. In particular, the initiation of holding was understood as a response to their children's needs.

Rosanna, Kitty and Leni valued the responsibility they felt toward their children during maternal holding. This manifested particularly in the navigation of relational needs.

In their encounters with and fulfilment of perceived children's needs, participants found some of their own important needs encountered and fulfilled as well. Feelings of love, comfort, safety, warmth and connection were all gifts that these mothers wanted to give to their children by holding them. In giving, mothers often received them in return. All participants recognized and articulated very important maternal needs (including maternal purpose) met by holding their children. Ultimately, both maternal and children's needs within relationship were identified and navigated during maternal holding.

Looking at maternal holding through the lens of purposefulness brought with it a range of difficulties and rewards. Each mother relayed experiences of guilt and a sense of failure when they felt that they had not navigated their children's needs appropriately. Each mother also felt satisfaction, joy and fulfilment when they believed they had navigated their children's needs well. Both difficulties and rewards manifested in the relationship during maternal holding and were understood from within the framework of the relationship on reflection.

Experiencing a sense of purpose while holding one's child might lend a reductive or focused quality to holding. The identification and management of needs — whether it be the child's or the mother's needs — might reduce experiencing in the moment to a focus onto a particular need. It might momentarily push aside other concerns and qualities in service of fulfilling that need. It may also draw focus onto one or the other member of the relationship and thus create a sense of separation between mother and child. As Leni described, maternal holding can create a "running commentary, running narrative" in one's mind and body: does my child need or want to be held in this place at this time? Do they need a gentle cuddle? Are they afraid? Do they need containment? Will they be embarrassed if I hold them now? Should I hold them more often so that in the future they will feel held even when I am physically not present?

However, for participants, purposefulness most often appeared as a deeply relationship-centric quality. The 'rewards' of fulfilling children's needs fulfilled mothers needs as well. This relational quality of needs does not mean that children's and mother's needs were the same, only that navigation happened within relationship.

Needs intermingled so that they appeared to arise from the relationship more so than from an individual member. While a mother could identify a need as her own or her child's, the ways in which these needs manifested were profoundly relational. Individual needs, during holding, became relational needs as they were now a part of the mother/child 'us' experience. This experience of 'us' was highly valuable and ultimately a rather more expansive than reductive quality of being.

How participants spoke about their knowing appeared to transcend the felt understanding of 'need' to incorporate a greater sense of mission, an overall orientation and a profound desire to care for, consider, develop and support their children *and*, though perhaps inadvertently, themselves and their relationship. This kind of holding was bound up with participants' identity as mothers, and their regular assessment of whether they aligned with or at odds with their maternal purpose. Maternal holding appeared to provide an opportunity for the needs and purpose of *both* mother and child to be noticed, navigated and met through and for the relationship.

### Holding and expansion into the mother/child 'us'

This finding was formed by an exploration of the relationships between three sub-groups:

- Felt experiences of expansion co-created by mother and child in relationship;
- Participants' movement from a sense of self to self-in-relationship;
- The expansion of lived time and space.

These themes spoke to qualities that represented an understanding of what I termed 'expansion'. The selection of this term was based upon the use of it by participants and the felt qualities of the term capturing enlargement, generosity, unfolding and increase.

Across multiple forms of knowing, participants conveyed feelings, images and ideas around: oneness, connection, growth, adapting, changing, flowing, energy, the threads that bind, hugeness and immensity. For example, Kitty often referred to scientific and religious imagery and metaphor to explain the profound sense of love she shared with Harley; Rosanna described a kind of "familial" holding that transcended the holding of one individual to include others, and Leni cherished the sense of "just us" she felt while holding her children. Holding provided moments that transcended these mothers' everyday notions of a bounded self to include emotions, understanding and artistic representations of *self-in-relationship*.

Participants described purposeful and deliberate expansion. In these instances, their expanded self-in-relationship was explicitly engaged as the mothers elected to develop ways of being with their children in order to navigate changing relational needs like those found in purposeful holding experiences.

At other times, a felt sense of expansion emerged spontaneously from moments of holding and engendered feelings of wonder, gratitude and love. This expansion was unexpected and not always easy to articulate. Visual representations contributed to our understanding of mother's shifting awareness from self to self-in-relationship during holding. The unusual and precious experience of expanded self-in-relationship was difficult to convey in language.

Experiences of self-in-relationship arose into awareness for participants during moments of optimal maternal holding. This expansion of self into 'us' was meaningful and valuable to participants. Sometimes it lingered after the holding was over, perhaps because it was so valuable but also so different from their everyday experiencing of self.

Lived time expanded during optimal maternal holding to include experiences of time that diminished, vanished, and 'thickened' with a sense of past and present at once. Lived space appeared to expand as well, diminishing or vanishing like time, a sense of space including more than one family member or holding across distances.

For a moment during holding, there was only an 'us'. This was not a diminishment or merging of mother and child into each other, but a strange and precious expansion of mother-in-relationship-with-child. This spoke to a deep awareness of the present relational moment.

## Holding and stories of us

This final finding was comprised of the following sub-groups; the first sub-group had two different story subjects within it:

- The storying of holding within the mother/child relationship,
  - a   Stories of shared history,
  - b   Stories of relational patterns;
- The rewards of storying maternal holding.

Story is defined as:

1   An account of imaginary or real people and events told for entertainment;
2   An account of past events in someone's life or in the development of something (retrieved from https://en.oxforddictionaries.com/definition/story)

I believe that story can take many different creative forms including written and oral stories, performances, drawing, painting, sculpture, movies, photographs and songs. The post-structuralist movement also drew attention to how stories are always in relationship with other stories including cultural and familial stories, and stories contribute to how we understand ourselves (Thomas, 2002).

I would suggest that participant's stories were shared to inform, explain, explore and also to make sense of their experiences. When asked to inquire into their holding experiences, all mothers conveyed those experiences as stories. These stories were often verbal but also included their visual representations. In the selection of colours, shapes and images; in their placement, and in the sequencing of their construction, representations also told a story or stories about maternal holding and the mother/child relationship.

When I explicitly inquired into discrete descriptions of experience – for example, a physical sensation, a series of emotions or a set of images that arose when participant's considered maternal holding – each response was quickly positioned within a contextual story. Discrete representations of experiential, artistic or conceptual knowing were never without the contextualization of a story. For Rosanna, Leni and Kitty, conveying stories of holding and relationship appeared to be a necessary element of our inquiry.

Each story about holding was nested within other more general stories of the mother/child relationship: their shared history and relational patterns. Plot and character were dominant features of our exploration into holding even if the plot and characters of mother and child described during holding represented only a few seconds in time. With plot and character, we could see the story of the mother/child relationship, we could see their relational dance as it occurred over time, we could empathise with characters and enter a plot with the possibility of teasing out subtleties and tacit knowing and potentially developing that story. Inevitably larger, extended relational stories 'held' these micro-stories of holding.

Stories conveyed what participants felt were tensions and harmonies within their relationship over time and during specific moments of maternal holding. Stories communicated what these mothers enjoyed, valued and nurtured in their relationship and what they found difficult, struggled with and managed within their relationship.

Purposeful holding was supported by re-engagement with important relational stories that explained what had been needed and how it had been attended to in the past, and also the rewards mothers felt they received when they met relational needs. When relational needs changed, new adaptive stories were developed. These were stories that explained and structured their ongoing relationship.

Stories also illuminated relational rewards; they described a sense of belonging, satisfaction, clarity, meaningfulness and conveyed the uniqueness of the mother/child bond. There was often great joy in the sharing of an 'us' story.

Storying knowing (in images and words) enabled sharing of that knowing, it gave us the opportunity to clarify, make sense, confirm, challenge and develop our knowing about maternal holding.

Holding was not fixed in a particular conceptualisation or experiential quality in the expression of these stories. Stories shared in sessions continued to evolve within the mother/child relationship and within the relationship between me and each participant.

Moments of maternal holding appeared to capture and provide fertile ground for the development and reinforcement of important relational stories of 'us'.

## Conclusion: maternal holding experiences were co-created by mother and child

This inquiry generated three findings that spoke to qualities of the maternal holding experiences that were common for all participants:

- Maternal holding was purposeful;
- Mothers experienced an expanded awareness of self-in-relationship during maternal holding;
- Mothers conveyed their holding experiences and knowing via stories of shared mother/child history and relational patterns of being.

There appeared to be an underlying theme in all three findings: experiences of maternal holding were co-created by mother and child.

The identification and navigation of relational needs from which maternal purpose emerged were created within the mother/child relationship. Purpose, need and reward were not necessarily experienced as the same by mother and child, but it could not be understood without reference to the relationship. Purpose, needs and rewards were generated and navigated *by the relationship*.

Participants chose to expand their ways of being in order to meet their children's and their relationship's changing needs. Experiences of expansion also spontaneously 'sprang' from the relationship. Expansion occurred in response to, and was generated by, relational experiencing in a moment of holding. Mother and child both necessarily contributed to that expansion in an ongoing dance of intersubjectivity.

Maternal holding afforded participants the opportunity to become aware of an expanded sense of self-in-relationship. This included changed and expanded experiences of lived time and space. The felt atmosphere of 'us' was cherished; awareness of this self-in-relationship provided valuable and meaningful moments of belonging, connection and an enlarged oneness.

Both findings around purposefulness and expansion were represented in stories (visual and verbal). Stories about the shared history of mother and child and their relational patterns contextualized and clarified maternal holding experiences. These stories communicated knowing about maternal holding in ways that could be shared, reflected upon and developed. Significantly, these stories arose from relational experiences; they were formed in response to relational experiences and played out within relationship. Stories may well have differed for mother and child, but they could not be told without reference to the relationship, they were of and for the relationship.

The lived relationship during moments of holding could not be predicted or controlled by mother or child alone. What occurred within the relationship was co-created by mother and child.

The three findings for this inquiry were significantly interrelated as touched upon in this chapter. In the next chapters, I will go on to explore these findings in relationship with other academic, artistic and literary voices and imagery across time and disciplines.

Bringing my findings into dialogue with other voices developed my relationship with them by:

- Placing them in relation to prior research, thought, imagery and theory;
- Posing questions to both the findings and other's voices that at times clarified and/or challenged my understandings;
- Demanding a developed, coherent, concise and evocative way of communicating my now enriched findings for a future audience.

Engaging with other voices to clarify and develop my findings can be likened to some therapeutic practices around what has been 'found' by client and therapist in any given session. In the first instance, practitioners constantly check in with clients to see if what has been articulated by therapist and client feels authentic and helpful. Practitioners also bring their 'findings' or experiences and emerging knowing to their supervisors and peers, and to relevant literature, in order to clarify and further develop their understanding. They bring this learning back to their client as well, to further their shared understanding of client experiences.

# References

Thomas, L. (2002). Poststructuralism and therapy: What's it all about? *The International Journal of Narrative Therapy and Community Work*, 2, 85–89. Retrieved from http://dulwichcentre.com.au/wp-content/uploads/2015/07/postructuralism-and-narrative-therapy-.pdf.

# 6 Holding is purposeful

## Introduction to purposeful holding

Purpose emerged as an integral quality of maternal holding. Participants experienced this purposefulness both in the moment of holding and on reflection as a sense of responsibility toward their child. In particular, the experience and conceptualisation of *need* underpinned purposefulness and involved the identification, navigation and management of needs.

Examining the locus of needs was perceived as valuable. While both mother and child's needs were potentially present at any one time during holding, some needs felt more clearly a mother's 'own', emanating from a time in her life prior to her relationship with her child. For example, how she understood and navigated her own past experiences of being held as a child might be examined or attended to before, during or after holding her child. There was a recognition that a mother's own needs were present within the relationship during holding. For those personal needs that appeared unhelpful to the relationship, each mother assumed the responsibility of navigating these as best she could outside of the holding moment.

Experiencing maternal holding through the lens of purposefulness, responsibility and need provided mothers with opportunities for rewards (like the satisfaction of meeting a need) as well as difficulty (like the pain and stress that can come with constantly adapting to the perceived changing needs of growing children). If maternal holding is in part about attending to needs and purpose, then the possibility of reward but also 'failure' and mistakes arises.

At first, purpose manifested as a focus on children's needs. As we, and later I, explored maternal holding it became increasingly clear that purpose and needs emerged from and were about the mother/child relationship, with the mother and child's needs appearing interdependent. We could not isolate a child's need without reference to the mother during holding and vice versa. Interdependence of needs did not mean mother and child experienced the same needs only that they were mutually encountered within the mother/child relationship during holding.

As we developed our knowing around the role of purpose and need in maternal holding three important qualities emerged:

DOI: 10.4324/9781003104094-7

1    A maternal desire to focus primarily on the child's needs;
2    An understanding that children are not immune to their mother's needs during maternal holding;
3    The lived experience that maternal purpose and needs navigation occurs within the embodied, emotional and psychological relationship of mother and child.

These mother's findings led to me engaging with literature in four key areas: the relationship between purposefulness and innate intentionality; the possibility of co-created and co-navigated needs; how attention to relational or intersubjective purposefulness may provide meaning and support for the mother/child relationship and the contributions of cultural norms to the experience of purpose within maternal holding.

### Maternal holding: a space for the meeting of philosophical intentionality and purposefulness

The purposefulness described and explored in this inquiry had at times a deliberate and explicit quality to it. At other times purposefulness appeared almost as a by-product of the mother/child relationship, it was felt to be an innate and unconscious result of 'the way things are' for mother and child. This led me to wonder if, in the first instance, maternal purpose was an innate or socially constructed phenomenon.

I discovered a key concept in philosophy and phenomenology known as intentionality. This describes the fundamental directedness or 'aboutness' of human experiencing: Our knowing is always directed towards and about something. This 'aboutness' does not describe everyday purposefulness or intention. It is a less conscious, generalised orientation toward the other. It has also traditionally been considered a cognitive quality: human 'aboutness' as a brain-based conceptual orientation. However, dialoguing with various definitions of purposefulness raised the possibility that purpose experienced during maternal holding might be an expression of our essential intentionality and intentionality might not be limited to the cognitive domain.

### A 'maternal intentionality' may arise during maternal holding as a sense of purpose

I quickly became aware that intentionality and purpose have served quite different functions in philosophical thought. Philosophical intentionality had traditionally (and contentiously) been coupled with the concept of mental representations. A mental representation is a theoretical means of representing experiences of phenomena in the brain. This rests on the notion that there is some kind of "resemblance" (Watson, 1995, p. 142) between that which is represented and the representation.

This was not the kind of 'aboutness' that emerged from the data and yet the idea of intentionality, of a fundamental maternal *orientation* to her child spoke powerfully to me (whether this orientation was positive or negative).

I was compelled to continue my search and found that intentionality might be embodied, emotional and deeply intersubjective as well as cognitive. This kind of intentionality spoke directly to the maternal purposefulness present in this inquiry.

As researchers and theorists supporting motor or embodied intentionality would suggest, we may be able to do away with the idea of mental representations all together in certain kinds of movement. Alternatively, there may be types of intentionality within human experiencing that play an interdependent role with one another such that mental representations are but a part of the many contributors to our 'aboutness'.

Philosophers, Hubert Dreyfus and Alva Noë have suggested we don't need to refer to mental representations to explain intentionality in all circumstances. Using the term "optimal grip" Dreyfus (2005) describes Merleau-Ponty's motor intentionality stating:

> When you're skilfully coping in flow, without thinking, without rules, your body and its skills are drawing you to get this optimal grip on the situation. And the situation is always completely concrete. It's something that you've never been in before and the other people haven't been in before and you'll never be in it again because having been in it this time has changed you.
>
> (para. 9)

And:

> When you perceive ordinary objects … you move around them … and you are led by the object calling on your body, it's just outside of what your mind does or could do, the object just calls you to get into the best relation to it.
>
> (para. 8)

Dreyfus' notion of 'skilful coping' emphasises an embodied intentionality rather than a cognitive one. In this approach, perception and action are connected without the need for an intervening mental process. Noë (2004) similarly describes perception as "not something that happens to us, or in us. It is something we do" (p. 1).

The participants in this inquiry had held their children so often over so many years and in so many different situations that their holding experiences frequently felt automatic, they simply knew how to be as they held their children, and how to fulfil whatever purpose emerged in the moment. Rosanna, for example, spoke about holding her twins and feeling "in the now" and Kitty referred to feeling "just still, one and perfect" at times when she held her daughter. These automatic ways of holding appeared even in the earliest instances of holding their infants without reference to a conceptual struggle with 'how' to hold them. They just held, as each mother's body found a way of getting into the 'best relation' with her child.

It is possible in these circumstances an embodied rather than cognitive intentionality is more at play. As Eagleman (2011) writes:

> Innumerable facets of our behaviour, thoughts, and experience are insepar-ably yoked to a vast, wet, chemical-electrical network called the nervous system," and "although we are dependent on the functioning of the brain for our inner lives … most of its operations are above the security clearance of the conscious mind.
>
> (p. 4)

However, Ungureanu and Rotaru (2014) argue: "it is possible that, in the process of gaining skills, the initial explicit representation of objects and rules are moulded into subpersonal representations for action," (p. 226). They refer here to mental processes outside of our awareness. They conclude that: "the idea of optimal grip is based on the thesis that the skilful coper is an embodied agent, emotionally involved in continuously improving his actions. But the emotional involvement does not exclude subpersonal … representations for action" (p. 228). This suggests that just because we are *unaware* of a mental process (for example, moments when we hold our children 'on automatic') it does not mean that mental processes or representations are not involved in the act of holding.

Originally, philosophical intentionality described "the directedness, aboutness or reference of mental states – the fact that, for example, you think *of* or *about* something" (retrieved from plato.stanford.edu, *Consciousness and Intentionality*, para. 1). However, as described above, there are already those championing *motor* intentionality as well as *affective* intentionality (Goldie, 2002; Slaby and Stephan, 2008), Songhorian's (2012) sub-personal inter-subjective affective intentionality and Tuomela's (2013) *collective* intentionality. All of these revolve around an essential 'aboutness' humans have towards things, environments and others. What is particularly relevant to maternal holding in these descriptions of multiple kinds of intentionality is that embodied, affective and collective intentionality are inherently purposeful.

Collective intentionality also refers to the 'aboutness' of a group of people towards an object, others or a state of affairs. This concept has been well described in Tuomela's (2013) book *Social Ontology* where he proposes a quality of human experiencing from a "we-mode" defined as "thinking and acting together as a 'we' to promote the interests of 'us'" (p. 5). Here, collective intentionality is coupled with purposefulness.

When Leni and Kitty referred to sometimes feeling at "one" with their chil-dren they were expressing a felt intersubjectivity. They might also have been expressing a particular quality of this intersubjectivity: a collective intentionality or a mutual purpose. They both talked lovingly and proudly about the feeling of 'us-ness' during maternal holding. In moments of optimal holding, purpose did not always feel one-sided or singularly directed. The 'oneness' they describe spoke to a deep mutual aboutness in the moment of holding; a sense that both mother and child were 'about' one another but also purposefully 'about' that particular holding, in that particular moment for them.

When I considered this mutual aboutness I recalled a classic image of maternal holding: Christian representations of Mary and the baby Jesus. These images often reflect an intense 'aboutness', an intentionality that is particular to that relationship, even a shared aboutness. This mother and child are typically haloed in light or gold, they are serene, and they are 'in their own world'. In that iconic moment of holding they appear to be about something that is theirs alone, something we cannot interrogate despite the many other stories attached to it.

Songhorian's (2012) sub-personal intersubjective affective intentionality describes how "a person can be directed towards another even though she is not conscious of her own direction" (p. 112). Cognition is not a necessary part of this kind of intentionality. She uses Scheler's ideas in the *Nature of Sympathy* (1923) to support how this kind of intentionality "represents the original presence of the 'us' within the 'I': it is the primeval basis of all these kind of acts" (p. 115). In this moment of 'us', aboutness and purpose cannot be separately located into two different bodies, it is of the *shared* space, body and time of mother and child together. It is possible that maternal intentionality may fall under a more broadly understood 'collective', intersubjective or relational intentionality.

Biologist and cognitive scientist W. Tecumseh Fitch (2008) proposed a fundamental cellular intentionality present within the eukaryotic cells (p. 3). At a "microanatomical" level (p. 3) these cells are "goal-directed" (p. 1). They possess 'aboutness' by virtue of being able to "rearrange (their) own molecules in a locally-functional manner" (p. 3). Fitch contends that

> when combined properly into large interconnected systems, this mass-action of cellular nano-intentionality yields intrinsic intentionality in the typical philosopher's sense, as well as both consciousness and the efficacy of our subjectively sensed self to move the body and perform other acts of will ('intentionally' in its general English sense).
>
> (pp. 9–10)

Fitch's nano-intentionality supports the intermingling of a generalised innate aboutness and a consciously experienced 'aboutness' or purposefulness.

Exploring different forms of intentionality in relationship with experiences of purposefulness during maternal holding arose because of a strong sense of the depth and innateness of this purpose, not only for participants but also for myself. Purpose felt fundamental to our holding and yet, when we explored it, we acknowledged that we were not always cognitively aware of it in the moment of holding. Purpose appeared as an embodied awareness and shone through in our aesthetic forming, it felt like we were essentially oriented to and 'about' our children and relationship in that moment.

Discovering that philosophical 'aboutness' was not limited to cognitive modes of being supported my idea that experiences of purposefulness might be manifestations of a 'maternal intentionality'. Participants and I experienced purpose as an essential orientation toward our children across multiple modes of being. However, this orientation had particular qualities that appeared to bring intentionality into awareness in a way that was best described as purpose. I explore these in the following section.

### Mothers are 'about' their children in a purposeful and particular way

When Leni reflected on her changing relationship with her daughter, she had the feeling "I have to do this right". In the first instance she was about her daughter, in the second she was about holding her daughter in the 'right' way. She had a wealth of experiences and knowledge that she referenced in order to determine what way of holding her daughter would in fact be 'right'. Leni wasn't only oriented to her daughter as she held her; she was directed toward her daughter in very particular, purposeful ways.

I have considered the presence of multiple forms of intentionality. I extend this understanding to suggest that during maternal holding our intentionality is value-laden and based on a shared mother/child relational history. This 'aboutness' is very specific, unique and particular to the mother/child bond, and it involves purpose.

In any holding encounter with her child there exists some kind of prior knowledge about the relationship. Even the very first experience of holding one's newborn often emerges from a 40-week experience of holding them *in utero*. This prior knowledge about the relationship includes information, judgments and values based on shared past experiences; it orients the mother to her child in a particular way. For example, when I held other people's children, I did not experience the holding in the same way. Leni, working as a family day carer, also explained that with other people's children: "there's no emotion to it so ... just a physical act". She would "comfort them" but it did not have the emotional depth that holding her own children had because the relationship she has with her children is one of "love". That love is particular to their relationship, it is not a free-floating generalised aboutness, it's an aboutness tailored to their relationship.

At its most basic level, maintaining the survival of one's child is (usually) a very important and valuable need, not only for the child but also for the parent. This 'aboutness' however is also very specific. These mothers didn't just know that they wanted their children to survive; they knew and enacted this in highly informed and attenuated ways: they knew their child or wanted to know them better, they knew, for example, what they liked and didn't like, when they liked it, and when to adapt how they held their children. For Leni, if she held her daughter "right" then she would meet what she felt her daughter needed in that moment and she would fulfil some of her maternal purpose. Holding her daughter 'right' had very particular criteria for Leni, criteria that were slightly different for her son and for the other participants as it depended on Leni's unique shared history with her daughter. These criteria were not necessarily cognitively salient in the moment of holding and yet were present in the way the mother/child relationship played out in that moment.

Leni noted that her "brain doesn't stop" when she holds her children. Even when she had those blissful brief moments of "squeezing love", where her thoughts were quiet, her aboutness was still value-laden – it was full of warmth, oneness and relaxation, it was full too of the ways that she understood her maternal responsibility. Her aboutness was comprised of emotion, sensation and quite often thought. It could not be divorced from her experiential knowing of her child which was ever and always particular to *their* relationship and their relational history.

Returning to the feeling of holding my son, I knew instinctively that holding him was not the same as holding others; it was textured with everything that made my relationship with my son, our shared history, our quirks, our hopes, holding was particular to 'us' (see Box 6.1).

---

**Box 6.1 Ariel Moy, *The Ways in Which We Hold*, poem.**

Holding you,
I remember the weight of infancy,
The collapse of tears,
The wrapping of arms around.
As you get older you meet me,
At eye level,
Cheeky, serious,
The holding evolves with us.
I cannot and do not wish,
To separate,
Who we were,
From who we are,
In this moment of holding,
Or remembering.
We are,
*We* are.
We were,
We hold,
In ways that are,
Ours alone.
Beneath choices and the present,
An inevitability,
A history of 'us',
Shaping and being shaped.

I suggest that:

> Purposefulness may be a quality of maternal intentionality that arises into awareness and is uniquely directed toward the mother/child relationship.

Further, purpose, as described by participants, most often manifested as a sense of needs identification, navigation and management (explored further in the next section). To manage need requires effort. In light of this I suggest that:

> Maternal intentionality involves the identification and navigation of needs and requires effort; it is value laden and responsive to mother/child shared history. These qualities bring maternal intentionality into a felt though not necessarily cognitive awareness as a sense of purpose.

There are a number of important considerations to take into account when suggesting a 'maternal intentionality'. First, experiences of purpose do not necessarily equate with helpful or healthy needs identification and navigation. Similarly, maternal intentionality does not necessarily signify a positive orientation towards one's child.

Second, maternal purpose may not emerge in *every* mother/child relationship. Some mothers may take time to develop a relationship with their child, some mothers may never develop a relationship and without relationship it is difficult to experience maternal purpose or intentionality.

Third, if there is a maternal intentionality it may manifest in multiple ways, a felt sense of purpose may be only one of its facets.

Finally, we need to take into account the cultural prescriptions and social forces at play in the experience of maternal purpose (explored later in this chapter).

In terms of therapeutic work, exploring the possibility of an innate maternal orientation to child in the form of purpose will illuminate a mother's sense of what is *fundamentally necessary* for her to feel satisfied with her mothering, her child's flourishing and her relationship with her child. From there we can explore how adaptive and beneficial this orientation is, what works and what doesn't, and what might be developed in order to grow relational health.

## Co-created and co-navigated needs and purpose during maternal holding

The relationship between purposefulness and maternal holding primarily manifested in experiences and conceptualisations of need. Need was articulated repeatedly by mothers over the course of our work together. To explore experiences of purposefulness it felt imperative to examine current understandings of need, needs identification and navigation within mother/child relationships, and the ways in which both mothers and children shape and are shaped by the relationship's needs within the moment of holding.

## Needs research: Maslow's hierarchy of need

Modern understanding of human needs owes a great deal to Maslow's (1943) conceptualisation of the hierarchy of needs. According to his theory, there are discrete kinds of different needs that are organised in the shape of a mountain: the bedrock includes basic physiological needs around survival building up to an apex of self-fulfilment and self-transcendence needs. In this scenario we develop from a necessary navigation of personal needs toward interpersonal engagement needs.

Maslow proposed a natural progression of needs and the motivations that accompany them. As lower-level needs are met, higher level needs are more likely to be met (Taormina & Gao, 2013). From clinical experience however, he noted that some levels in the hierarchy appeared more important than others for individual patients (Maslow, 1943). In these instances, creativity, for example, may appear as a more significant motivator than love for some individuals despite its appearance higher up the 'need mountain'.

Maslow considered need a primary motivator and in particular, recognised that basic needs were focused on an end result, as such they were often more unconscious motivators than conscious. He also acknowledged that need was only one significant contributing determinant of behaviour along with biological, situational and cultural contexts.

In 1971, Maslow changed his motivational mountain (Maslow, 1993): 'Self-actualisation' (or fulfilment) was superseded at the peak of the mountain by 'self-transcendence'. This reflected the fulfilment of a need that was directed beyond the self, a motivation to satisfy *another's* need, be it another person with whom one was in relationship or a larger community. This interpersonal or supra-personal realm of need and purpose clearly manifested itself in participants' desire to attend to their *child's* needs as opposed to their own. In doing so however, participants also experienced fulfilment of their own self-transcendence needs and, lower down the hierarchy, their needs for belonging, love and esteem.

A difference in awareness of needs may contribute to participants' belief that they were 'about' their children rather than about their own needs. Operating at the peak of the needs pyramid by choice, electing to put one's child first, might temporarily obscure a mother's awareness of the presence and engagement of her own needs and how they are/are not being met. On reflection, however, participants were aware of the presence of their own needs during maternal holding. This speaks to a difference in focus rather than presence. During maternal holding, mothers initially felt that they were attending to their children's needs but as we delved further into their explorations of holding, they noticed the inevitable interaction of their own needs with those of their children.

While Maslow's needs hierarchy has proved an influential approach in many research designs and assessments, alternative theories and forms of assessment have emerged since. The placement of needs in a hierarchy is not necessarily helpful as multiple needs may be operating at any one time (Tay & Diener,

2011). As described above, awareness of needs can also fluctuate such that some appear to be dominant when others are also at play. Additionally, Maslow based his theory on white Western patients with their own particular cultural values and habitual concerns, including an orientation toward individualism. Some authors emphasise relatedness (Hanley & Abell, 2002), some recognise the role of one's cognition and perception of the fulfilment of needs in time according to a systems theory approach (Heylighen, 1992) and some have placed needs (like shelter and food) outside of the needs hierarchy as they are not so much needs as fundamental "satisfiers" for existence (Max-Neef, 1992, p. 199). All approaches however recognise a need for relationship.

### The need for relationship: attachment, patterns of being together and maternal holding

As we explored meeting and navigating their children's needs, participants and I could not conceive of holding our children without a sense of our mother/ child relationship, and further, of our *need* for that relationship.

Much has been written about the mother/child relationship and the navigation of relational needs through the lens of attachment theory. According to attachment theory the earliest intimate relationship (between primary caregiver and infant) shapes a child's later relationships as they mature (Ainsworth, 2005; Bowlby, 1969; Fraley, 2002). Attachment processes focus on how mothers help children navigate and meet their needs through the primary relationship, in particular, needs around security. A mother's own attachment style (built with her primary caregiver and possibly re-shaped as an adult) contributes to how she meets or does not meet her child's needs as well as her own. Maternal holding, as a key behavioural component of attachment, contributes to how children's needs are met.

Attachment theory was pioneered by psychiatrist John Bowlby and originally based upon his observations of children in the Child Guidance Clinic in London in the 1930s (Bretherton, 1992). Bowlby noticed what appeared to be damaging psychological and behavioural consequences of separating a child from her mother. His subsequent theory highlighted the profound importance of infant-mother relationship for later development.

Bowlby (1958) wrote that infants display behaviours that promote closeness to their caregiver. This helps ensure that the relatively helpless infant meets basic needs for safety, warmth, nourishment and survival. Pearmain (2001) writes:

> How infants feel and how they pick up how others feel is central both to learning and creating a sense of self as memory ... in other words, information that is not mediated by a personal way of relating to the infant has no intrinsic meaning and is not utilised by the infant.
>
> (p. 22)

Goleman (2006) adds:

> This ability of an infant's cries to trigger on-target care-giving – a phenomenon seen not just in mammals but even in birds – suggests that it is a universal template in Nature, one with immense and rather obvious benefits for survival.
>
> (p. 215)

Without a relationship providing nourishment and safety as well as touch and care, an infant cannot survive.

Even with their limited physical and verbal autonomy, infants are active in their relationships with their caregivers and the meeting of their needs. What infants do have at their disposal – such as their ability to direct their gaze, form facial expressions, vocalisations, body tension/relaxation and body position – they bring to their relationship with their caregiver and use within that relationship.

Stern (1977) writes: "both mother's and infant's behaviours could largely be explained as mutual attempts to regulate the baby's momentary state" (p. 2). I would extend this by saying that holding a screaming or a cooing child impacts the caregiver's experience or state as well. The infant as experienced within relationship alerts the caregiver to the presence of their infant needs but also the caregiver's own, for example, the need to calm the baby so that the caregiver as well as the baby do not feel distress. Kitty, for example, described holding as a "circuit breaker" for both mother and child. As Stern, Bruschweiler-Stern and Freeland (1990) write: "the rich choreography between (the infant) and his mother" (p. 8) is a relational dance where needs are navigated together.

With the advent of attachment research relationship became identified as a means of meeting basic needs for the child and it was also understood as a basic need *in itself*. Proximity-seeking behaviours were considered to be innate rather than learned as had been proposed in the dominant attachment theory of the time (Dollard & Miller, 1950).

Touch and holding have been explored within attachment research. Psychologist Harry Harlow and colleagues famously (and controversially) observed that infant rhesus monkeys provided with 'surrogate' mothers at birth (one made of wire, one covered in cloth) would cling to the 'cloth mother' the majority of the time, irrespective of whether that surrogate provided food (Harlow & Zimmerman, 1959, p. 431). They concluded that caregiver comfort and touch (in the form of a soft surrogate to cling to) was most important for the infant: more important than food (p. 428).

The historical and theoretical link between attachment and needs research and theory is explicit. Harlow became Maslow's graduate adviser (Kenrick, Grisckevicius, Neuberg & Schaller, 2010). Earlier behaviourist views of needs had focused on primary needs such as thirst and hunger and secondary needs were considered for those conditions associated with the meeting of primary needs. Touch, comfort, and relationship were thus considered secondary needs.

Harlow's discovery that needs for touch, comfort and relationship were *independent* of needs for food and drink provided a significant challenge to traditional conditioning theories of need. With Harlow's work, Maslow and others were inspired to consider multiple sources of fundamental human needs beyond the purely physiological, recognising that the need for relationship appeared to be as significant as the need for nourishment and rest.

Psychologist Mary Ainsworth (who worked with Bowlby in the 1950s) expanded on his Attachment Theory in one of many ways by creating, along with B. A. Wittig, a specific scenario in which infant-mother interactions and the consequences of those interactions might be observed in a clinical setting (Ainsworth & Wittig, 1969). This *Strange Situation* involved the careful observation of mothers and infants in stressful situations, noting infant behaviours when the mother was present, when a stranger was also present, when the child was left alone with the stranger, when the child was left completely alone and then when the mother returns. Based on observations of the child's response to comfort provided by a stranger and their mother, Ainsworth and colleagues progressively described four attachment styles: secure, insecure – avoidant, insecure – ambivalent/resistant, (Ainsworth, Blehar, Water & Wall, 1978/2005) and later disorganised/disoriented attachment (based on an extension of Ainsworth's work by Main & Solomon, 1990). Each style reflected how the children communicated and coped with stress and regulated their emotions (Zimmer-Gembeck, Webb, Pepping, Swan, Merlo, Skinner, Avdagic, & Dunbar, 2015).

In 1985 George, Kaplan and Main created the *Adult Attachment Interview* (AAI) to inquire into *adult* attachment styles and their relationship with attachment styles from infancy. This included a study showing the predictive relationship of early attachment behaviours (at infancy) to those coded in interviews with the same children at six and 19 years of age (Main, Hesse & Kaplan, 2005). Primary caregiver/child relationships were so influential that the style of relationship one had as an infant deeply impacted the style of relating one possessed as an adult.

Attachment infant/caregiver interactions are peppered with frequent, necessary and intimate moments of maternal holding. In keeping with this observation, influential psychoanalyst Donald Winnicott emphasised the importance of "holding" and the "holding environment" (Winnicott, 1965, p. 53). He describes holding, especially physical holding, as "a form of loving. It is perhaps the only way in which a mother can show the infant her love of it" (p. 49). This holding includes behaviours such as attending to a child's bodily and emotional needs (feeding, bathing, rocking, vocalizing and playing) (Winnicott, 1965, p. 43). Holding significantly contributes to the maturing child's growing experiences of dependence/independence, personal agency and safety within their own bodies, in their relationships and in their environment (Winnicott, 1960, p. 590). I would suggest that emotional and psychological holding based on a history of physical holding provided by mothers are also forms of "loving".

Winnicott (1953) described a healthy parent-child bond as including "the good enough mother (or parent)," (p. 94). This mother showed her child that she would stay with them, continue to 'hold' them, even when they were angry, frustrated and sad (Winnicott, 1958, p. 202). She would identify and adapt to her child's changing needs, fulfilling them initially (in infancy) almost completely but gradually fulfilling them less and less as the child became more aware of themselves as a separate agential individual in the world.

There has been significant discussion and exploration of Winnicott's theory of maternal holding and its importance for the child, including criticism of its white male, 20th century, idealizations of a "self-effacing, all-nurturing mother," (Kraemer, 1996, p. 766). As Ogden (2004) writes, Winnicott's conception of holding "is strongly evocative of images of a mother tenderly and firmly cradling her infant in her arms" (p. 1350), much like the Christian Madonna and Child imagery. Unsurprisingly, given this focus on the 'self-effacing' mother, less attention has been paid to *mother's* experiences of holding.

In this inquiry participants were not 'self-effacing' and 'all-nurturing'. Their experiences did reflect a desire to put their children's needs first (this may have been contributed to by cultural prescriptions around mothering explored in the next section). However, on examination, participant's experiences also revealed a profound involvement and investment in the *shared* mother/child holding experience and the *relationship's* needs, including their own needs. As we explored mother's holding experiences it appeared that holding was as much for them as it was for their children. For example, Kitty related experiences of holding her daughter when it was the last thing she wanted to do. She held Harley for Harley's sake, but the result was a "circuit breaker" for them both; emotions were regulated and calmed for each of them as a consequence of the holding. On the one hand, Kitty put Harley's needs first, but on the other, Kitty also had important needs for a happier mother/child relationship and less distress for herself met as well. These maternal needs were even more explicitly present when each mother discussed their maturing children and the perceived distancing between them and loss of holding once their children were adults. Each of the mothers experienced pain at the thought of or the experience of that loss because holding gave them to them as well, their needs were also attended to.

Kraemer (1996) writes:

> Recognizing the mother's subjectivity requires that we recognize the ways in which the baby serves as an object to the mother's needs. This includes fully acknowledging the critical ways in which the mother is nourished by her baby's confirmation of her usefulness.
>
> (p. 781)

All participants spoke about the qualities of what they received from holding their children, it was an essential part of their holding experiences. Researchers have inquired a great deal into the attachment experiences of children, both theoretically, from observation and interviewing those same children as adults. Attachment research has found that mother's attachment style (and thus their previous attachment experiencing) contributes to their children's attachment. However, if a mother is an essential part of the attachment process for a child, it seems quite possible that a child might also be a significant contributor to their *mother's* relational needs and experiencing as well.

Kraemer (1996) notes that recognizing her own needs as well as recognizing, adapting to and meeting the needs of her child:

> Demands an extraordinary degree of emotional and psychic flexibility. She has to embrace and move between ways of experiencing and knowing herself that are essentially and painfully incompatible, without feeling she has to reject any of these various possible mother-selves.
>
> (p. 785)

Like the expanding sense of self described by participants, Kraemer notes that being able to hold these at times disparate, incompatible and intense feelings around maternal and child needs requires of mothers an "expansion of her experience of herself" (p. 785). This is an expansion that identifies and navigates needs within the mother/child relationship more so than within either child or mother alone.

Kraemer (1996) captures qualities of this kind of maternal experiencing around relational needs with the seemingly simple act of putting one's child to bed:

> Betwixt the dark and the daylight, the mother finds herself on the threshold; poised to tiptoe away towards claiming herself, drawn back to check, just once more, her sleeping child ... she may wonder what she will encounter within herself: Will it be a skirmish or a rendezvous? And how will she feel about what she finds there?
>
> (p.788)

The entanglement of maternal and child needs within relationship can be hard to navigate. Needs constantly change and thus maternal purposefulness, at its best, evolves. Attending to a child's needs as well as her own requires relational work, it requires a 'flexibility' around one's sense of self and self-in-relationship. Attachment theory, with its focus on the child's needs can miss the dynamic, complex interplay and development of *both* mother and child's needs within their relationship.

In the first few years of holding my son I was aware of wanting to hold him in a way that felt right for our relationship; this was similarly expressed by participants. My explorations primarily took the form of drawings and later discussions around those drawings.

I noticed a number of things about what holding was like for me as I drew. At the beginning of my art making inquiry, *my* past experiences of being held and not held were at the forefront of my representations (see Figure 6.1). My mother and father both left when I was 18 months old and I lived with my paternal Nan and Pop (see text below, 'How my nan held me' sourced from www.holdingmatters.com). I formed a powerful and beneficial attachment

*Figure 6.1 How Can I Hold Myself with You?* Pencil on paper, 295x210mm.

with my Nan in particular (my father returned when I was four and I saw my mother again when I was 13).

*How my nan held me*

> I remember her hands. She was a fierce knitter and her hands were always click-clacking on a new project but as we both grew older my nan's hands grew stiffer and she couldn't knit anymore. I would sit on her lap and she would place her hand on mine and even though her hands were still, even though the magentas and teals she'd whip into a scarf had vanished, I felt safe and loved.
>
> Her hands were covered in sunspots, gnarled with arthritis but what I saw was her sapphire ring, the way she would have carried herself in the 50s, a young Liz Taylor. Her ring spoke of grace and steely strength. Perhaps because she had these gold-edged ceramic swans on her dressing table, I always likened her to them, elegant above the surface, busy underneath.
>
> I realise now she must have been in pain but back then all I knew was the comfort of those hands, how they'd sneak a biscuit out of the tin, play hangman with me, make her famous trifle, a staple at my Aunty's Christmas table.
>
> I know that my Nan used to carry me around because I remember the day she could no longer do it. I'd gotten too heavy and she'd had heart problems. She walked me to bed instead, using those hands to tuck me under the covers and turn out the light.

*Figure 6.2* Ilma Irene Sinclair, personal photo.

Nan always took my hand as we 'went up the street', dressed up in her heels and frock, her brooch and lipstick and black hair curled and set. When we'd chat to the butcher lady and she'd treat me to some mortadella, Nan would stand beside me as if I were a part of her; when a tall bejewelled lady at the bank said I was so good to stand so quietly and wait, Nan beamed. Nan's holding, her hugs, her touch told me that I mattered to her, that I mattered.

You might think this kind of touch stopped when I was a teenager, those years of sorting yourself out and putting distance between yourself and those who've raised you, but even as well-advanced in my years as I am now, I still haven't achieved 5 foot and back then I was tiny. As a 15-year-old I was able to sit on Nan's knee before saying goodbye, me with braces and a late 80s perm growing out, acid wash jeans and the odd pimple, she weathered all of my sartorial and otherwise faux pas.

We spent a lot of time sitting side-by-side on her bed, looking at her dark wood drawers filled with costume jewellery, strings of pearls, medicines and various shades of pink rouge. Somehow, I always discovered new things to hold and wonder about, I must have driven her nuts.

We'd open up old photo albums and I'd listen as she told me stories about her youth before the second world war, the times later when my Dad was young and Pop worked up the hill at the asylum, and the apple orchards the family owned. Photos of Pop in the Army, of our trips to Beechworth when all the Christmas beetles settle on my arms as we sat on the porch at night, and even the odd wedding photo of my mother and father.

In that strange way children have of mixing things up, the only thing I knew of my mother back then was that she'd left. Nan had received a sky-blue vase from my maternal grandmother, and it stood in the little hall with thick coloured feathers erupting from it. A gift from a trip to Japan. In my mind that vase told a story: my mother had left to travel and that made sense to me.

Of course, I took for granted what I had with Nan: her hugs were normal, her attention was a given. The way her body slowed and curled as she got older just meant adjusting the way we were together. She didn't dress up for the street as often. Playing poker at the coffee table slowed down and I did the card shuffling. She watched daytime TV more while Pop listened to the radio in the kitchen and there were a few less of her famous pies. We'd go to the shopping centre with my aunty and cousin, who was like a sister to me, that way my aunt could drive. We'd walk a bit slower. She never ever showed me she was in pain or unhappy. Nan had a lot more appointments with specialists and then I was in my last years of high school followed by uni and I was busy, so I saw a lot less of her, preoccupied with getting good grades.

The morning Pop called my dad to say nan had collapsed, we sped to her house. She'd had a few heart attacks by then. In the drive-way Nan and I always walked down to go to the bakers and newsagent, there was an ambulance. We ran into the little unit Nan and Pop had shared for decades, the only one of their homes I knew, and Nan was laid out on her bed.

Soon to turn twenty with the un-wavering knowledge that Nan would always be there, the next minute played out like someone else's story. This time it was my hands that touched her face, still warm as if she were sleeping. I lent down toward her closed eyes and gently placed my arms around her. She couldn't hold me, but we still held one another all the same.

In that last touch crowded two decades of memories that felt so new they sizzled between us. I could hear her voice narrating this moment: "as much as if to say, it's okay pet".

Those stories of us still burn today. The way Nan held me, and I was held; those moments were baked out of all those little things we did together, all those moments she gave to me and I hope, I gave to her. The touch of her hands is with me as I type, it's so much a part of how I hold myself in the world that I barely notice it but without that touch, without our history, I would be a very different person today.

Over the years I've realised that Nan's knitting didn't stop when her hands grew too painful for the fine skills required: she was knitting us together, and in the odd stitch here or there, our moments of touch and holding sparkle like sapphires amidst the wool, our story still a warmth no winter can chill. And some of that yarn, a thread of royal blue, is woven into the ways my son and I knit our stories together, of the way I hold him, and he is held.

The pain associated with these experiences powerfully arose when I gave birth to my son and I wondered if I would be capable or worthy of caring for him as he deserved.

As my drawing evolved I also saw how I gave to my son in ways that appeared unique from my personal past. Then I started to see how much I received from my son (Figure 6.3) during holding; the intensity and goodness of how much he gave, and how much we gave one another.

As my series of drawing continued what stood out for me was how much we uniquely created *together* during holding. My past was a part of the holding and so was my son's past, but these were not separate individual forces within the holding; the energy in our holding moments was ours. What we brought to holding was shaped within the holding by us. So, what holding was like for us was *new* as Kitty had described, and unique and, like Leni said, ours alone. Exploring what needs I brought to our holding also enabled me to attend to what wasn't helpful in our relationship, those needs that originated from my personal past. And outside of our holding moments, I had the opportunity work with these unhelpful needs. Within the moment of holding, I also had the opportunity to experience what positive attachment and loving holding was like. I as a mother received that love from the holding.

The participants and I felt that our children's relational patterns of being with us were shaped by the many ways in which we held them including our personal past. However, in turn, *we* were also shaped by our maternal holding

*Figure 6.3* Ariel Moy, *I Love You* felt tip pen on paper, 295x210mm.

experiences with *them*. All participants conveyed that their new mother/child experiences impacted upon their understanding of relationships and their experiences of relationship with their child. As Kitty said she learned that she had the "capacity, and that I could actually love something and find out what it was". The differences in the way Kitty mothered her daughter compared to her own mothering experience were stark, some of the changes she made to ways of relating were deliberate, but she felt that most were "new", and they arose organically from the particularity of her relationship with Harley.

Lucas & Dyrenforth (2006) emphasise that while relationships are important, the quality of the relationship is even more important for subjective wellbeing. These mothers engaged in *new* relationships when they held their children, relationships of a significantly different quality to their own relationships with their mothers. What they experienced within the mother/child relationship and maternal holding emerged as more important in our inquiry than what they had experienced in the past with their own mothers. This was perhaps because each of these mothers (including myself) were already aware of our past difficulties as well as strengths gained from our relationships with our mothers. This awareness did not preclude the involvement of prior attachment behaviours during holding, but it did mean we'd already worked and continued to work on identifying and modifying any maladaptive patterns of being with our children. The important understanding was that no matter what we brought or tried not to bring to the relational moment of holding, that 'material' was present and *reshaped* by the relationship, by mother and child together.

While participant's past relationships with their own mothers arose in our inquiry, we did not explore these in depth for a number of reasons. First, we had made a choice to focus on whatever emerged as most important for participants during our sessions: the inquiry was led by the data. Some data referred to mother's experiences of being mothered (as mentioned above) but most of the data focused on the present mother/child relationship. That is, participant's descriptions of the difference between mothering now and being mothered as a child focused on qualities of what it was like to hold their children now, rather than an exploration of what is was like for them being held as a child. Participants described the qualities of holding that they experienced with their children, some of which were initially deliberate reactions to their own experiences of being held but many of which were simply unique to the present mother/child relationship.

Second, though maternal holding is considered an attachment behaviour, this inquiry was not undertaken through the lens of attachment theory but rather through the lens of lived experience as re-constructed from memories. If we had explored maternal holding via attachment theory, it would have made sense to deliberately explore each mother's own attachment styles and thus their experiences being mothered as well as utilise attachment measures. With a broader lens governed by values rather than a theory, we chose to remain open to what emerged as important around maternal holding.

Third, there have been reconsiderations or modifications of attachment theory that appear relevant to participant's (and my own) experiences of relationship and holding (Rutter, 1995, Field, 1996, Mercer, 2011). These relate to the impact of maternal attachment styles upon a new mother/child relationship as well as my suggestion that the mother/child relationship not only attends to children's needs, but also attends to mother's needs and thus may have the power to re-shape mother's own attachment styles.

For example, attachment to a primary caregiver may be only one amongst many influences on relational patterns in adolescence and adulthood, including upon the new mother/child relationship. Participants mentioned other relationships that contributed to their understanding of their relationship with their children (spouse and friends, or in my case, my Nan) and explicitly described how holding their children changed their understanding of what was possible within relationships. Supporting this, it has been suggested that attachment occurs across the lifespan posing a challenge to the notion that there is a time critical period for attachment from infancy to four years of age (Field, 1996). It has also been suggested that attachment can occur across multiple relationships (Field, 1996). Field suggests that "a parsimonious model of attachment would need to accommodate multiple attachments to a variety of figures at different stages of life" (p. 545). This would suggest that attachment (or as I describe below 'patterns of being together') may be potentially as significant for mothers as for their children.

Another reconsideration of attachment theory describes how the concept of attachment may reduce the complex domain of significant relationships to the presence, complication or absence of security. Rutter (1995) writes that "attachment is not the whole of relationships. What is needed now is a bringing together of attachment concepts and other formulations of relationship so that each may profit from the contributions of the other" (p. 566) including contributions of "connectedness, shared humour, balance of control, intimacy and shared positive emotions" (p. 557). There are also socioeconomic, genetic, environmental and cultural contributions to relational styles.

While I refer to attachment literature, both the decision to be led by the data rather than a theoretical lens, and some of the critiques of attachment theory, guided my decision to not explicitly inquire into participant's own attachment styles and relationships with their mothers. In keeping with this, I chose to refer to the significance of the mother/child relationship as *patterns of being together* or *usness* (explored in greater detail in Chapter 7) rather than as an attachment style. The *need* for relationship remains but these needs manifest within a complex, dynamic mother/child pattern of being together not confined to ideas of attachment and security alone. Irrespective of the research lens, what appeared in the data was the presence of needs and maternal purpose around fulfilling those needs. One of those needs was identified as a need for relationship as mothers normalised affection for their children, this need for relationship however was also experienced by the mothers.

I suggest that, just as children's relational patterns of being together with their mothers are significantly shaped by their mother's successful identification and navigation of the child's needs, it is also possible that a mother's own needs, in particular, the need for relationship, are significantly (re)shaped with her child. I will explore this in more detail in the following section.

### Needs in the mother/child relationship are co-constructed and navigated

> The real failure: that he couldn't be the sort of father he wanted to be, a man who had transcended his ancestral muddle and offered his children unhaunted love.
>
> (Edward St Aubyn, 2014, p. 654)

> (Through my children) I have uncovered stockpiles of meanness, paroxysms of infantile rage, the ache of separation. Sometimes I am again the vengeful older sister. At others the hard-done-by child. These regressions are not dignified.
>
> (Kate Cole-Adams, 2009)

Participants and I explicitly wanted to offer our children 'unhaunted love', even if that hope was not entirely possible. This rested on an assumption that we brought to our relationship with our children our past history, but we also recognised the ways in which holding our children in the present shaped our experiencing as well. A mutual shaping of experience was understood as a given in the intimate act of holding.

Historically the focus of needs and attachment research was upon the infant, the mother a ghostly counterpart; maternal navigation of children's needs populated her purpose, a purpose about and directed toward her child.

While mother's contributions to the attachment relationship were explored, *maternal* experiences of the attachment relationship as well as the navigation of needs within that relationship were not. And yet, as the above quotes demonstrate, parents bring their attachment experiences into their relationships with their children, they too feel and have needs met or frustrated within that relationship, they too might grow and develop because of that relationship. Given attachment relationships are so important for the child, it is possible that this new attachment experience is important for the mother as well.

An exploration of the *maternal* experience of holding (an attachment activity) and relationship may be as valuable as our previous focus on the child's experience, as it recognises what both parties give and receive within the relationship and that it is possible for both parties to develop their relational styles with each other. What has generally been understood as a focus on children's needs may be reconsidered as a co-creation and co-navigation of child and maternal needs *in relationship* with one another.

Kim, Leckman, Mayes, Feldman, Wang and Swain (2010) found that for new mothers (2–4 weeks and 3–4 months postpartum) fMRI images showed increased grey matter in areas of the prefrontal cortex, midbrain and parietal lobes. They also found that the increases in the midbrain including the amygdala and hypothalamus were "predicted by a mother's positive perception of her baby at the first month postpartum" indicating that perhaps the mother's positive feelings about her baby may "facilitate the increased levels of grey matter volume".

During the early years of children's attachment construction mothers also experience changes in the activation of oxytocin and dopamine. As Bartels and Zeki (2004) write:

> We conclude that human attachment employs a push-pull mechanism that overcomes social distance by deactivating networks used for critical social assessment and negative emotions, while it bonds individuals through the involvement of the reward circuitry, explaining the power of love to motivate and exhilarate.
>
> (p. 1155)

These neurological and hormonal findings demonstrate that changes occur at a cellular and hormonal level for women as they become mothers and hold their children.

Choi and Goo (2012) explored mothers' child rearing attitudes and mother/ child attachment. They found that after participating in group art therapy sessions in a Winnicottian 'holding environment' (an environment that 'held' the mothers psychologically and emotionally in a maternal and supportive manner) the mothers felt it was possible to change their nurturing attitudes toward their children, including expressions of affection like holding and touch. Children are not the only ones in the mother/child dyad to change and evolve.

As Siegel (1999) writes, "interpersonal processes can facilitate integration by altering the restrictive ways in which the mind may have come to organise itself," (p. 336) for infants, children *and* adults across time. Experiencing within relationship encourages "connections between minds" which Siegel describes as "a dyadic form of resonance in which energy and information are free to flow across two brains. When such a process is in full activation, the vital feeling of connection is exhilarating" (p. 336). These connections between minds (and bodies) impact both people in relationship.

Siegel (1999) has proposed the malleability of adult attachment styles. Through therapeutic work adults can "earn" (p. 92) changes in their attachment styles. In Session 2A Rosanna read from her journal about a new "insight" and "clarity" she had come to through considering holding. Her own mother had "no boundaries" and this led to her being:

> Judgemental and critical of everyone ... over the years I have learnt that to give her information is to put myself in danger.... I do not want her to touch me. I don't want to touch her. I have to place the boundary between us and maintain it ruthlessly because she violates me psychologically.

The attachment style between Rosanna and her mother was experienced as highly damaging and yet through new relationships, education and her own prior therapeutic work, Rosanna's attachment style or patterns of being in relationship changed over time with her children. She did not repeat the ways of relating she had learned from her mother, she learned something new from her life experiences including her relationships with her children.

From within a relationship with one's child, a woman's experiencing changes, and thus what she can conceive of as possible for relationships also changes. I have been shaped by my relationships with my parents, my aunt, my partner and my Nan, but I have also been shaped by my relationship with my child. No love can be 'unhaunted' by relationships past, but new and different relationships can also shape and re-shape mothers in relationship with their children in the now.

### Paying attention to how mothers and children both give and receive during maternal holding

All mothers spoke of their children's active participation in the atmosphere of maternal holding: their children's needs were present, but their children also responded to their mother and her needs.

Maternal needs contributed to the relationship's emotional and behavioural state. Leni needed to feel more independent from her children when they were infants so that she felt safe from hurting or damaging them in the way she had been damaged. Kitty needed Harley to feel like she was the focus of attention when they visited Kitty's grandmother's house and was annoyed by her grandmother's desire to be centre stage. A child is unlikely to be immune to the emotional and physical atmosphere present in the mother/child relationship. If a mother is upset, frustrated or afraid, the child, being human and being intimately held by their mother (physically, psychologically and emotionally), is likely to respond to emotions and sensations present. The intimate quality of an important relationship reflects familiarity and access to the other, part of which is a sense of their needs and how these function in the moment of holding.

For example, when I asked Leni where *she* was in the postcard she had selected to represent her relationship with Lucy, she struggled to identify herself. She explained: "Well see … I find it hard to differentiate … to me that is *us* (the postcard)." When I asked her what it felt like being in this relationship, she took time to find the right words: "I feel half of something? When I think about me. If I was to say that is the relationship, *I* am half of that". Despite conceptualizing holding as an activity that was about her children's needs, Leni's experiential and presentational knowing signalled a profound intersubjectivity: she and her children were more than just themselves in relationship with one another; they experienced, gave and received in ways that could not be definitively located in mother or child.

Infants are also other-oriented and aware of others' needs. Koster, Ohmer, Nguyen and Kartner (2016) suggest that a pro-social orientation may exist within 9–18-month-old children even before (or irrespective of whether) they can express that behaviourally (p. 546). They tracked 71 infant eye-movements as they watched different animated picture stories showing two characters who were able to achieve their goal, two characters who could not reach their goal, and a third scenario in which a helper was present; in this last scenario there was a time lag of three seconds in order to see if the infants demonstrated "anticipatory looking behaviour" (p. 544). Sometimes the helper helped the character in need, and sometimes they did not. Koster et al. found that "the infants in all three age groups (9–11 months, 12–14 months, 15–18 months) expected the helper to help the individual in need" (p. 546). Koster et al. stated that "understanding the needs of other people is a necessary precondition for early helping behaviour" and it appears that the infants in their study understood the presence of another's need (p. 547).

A recent study by Hepach, Vaish & Tomasello (2017) found that two-year-old children's body posture was "more elevated" (p. 106) when children achieved their own goal or helped another achieve their goal (it also decreased when they did not achieve their goal or help another achieve *their* goal). Children's bodies reflected their ability to identify and manage need and purpose both for themselves *and* for others.

In another study, De Haan, Belsky, Reid, Volein and Johnson (2004) explored the relationship between infants' responses to emotional facial expressions and their mothers' emotional disposition and found that those infants that had more experiences of positive maternal emotional expression would spend longer looking at negative, and therefore novel, facial expressions. These seven-month-old infants were aware of and influenced by their parent's emotions and behaviours.

Participants were aware not only of what they gave during the moment of holding, but also of what their children gave. They were aware of the 'rewards' they received while holding their children. When we talked about her final representation Rosanna reflected that "thinking of my children … I can feel the sunshine"; Leni said "a cuddle from them … I have earned it … it's like a praise … a thank you", and Kitty said "when I think about this stuff it makes me very teary but it makes me stand up tall … like, push my heart forward". These mothers described the positive feelings *they* experienced when they held their children and, recognised that (as Kitty said) holding "gives to me as well".

Mothers differ on the degree to which they can and do navigate relational needs and acknowledge rewards. For example, maternal 'mind-mindedness' research explores the differences in mother's allocation of meaning to their child's behaviours, vocalisations and expressions. Those that do ascribe meaning are more likely to pay attention to their children's behaviours, vocalisations and expressions (Meins, Fernyhough, de Rosnay, Arnott, Leekam & Turner, 2012; Illingworth, MacLean & Wiggs, 2016). Mind-mindedness has also been linked to increased maternal self-awareness (Hill & McMahon, 2016), that is, paying attention to how one experiences the relationship with one's child.

In session, when we inquired into their experiences, participants absolutely allocated meaning to their children's behaviours, they were acutely sensitive to their children's expressions, words, movements and posture. With this 'mind-mindedness' they were also able to acknowledge the rewards their children but also, *they* received from holding their children. For example, Kitty noted that between our sessions she increasingly appreciated how valuable holding Harley was for her: "I think about it a lot more. Even this morning, I was thinking about it (holding) when she came into our bed and I was holding her and, I thought: 'you haven't done this for such a long time'". Attending to her relationship increased her awareness of how much she received from it.

Daphne de Marneffe (2007) writes:

> When she relinquishes control over her time, forgoes the satisfaction of an impulse, or surrenders to playful engagement with her child even as she feels driven to 'accomplish something', the surface quality of capitulation in these decisions belies their role in satisfying her deeper motives and goals. These deeper goals have to do, ultimately, with the creation of meaning.
>
> (Chapter 41, Section 2, para. 8)

This illuminates the intersubjective quality of needs navigation and reward. de Marneffe continues:

> This process can be one of extraordinary pleasure. There is the sensual, physical pleasure of caring for small children … taking care of their needs; the delight in being able to make our children happy and in being made happy by our children.
>
> (Chapter 41, Section 2, para. 9)

As mothers, participants had powerfully experienced reward from within the mother/child relationship. Sometimes the successful adaptation to a child's new need is a reward in itself. Kitty said she was always "catching up" to her daughter but as she did so she felt good about having the "capacity to change" with Harley.

Oftentimes the rewards could not be anticipated: Rosanna described the joy she felt in being able to hold her grandchildren and model holding and mothering for her daughters. Leni's happiness in experiencing relationship with her children, summed up in the description of "just us", was new, she had not had this kind of relational feeling before. Lafrance (2015) wrote: "the artist Sarah Walker once told me that becoming a mother is like discovering the existence of a strange new room in the house where you already live" (para. 1). Needs and rewards were not entirely a mother's or child's own in the mother/child dyad as new needs and new rewards arose within relationship and were understood within the space of the mother/child 'us'. These needs and rewards were co-constructed by mother and child and shaped relational purpose.

Studies have explored parents' experiences of holding their pre-term or newborn infants with Kangaroo Care (KC) where there is skin to skin contact as the infant is held upright against their caregiver's chest. What began with attempts to benefit children resulted in benefits for both children and parents. KC was initially employed in neo-natal intensive care units to better infant's chances of development and survival (Hall & Kirsten, 2008) but is now more often used to "provide benefits such as bonding and attachment, physiological stability of new-born babies ... [with] positive effects on infant development" (Zhang, Lip, Yim & Goh, 2014, p. 142). In a two-part 2014 meta-study into 29 qualitative papers "reporting experiences from 401 mothers and 94 fathers" (Anderzen-Carlsson, Carvahlo-Lamy & Eriksson, 2014a), it was found that in a supportive environment KC was associated with increased parental self-esteem. Similarly, a 2013 study found KC to contribute to a sense of "meaningfulness", "calm and relation", and increased confidence in abilities (Heinemann, Hellstrom-Westas & Hedberg Nyqvist, 2013, p. 699). This kind of explicitly purposeful holding has been shown to provide rewards for both children and parents.

Holding is not a solo activity, it involves two people, and in the mother/child relationship, holding involves two people in a long-term intimate relationship. When I hold my son there are moments where I feel as if the needs, rewards and purpose of my holding originate not so much in me but in our relationship. This can be a sensation of blurred physical boundaries or a sense of shared pressure or warmth in the body, it can be a flowing of emotions that feels as if it emerges from 'us'.

In coupling innate 'aboutness' with experiences of relational purpose, I suggested the presence of a 'maternal intentionality'. This intentionality manifests as a sense of purpose for mothers in relationship with their children. However, in this section I have explored how relational needs and purpose are less a mother's own, and more of a relational *ours*. Mother and child together, mutually *about* their relationship, experience need and purpose from within that relationship in the moment of holding and these experiences can be understood on reflection.

Perhaps maternal intentionality or purpose might then be more aptly renamed *mother/child intentionality* or *mother/child purpose*. The reason these qualifiers are important is because the research showed us that purpose and needs were of and about the mother/child relationship.

Further, if something arises from a relationship, we have increased access to information about that quality. For example, exploring maternal experiences of holding we noticed that purpose appeared as thematic. We inquired into the mother's experience of purpose but in doing so we discovered aesthetically, symbolically, experientially and conceptually how each mother also saw her maternal purpose *affect her child*, how her *child effected that purpose*, and how that purpose played out in their *relationship*. We have multiple points of view from which we might examine holding and purpose.

Barad (2007) writes that "intentions are not pre-existing determinate mental states of individual human beings" (p. 22–23) but should instead be described as "an entangled state of agencies" (p. 23). Deeply felt qualities of purpose and need experienced during holding originate from an 'us' rather than the two 'I's of mother and child. Purpose manifesting during moments of holding and on reflection allows us precious glimpses into relational experiencing of the mother/child 'us'.

**Purpose provides the mother/child relationship with structure, reward and support over the long term**

> It is true that life has no meaning, if by that we mean a supreme goal built into the fabric of nature and human experience, a goal that is valid for every individual. But it does not follow that life cannot be *given* meaning.
>
> (Csikszentmihalyi, 1990, p. 215)

As described above, participants and I were aware of and cherished the 'rewards' we received during holding. Purpose and its many micro-fulfilments provided us with deep satisfaction and included a sense of valuable relational needs well negotiated and met. It also provided us with a guide and support in our constantly changing relationship.

Sartre (1946) famously said: "man is condemned to be free" (p. 5). If nothing is determined or 'meant to be' then it is up to us to create our own meaning. As Bakewell (2016) writes: "not surprisingly, this radical freedom makes people nervous," (p. 154). This philosophy lays the responsibility for purpose and meaning squarely at the feet of each human being.

Sartre's response to the inherent meaninglessness of our existence is to *create* meaning or 'necessity' of our experiences. So, for example, a mother might consider holding her child to be valuable, meaningful and necessary: holding her child provides positive attachment experiences for them, holding her child keeps them safe, it is something she needs to do, it is a part of her maternal purpose, mothering her child is a fundamental part of who she is in the world and what she does. All participants held their children, as Leni said: "for a reason" and reason lends meaning and structure to their holding experiences.

There are huge benefits to creating meaning and purpose from an experience. For example, they have been positively linked with well-being across age-groups (Steger, Oishi & Kashdan, 2009); well-being for those experiencing social anxiety disorder (Kashdan & McKnight, 2013); well-being for secondary school boys (Riedel, 2014); reduced "risk of mortality from stroke, CVD and all causes" (Koizuma, Ito, Kaneko & Motohashi, 2008); higher income that continued to increase over the nine years between researcher's assessments (Hill, Turiano, Mroczek and Burrow, 2016) and a reduction in the risks of burnout for firefighters (Krok, 2016).

A part of psychological wellbeing is the recognition and appreciation of rewards (Froh, Sefick & Emmons, 2008; Watkins, 2004; Emmons & McCullough, 2003). As described previously, when one views maternal holding through the lens of purpose, and in particular, the lens of need, successful need fulfilment during holding affords opportunities for satisfaction. As conveyed by participants, holding can be incredibly rewarding and so too a sense of purpose during holding.

Seligman (2002) notes:

> Positive psychology takes seriously the bright hope that if you find yourself stuck in the parking lot of life … there is a road out. This road takes you through the countryside of pleasure and gratification, up into the high

country of strength and virtue, and finally to the peaks of lasting fulfillment: meaning and purpose.

(p. xii)

As Kitty said, having Harley was the "best thing that ever happened to me",
Leni noted that: "maybe I get more from it [holding] than they do" and
Rosanna placed a bright red postcard in her final representation that read: "I
can't live without you". Each mother in this inquiry linked their experiences
of holding and having their children with a significant degree of subjective
wellbeing, meaning and purpose.

Meaning and purpose are profoundly entwined. One way of approaching
such a complex and important term is by breaking it down into two components: the 'what' and the 'why' of meaning. Proulx, Markman and Lindberg
(2013) write: "while a sense of the *what* organises our epistemic understanding
of reality, a sense of the *why* directs us in how we should conduct our lives and
provides explanations for the events that constitute our life story" (p. 10). They
write: "meaning' deals with the *what* and 'purpose' deals with the *why*" (p. 7).
Meaning represents what we understand and value about our reality; purpose
provides us with a "guide for living" (p. 10) in that reality. Similarly, Wong
(2012) describes purpose as the "motivational" (p. xxx) component of meaningfulness and Martela & Steger (2016) define purpose as providing the "core
goals, aims, and direction in life" (p. 531).

Kitty said that her love for Harley and her experiences of holding her were
"of this universe" and of "profound importance": this recognized the 'what' of
meaning – her love for Harley and her experiences of holding her are fundamental to Kitty's understanding of her reality. When she said that she can see a
"structure" in their relationship and that she is "having to change" and "having
to let go" she is expressing her 'why' or purpose: she knows what she will have
to do to live meaningfully and fulfil her sense of purpose with her daughter as
she matures. By providing an understanding of and a guide for mothering,
purposefulness serves a significant function during maternal holding.

Purpose also provided support during difficulties and over the long term.
Kitty described the well-known torture and challenge of sleep deprivation with
her infant daughter. She remembered a "big moment"; the first time she got to
hold Harley as they fell asleep peacefully together (explored in her first representation Figure 4.1). That experience of holding was a reward, a golden
moment that she could return to as a reminder of how calm, blissful and
meaningful holding could be. That holding moment not only felt meaningful
and purposeful for Kitty but it *reinforced* her ability to continue on during
harder times.

Finding purpose in maternal holding experiences may contribute to mothers'
ability to weather the storms, exhaustion, contrariness and monotony of caring.
Given the long-term commitment required of caregiving, a sense of purpose in
the everyday and frequent act of maternal holding may well serve a supportive
and protective function. The relationship between purpose and meaning, and

their relationships with well-being, appear to be actualized in participant's understanding of maternal holding: with a sense of purpose they can hold their children even in the face of what they considered uglier, harder emotions like anger, boredom, fear, disappointment and dislike. All participants felt they had 'failed' their children at times with accompanying emotions of guilt, anger, regret and sadness but they most often chose to continue holding or offering to hold their children despite this. With difficulties came rewards, a sense of purposefulness mitigated those difficulties and drew attention to the satisfying qualities of holding children.

Participants noted that mothering and holding their children required effort. Mothering for Leni was a "job I have to do" and purposefulness shaped her "work". It was not the only motivation or guide for maternal holding, but it did appear to be a significant one. Perhaps speaking about the effort of motherhood, the work and purpose involved, reflects the legitimacy and seriousness these mothers and I place upon mothering including holding our children. In a world where work has traditionally been associated with paid employment and the many positive values attached to that, applying some of these values to mothering expands the possibilities for maternal recognition and respect both personally and in the community.

It has been noted that "high reward mothering" can mediate the effects of "maternal stress on depression and social functioning" across cultures (Lanza di Scalea, Matthews, Avis, Thurston, Brown, Harlow, & Bromberger, 2012, p. 481). In general, immediate rewards and their associated positive feelings also contribute to the pursuit of long-term goals (Wooley & Fishbach, 2016; Berridge, 2001; Custers & Aarts, 2005). The immediate reward of an optimal holding experience may contribute to long-term mother/child purpose.

As Carl Jung (1983) wrote: "meaninglessness inhibits fullness of life and is therefore equivalent to illness" (p. 373). Meaning is at the core of what it is to be alive – from the meaning attached to the fulfilment of basic bodily needs through to, as psychiatrist, neurologist and Holocaust survivor Victor Frankl (2011) describes, the relationship between meaning, happiness and "the capability to cope with suffering" (p. 113). This is particularly relevant to maternal holding – holding one's child is not always pleasant or desirable, it can be highly stressful, it can include feeling like we've missed the mark or that we've been forced to do something we do not want to do (all experiences described by participants). An abiding sense of purpose associated with holding helps mitigate these more troublesome or painful holding experiences.

The beneficial functions of purposefulness experienced during maternal holding do not serve the mother alone; they serve the relationship. All participants were motivated to make sure their children's experiences were different to their own. Their purpose included a focus on their children's needs but also on their own – their need to give love, as Leni said, "the right way"; to model love the right way, to experience mother/child love the right way.

To understand maternal holding through the lens of co-created purpose and needs navigation, is to gift that experience with three qualities: the provision of a structure or 'guide to living'; the ability to reward the mother/child relationship regularly by satisfying relational needs and, with these rewards or 'golden moments', to provide support to the relationship over the long term, particularly during the painful, confronting or stressful times. Most importantly, understanding the relationship through an intersubjective lens provides *relational agency* and a supportive sense that the mother is not alone in what can at times be a very painful and challenging relationship. Though mother and child bring different qualities and needs to the relationship, they are in it together. More than Winnicott's 'good enough' mother, we might consider explicitly conceptualising and supporting a good enough mother/chid relationship.

## Cultural uses of coupling maternal holding and purpose

> Master narratives, or prevailing cultural storylines, of motherhood provide a framework for new mothers to make sense of their experiences and to develop a coherent maternal identity.
>
> (Kerrick & Henry, 2017, p. 1)

> Women feel they have to grow the bacon, cook the bacon, look sexy while they serve the bacon and make sure the bacon is free-range, organic and nitrate free, as well as bring it home.
>
> (Janella Purcell in Hawkes, 2016)

When describing holding experiences, the support they did or did not receive, the meaning they made and the judgments they navigated, participants regularly referred to family, friends and their cultural milieu. We were all aware of experiencing holding within a particular society at a particular moment in time. Leni brought up parenting books that caused her distress, Kitty noted cultural pressures around physical intimacy particularly between mothers and their maturing children and Rosanna considered her Anglo-Saxon background when describing what she found most interesting about holding.

Cultural prescriptions are conveyed as much by imagery as by words. When I started my inquiry into maternal holding, I began by making visual representations and at the same time, I searched for imagery of maternal holding. A Google search revealed two dominant streams: representations of the *Madonna and Child* and Stock Photo imagery. Both of these streams of images reflect cultural ideologies.

In the Stock Photos imagery, a mother holding her child (most often an infant) is usually dressed in or framed in bright white. For advertising purposes, these photos convey a sense of calm, child-centric purpose, clarity, innocence and/or safety. Mother is loving, in control, and utterly focused on her peaceful and joyous child. As representative of a common understanding or an ideal, these white, bright mother and child photos do not appear to cover the wide range of actual mother/child experiences. Even when a more specific instance of holding is used as a search term, for example, "mother holding screaming child", white still appears to be the dominant hue.

The culture/s we are born into have a profound impact on how we process and make meaning of our experiences, they inform how we think, feel and behave. Cultural, societal and familial voices all have much to say about mothering and purpose. Some ideas about parenting are so imbedded in our culture we barely notice them while others may be frowned upon in the present only to become the 'right way' to parent a few years or decades later. Leni was bombarded with "other voices" about what she should and should not do as a parent, as other people significantly contributed to the 'framework' upon which she built her maternal identity.

Different cultural models of motherhood both limit and expand the experiences of caregiving available to individuals. Speculative fiction has long explored utopias and dystopias based around women's fertility, mothering rights and responsibilities. These include Charlotte Perkin Gilman's *Herland* (1915), Margaret Attwood's *The Handmaid's Tale (1985)* and P. D. James' *Children of Men (*1992). In a society, for example, that does not encourage mother/child attachment and individual bonds, how might a sense of purposefulness while holding a child manifest? The needs a mother fulfils, the qualities of her purposefulness and what she appreciates about maternal holding may differ depending on the norms and expectations of her culture.

From a cultural standpoint, mothering has served many purposes beyond the simple continuation of the species (though this is a highly significant and loaded purpose). It has, and continues to provide, fertile ground for current cultural, political, religious, familial and individual beliefs. As Shari L. Thurer (2009) writes: "the good mother is reinvented as each age or society defines her anew, in its own terms, according to its own mythology" (Chapter 21, Section 1, para. 13).

### Mothering, purpose and work

Leni often referred to holding her children as a "job" she "needed to do". It is possible that the way she viewed holding her children in this respect and the value she placed on it may have come from the stories and symbols of work employed in our present culture.

Katz Rothman (2007) writes of three dominant ideologies in modern Western culture (capitalism, patriarchy and technology) and how these dictate our experiences and understanding of motherhood:

> When we think of our relationships with our children as a job to be done well, we are invoking the ideology of technology ... to do these parenting tasks efficiently, we divide them up into their component parts, organise them, systematize them, rationalize, *budget* our time, *order* our day, *program* our lives.
>
> (Chapter 24, Section 2, para. 1)

In a study that looked at Australian indigenous mothers' experiences of an early-intervention program and their ideas of motherhood, one mother summed it up: "I have purpose now," (Ussher, Charter, Parton, & Perz, 2016, p. 5). Another noted: "We want to give our kids a better life and that needs to be recognized," (p. 5). Being a 'resilient mother' and being a 'good mother' comprised one of two main themes of experiencing that emerged from the study. Resilience and goodness speak to the sense of purpose, meaning and *effort* put into mothering – and the capacity to bounce back when challenges are experienced. These mothers recognized the stresses they had to manage and overcome and the long-term goals of giving their children a better childhood experience than they had – their parenting had purpose and meeting that purpose required work and effort.

Ruddick (1989) writes that the idea "of mothering as a kind of caring labour undermines the myth that mothers are "naturally" loving" (p. xi) and moves the idea of mothering away from "a form of identity or a fixed biological or legal relationship" (p. xii). In 1995, when historian Molly Ladd-Taylor wrote her book *Mother-Work*, she found that most people assumed it referred to working mothers but, she was referring to the work of creating a life and caring for children, all generally unpaid work. This notion of motherwork "still seems to many like a contradiction in terms" (p. 8). That mothering and work might experientially overlap came as no surprise to me, embedded as I am in 2019: my cultural milieu tells me that mothering requires effort, it takes a great deal of time, it requires 'juggling', compromise and self-development. This kind of purposefulness makes sense when it emerges from a society and time that tells these kinds of mothering stories.

### Maternal purpose and mother-blaming

Participants and I felt a pressure to mother the "right way" (as Leni said). Like participants, I too had held my son in ways purposefully different from my own experiences so that I wouldn't 'make the same mistakes'. Again, while this particular purpose was not always cognitively conscious, it was felt at times during the moment of holding and definitely on reflection.

Pascoe (1998) writes in *Screening Mothers* "mother-blaming theories came to play a critical part in child psychology and psychoanalysis after the Second World War" (Chapter 2, p. 3). One possible 'use' for this blame was to place newly liberated women back into the domestic setting and out of the work force so that men could return to work. This was the time when Winnicott's maternal holding and the 'good enough' mother as well as attachment theory emerged.

A development in mother-blaming voices can be found in the more recent cultural phenomenon of the 'Mommy Wars'. 'Mommy Wars' refers to the practice of women hating and judging one another's parenting approaches. However, as Kasey Edwards (2016) writes: "labelling the judgement and criticism that mothers face on a daily basis as a 'mommy war' reduces a complex social and economic problem to a simple matter of women not knowing how to behave themselves" (para. 13).

All participants conveyed guilt, regret or displeasure around maternal holding. Rosanna felt at times she did not give her eldest daughter as much holding as she needed, Leni felt like she should have a calm and "in the moment" experience while holding her children but that this was rare. Kitty's only representation of painful and difficult qualities of holding (Figure 4.5) was also the one that she ultimately felt was least representative or valuable. Her holding experiences in general were: "so outside of that, it's so not tainted by that".

It is possible that cultural mother-blaming was at play in participants' negative appraisals of their maternal holding. In Kitty's experience of her representation she had voiced her own needs and difficulties, her own concerns around losing Harley, she represented some (though not a great deal) of the negative qualities of holding her daughter and did not wish for these to take centre stage in our inquiry. Rosanna had an idea of the 'amount' of holding her daughter deserved though whether this amount was a product solely of her own consideration or of societal expectations it is hard to know. Leni explicitly referred to the "whole earth mother" imagery and concept as an ideal not truly achievable nor desirable, but still felt she should have certain earth-mother experiences during holding.

Perhaps Kitty was tapping into the 'suffocating' mother stereotype with all its negative sequelae for children. The 'smother mother' (Warner, 2012) is a new mother-shaming label applied to women who will not 'let go' of their children and infantilise them. It is linked to the 'intensive mothering' approach/label explored below. Kitty didn't want to focus on her fears around loss because they were painful and not representative for her of her holding experiences in general. But Kitty also didn't want to appear as a smothering mother, by holding onto Harley when her daughter might have wanted more freedom to receive and give affection elsewhere. Kitty reframed her painful experience, challenging a cultural norm around maternal affection and 'smothering' or co-dependence. She chose to cherish the moments they did hold one another and keep offering holding and affection even if she received a 'no' from her child. She challenged the assumption that associated independence and agency with separation. In both cases, cultural prescription and Kitty's understanding associated purpose with mothering and holding; both provided structure and guides within which to live, but Kitty chose to adapt her guide to fit with her unique relationship with her daughter.

Participants were aware of mother-blaming, they all described moments of holding where they felt they were not good enough or were at fault in some way. Yet they also recognised that this fault was an opinion, that it could be examined and re-framed within the context of their relationship with their child. What occurred between mother and child was theirs and thus a mother's interpretation of her experience was not hers alone, it was always open to what the *relationship* brought to holding in the moment and over time. Cultural norms prescribed purpose into experiences of holding but these mothers nevertheless shaped that purpose according to what appeared to fit the particular mother/child 'us'.

### Maternal purpose, intensive mothering, the supermum and alternative voices

Kitty wished to spend all of her time mothering Harley before she went to school. As she explained to her partner:

> I'm certainly not going to stay at home and clean!... I remember having that argument with (her partner) that I didn't stay *home* to be a housewife, I stayed at home to look after Harley, so "if you want me to look after her and develop her brain and everything, that's what I'm going to do". Otherwise, she can sit in front of the TV all day and I can clean all day.

This desire reflected Kitty's beliefs and values around mothering; a kind of mothering that was child-centric, that required significant effort and care, that was highly valuable and intensive.

The modern practice of 'intensive mothering' appears to be a dominant cultural construct and is as relevant now, if not more so, as it was in the 1990s (Ennis, 2014). As Hays (1996) writes: "the ideology of intensive mothering is a gendered model that advises mothers to expend a tremendous amount of time, energy, and money in raising their children" (p. x). This kind of mothering requires a stay-at-home mother, constantly monitoring and enriching her children. It can employ both notions of mothering as work or vocation and mother-blaming.

Anderson (2007) reflects on how Native American women, while being influenced by modern Western culture, have also protected and "revived their own distinct ideologies of motherhood" (para. 1). This mothering encourages collective care of a child. Anderson writes: "the welfare of women and children was thus linked to interdependencies between families, and between networks of women" (Section 2, para. 3). It is possible that in a society like this the relationship between purposefulness and maternal holding would manifest differently to modern Western culture.

Despite cultural diversity, it appears that intensive mothering ideals have been found in countries other than Australia, US, UK and Canada including Korean mothers (Chae, 2015), single, low-income African American mothers (Elliott, Powell, & Brenton, 2013) and Chilean lower and middle-income mothers (Murray, 2014). It might also be noted that many East Asian countries, heavily influenced by Confucianism, also display intensive mothering ideals and values. For example, in these countries, "childrearing has been the main duty of women. Motherhood is an absolute value beyond controversy, and a mother who sacrifices everything for her children's needs and success is idealised" (Chae, 2015). Purposefulness and motherhood go hand in hand in cultures that value intensive mothering.

What a mother defines as the most important of her child's needs can also dictate how intensive mothering and purposefulness manifest and can appear quite different from mother to mother. Intensive mothering was originally defined as "child-centred, expert-guided, emotionally absorbing, labour intensive and financially expensive" (Hays, 1996, p. 8). If a mother values, for example, her child's self-esteem above other qualities she will attend to these needs with commitment, education, and emotional, behavioural and intellectual absorption. If, however, she values self-efficacy and a disciplined mind-set above other qualities, she may manifest her intensive mothering in a 'tiger mom' style (referring to Amy Chua's memoir *Battle Hymn of the Tiger Mother*, 2011). These approaches, however intensive, would be very different based on their different values and the purposefulness of holding may be experienced differently too.

As a modern approach to parenting, 'intensive mothering' is accompanied by a wealth of reference materials used to 'educate' mothers on their role and responsibilities. This moves the idea of mothering as relational toward mothering as vocation or full time, skill-based activity: something done by the mother *to* the child, not *with* the child. Purposefulness is certainly present in this paradigm but is placed solely on the mother's shoulders, it is not mutual, and the wisdom necessary to fulfil this purpose is outsourced to experts.

All participants located purposefulness within themselves and not their children, but this was mitigated by their experiences of expansion, of a purposeful 'us' during holding. This will be explored in depth in the next chapter. However, if purpose is an intersubjective relational experience then, just like the co-navigation of needs, cultural norms would be co-navigated by mother and child. A mother may bring cultural influences into her moment of holding, but her child also brings experiences and influences as well, and in the alchemy of the mother/child moment no one cultural experience or understanding can entirely dominate.

At the same time the image of the 'supermum' has appeared. As Hall and Bishop (2009) write in *Mommy Angst* the "supermum" is "the mother who could do it all, with a smile, with a perfect figure, and on a budget (this) was the cultural ideal" (p. xi). One only has to look at popular women's magazines to observe the radical transformation of proud 'yummy mummies' from huge bellied to svelte in a matter of weeks (both to acclaim and condemnation). The 'supermum' can work, stay home, devote herself to her child and keep physically fit, attractive and satisfied all at once. Holding a child is but one of the many tasks she successfully juggles and fulfils. In this approach, purposefulness makes sense: holding her child is one of the many constant tasks she needs to fulfil as part of her role as mother. The expectations around the 'supermum' ideal may have indeed contributed to Leni's early box-ticking, the need she had to "get things done", torn between ideals of being able to complete domestic and other duties but also having to hold her infants.

As Warner (2005) writes in *Perfect Madness: Motherhood in The Age of Anxiety* attempting to mother today creates feelings of stress, anger, guilt, anxiety, resentment and regret: "that caught-by-the-throat feeling so many mothers have today of always doing something wrong" (p. 3). In an age of intense, conflicting and prolific prescriptions for how to mother – given our advice and consumption culture – it is easy to feel the "too-muchness" (p. 4) of it all. So pervasive is mother-blaming and mothering advice in our modern age it would be hard to find an act of love between mother and child that has not been analysed, championed or condemned.

In a world where we are bombarded with visual and verbal stories about what we should do, how best to mother, what our child needs and what a mother/child relationship should look like, maternal purposefulness (in its many manifestations) is built into every act of mothering. Thurer (2007) writes:

> Popular mother culture implies that our children are exquisitely delicate creatures, highly vulnerable to our idiosyncrasies and deficits, who require relentless psychological attunement and approval. A sentimentalized image of the perfect mother casts a long, guilt-inducing shadow over real mothers' lives.
>
> (Chapter 21, para. 1)

In my exploration of cultural prescriptions and purposeful holding I wondered how mother blaming, intensive mothering and 'supermum' labels might also speak to images of babies who are held in a way that doesn't sit with these values. On the one hand we have the imagery of Madonna and Child and stock photographs mentioned above. On the other hand, I found Banksy's re-working of a Renaissance painting entitled *Silent Night Madonna with Child and iPod* where the maternal gaze shifts from a haloed child to the iPod or somewhere inbetween her own hands and her child's. Perhaps this represents a successfully multitasking 'supermum' or a mother who rejects the need to intensively focus on her child every moment of every day, maybe purpose is present in this image and is focused on the object shared between mother and child or perhaps it is a comment on the proliferation and domination of technology imposing upon relationships.

Similarly, Diane Arbus' (1967) black and white photograph *Mother Holding her Child* shows a mother placing her child directly in front of herself and the camera's lens. The child cries and dribbles in distress. This is a rare image of maternal holding that isn't serene, that doesn't show a mother beatifically fixated on her child and who's maternal purpose is ambiguous.

Salvador Dali's (1949) *The Madonna of Port Lligat* paints a fragmented holding 'full of empty spaces' between mother and child and Egon Schiele's (1908) *Mother and Child* casts a pale Jesus in the foreground with a red Madonna, taking up the rest of the painting behind, holding her left hand up to his lips. These images may represent how mothering and holding one's child can also be, amongst other things, confusing, possessive, distressing, boring and challenging.

A wealth of books give voice to the more difficult, ambivalent and unpleasant sides of motherhood (as well as the joys) including Fiona Shaw's post-natal depression memoir *Out of Me* (2001), Maggie Nelson's mix of autobiography and theory *The Argonauts* (2016) and Kasey Edward's *Guilt Trip* (2017). With the internet there has been a rise of support groups, blogs, vlogs, social media accounts and websites for domain specific parenting experiences including support for single, rural, working, lesbian and/or depressed mothers to name a few. What these groups reflect is the incredible diversity of mothering experiences that cannot (and should not) be easily subsumed within one particular mothering ideology. As Arendell (2000) writes: "mothering is neither a unitary experience for individual women nor experienced similarly by all women" (p. 1196). These newer voices challenge notions of traditional maternal purpose and provide alternative ways of shaping purpose, to these I add a mother/child relational purpose shaped by both.

Culture impacts what can and cannot be said about and enacted by mothering. While people may understand that some ideas about mothering are culturally constructed "many *also* believe that other aspects are sacred, inviolable or at least common-sensical and that they follow from the natural propensities of mothers or the absolute needs of children" (Hays, 1996, p. x). Peggy Orenstein is quoted as saying of her female interviewees (in her book *Flux*, 2000):

> It was almost furtive for them to admit motherhood is not fulfilling.... It's like being anti-American. Motherhood silences women. The Kryptonite words for women are fat, slut, bad mother and selfish. The words make us lose our powers just like Superman loses his in the face of Kryptonite.
>
> (Almond, 2010, pp. 3–4)

This may speak to why participants did not focus on their negative experiences during the inquiry. If certain 'sacred' expectations around holding were *not* met, mothers' negative feelings around this 'failure' may be compounded (or constructed) by the displeasure of the cultural milieu.

Cultural prescriptions can easily be mistaken for an inner instinctive voice. There were countless times in my son's first few months when I responded to a blaming prescriptive voice, not questioning its origins; I took it to be the articulation of my own well-thought-out understanding. I conveniently forgot that cultural norms are fickle voices that change across time and circumstance, and that do not necessarily have anything helpful or truthful to say about my child and my own experience.

Psychoanalyst Lloyd De Mause (1974/1995) and psychologist Robin Grille (2005) draw our attention to child-rearing practices of many cultures prior to the modern age. Ideas of the intrinsic value of children, a mother's particular purpose and the special mother/child bond have not always held sway as dominant understandings and to this day remain complex. Infant and child mortality used to be very high (Orme, 2005), there was no contraception readily available and women's and children's places in society were up until the last 100 years or so, precarious. O'Malley (2005) points out that our modern idea of children as requiring care and attention over longer periods of time had a lot to do with the emergence of the "middle class" (para. 2) in the 18th century.

It is possible that in an age where the dissemination of information and opinion is so easily accessible, the power of any one maternal paradigm or cultural ideal may diminish in the face of so many voices. Fuchs (2016) writes: "social media … can both play a role for exerting control, exploitation and domination as well as for challenging asymmetric power structures of domination and exploitation. And in actual reality they do both at the same time" (p. 21).

While cultural ideologies have contributed to findings on the role of purposefulness in maternal holding, it is unlikely that they constitute an entire explanation. Participants entered the inquiry with different life experiences, at different stages of parenting with children of different ages and life experiences as well. Needs identified and attended to were not uniform across all mothers. It is possible that qualities of purposefulness emerged not only from the cultures these mothers and I participate in, but also from the navigation of *unique* mother/child needs, that are co-created from the mother and child's shared history and ways of being together; their own 'sub-culture', their own purpose.

A therapeutic exploration of cultural, social and familial 'voices' as well as the voices of the mother/child 'sub-culture' is highly valuable because it sheds light on the kinds of thoughts and ideas that often shape relational experiences beneath the surface and outside of everyday awareness. Bringing them into awareness provides mothers with more information and more agency.

## Purposeful holding: summary

I have made a number of suggestions about the relationship between maternal holding and purposefulness, summarized below:

1   We can be exquisitely 'about' our child in moments of maternal holding. Purposefulness may be a manifestation of 'maternal intentionality' that arises into awareness and is uniquely directed toward the mother/child relationship.
2   When one has a valuable, considered and specific 'aboutness' then that intentionality is more likely to emerge into awareness or be readily available to awareness upon reflection. Maternal intentionality requires *effort,* particularly in order to identify and navigate needs. It requires effort in order to be enacted in a specific way and effortful enterprises are more likely to appear in awareness.
3   Maternal holding cannot be experienced nor understood without reference to the mother/child relationship. Mother's and children's needs and purpose experienced during maternal holding are co-created within relationship. This does not mean that a mother or child's experience or conceptualisation of needs and purpose are the same; only that they always arise from and return to the relationship.
4   Attachment studies have focused on what children need and receive from attachment processes within the mother/child relationship. However, attachment is malleable in adults: just as a child's patterns of being in relationship with their mother are forming, a mother's patterns of being in relationship with her child also develop and change her own attachment style. The mother/child relationship is unique and new; it brings with it its own power to grow and develop mother *and* child.

5  Purpose and needs were identified as arising from, navigated within and returned to the mother/child relationship. Deeply felt qualities of purpose and need experiencing during holding originate from an 'us' rather than the two 'I's of mother and child. Maternal intentionality or purpose might be more aptly termed *mother/child intentionality* or *mother/child purpose.*

6  If purpose arises from the mother/child relationship, we have an increased number of vantage points from which that purpose may be noticed and worked with.

7  Navigating this long-term bond is not easy. Mothers found ways of supporting their relationship with their children by ascribing a sense of purpose to it. By successfully navigating relational needs during maternal holding mothers and their children co-created regular opportunities for a sense of satisfaction and reward. Reward, purpose and meaning have all been linked to well-being and the ability to keep going: to support relational strength in the face of difficulty.

8  Modern Western culture promotes a number of stories around mothering, including mothering as work, mother-blaming, intensive mothering and notions of the 'supermum'. Each of these encourages the view of motherhood and maternal holding through different prisms of purposefulness, though none of these alone account for the presence of purposefulness in maternal holding.

9  If purposefulness is co-created within the shared space of mother and child, then cultural prescriptions play out and are navigated within the mother/child relationship, they are shaped and reshaped by the unique qualities of that relationship and its history.

A relational or intersubjective mother/child purpose cannot be shaped, navigated or satisfied solely by the mother *or* child; it is the relationship that co-creates needs and rewards. The purpose and needs mothers bring to maternal holding are immediately, within the relationship and the moment of holding, intermingled with the purpose and needs the child brings to the relationship be they conscious or beneath awareness. This manifests in an ongoing dance of relational purpose and need as mothers hold their children and are in turn, held. What emerges as purposeful is of and for the mother/child 'us'.

Holding associated with a sense of purpose appears to have a protective and supportive function for the mother/child relationship. Bringing attention to co-created purpose and needs navigation, to the rewarding and rich experience of the mother/child 'us' reminds mothers that they are not alone in this significant relationship. There are mutual though different strengths, meaning and pleasures that can be found for both mother and child in moments of physical, emotional and/or psychological holding if we pay attention to them. All of this contributes to the possibility that a shift in focus in therapeutic work from the 'good enough' mother to the 'good enough' mother/child relationship might support, develop awareness of and advocate for the profoundly intersubjective qualities of maternal holding and purpose.

**Box 6.2 Ariel Moy, *A Nugget of Gold*, poem.**

What is mine in this moment?
What is yours?
Or rather, what is ours?
Smooth then rough,
Flowing then arrested with surprise,
I sense 'we',
And then it is gone.
Each moment a glimpse,
A nugget of gold,
Enduring, tough, real,
When I'd thought 'we' were just a
quick embodied quirk.
I'm trying to understand.

## Considerations for therapeutic work

Below I provide some ideas and questions that may be incorporated into therapeutic and supportive work for mothers and children. They are essentially about attending to qualities of purpose and need that may be present during moments of holding and that arise within the relationship. This will include an exploration of the cultural, social, and familial voices that might contribute to how a mother understands her relationship with her child particularly as it manifests around purpose and needs.

The work may begin with an arts-based exploration of intimate moments of affection like holding (as described in Chapters 1 to 4).

Once a representation has been made you can then co-explore the representation/s in an open and curious way before directing your inquiry to the suggested areas below. Holding and maternal purpose can be engaged with via talk therapy but will be significantly enriched by accessing non-conceptual knowing. As suggested in Chapter 1, it is beneficial if possible, to come to some kind of synthesis or understanding (for now) at the end of each session. All of these questions can be directed to experiences of holding and/or the representation of those experiences.

- Explore your client's sense of purpose during holding and within the mother/child relationship.

  What is this sense of purpose like?
  Does their sense of purpose involve need?
  What needs does she attend to during holding? What does she give?
  What needs of her own are present during holding? What does she receive?

- Explore your client's way of being with her child – what attachment or relational patterns of being do you both notice during holding?

  What elements, if any, of the mother's relationship with her child feel familiar to her from her own childhood? What is the same and what is different?
  Are there other significant relationships in her life that involve similar patterns of being to the way she interacts with her child?
  What patterns of being work well for their relationship? What would she like to change?

- Inquire into the ways in which this mother/child relationship feels new.
- You may wish to explore the possibility that what this mother gives to her child, the attachment developed between them, might be also received by her. That is, a mother's own attachment style may be reinforced, challenged and/or developed by this new attachment to her child.
- Investigate how other voices and imagery shape, limit and expand her experience of mothering and how these might manifest as she holds her child and when she reflects on that holding.

  Where are the 'shoulds' in her holding experiences?
  Does she feel that these other voices are contradictory or confirming of her own experience? Are they helpful?

- Inquire into the ways in which your client experiences *both* mother and child's needs and purpose within the relationship.

  As you dig deeper into needs or purpose, do they appear interconnected? Can a sense of her child's need ever be present without a sense of her own needs?
  When she successfully navigates her child's need, does she also navigate some of her own? This draws attention to the ways in which your client is not alone in the relationship, what she and her child have, they make together.

- Paying attention to the successful navigation of needs and purpose during holding brings experiences of satisfaction and rewards into awareness. Explore any sense of reward or satisfaction your client may feel during holding.
- Find examples of optimal holding experiences, consolidate and amplify them by representing them with art-making and creative expression.

  Is there, for example, a visual, textural, audible or aromatic shortcut a client might create or imagine that will take them to those optimal experiences, like Kitty's 'golden moments' or Leni's 'us'?
  Together you can explore and create a shortcut, it might be found in a child's soft toy or item of clothing, a drawing, an image, a particular perfume, a hot cup of tea, a heat-pack or a snippet of music. Your client might continue inquiring into and amplifying that shortcut at home.

- If the mother does have a short cut to positive and meaningful moments of connection, perhaps they can carry a small picture, an item of jewellery, a particular perfume etc that represents it or have it available for quick access in their home for when times are difficult. You can work on developing this together.
- Consider the ways in which positive moments can support the mother/child relationship during the harder times.

# References

Ainsworth, M. D. S., Blehar, M. C., Water, E., & Wall, S. N. (1978/2005). *Patterns of attachment: A psychological study of the strange situation.* New York, NY: Routledge.

Ainsworth, M. D. S., & Wittig, B. A. (1969). Attachment and exploratory behavior of one-year-olds in a strange situation. In B. M. Foss (Ed.), *Determinants of infant behavior IV,* (pp. 111–136). London: Methuen.

Almond, B. (2010). *The Monster Within: The Hidden Side of Motherhood,* Berkeley, CA: University of California Press.

Anderson, K. (2007). *Giving life to the people: An indigenous ideology of motherhood. In A. O'Reilly (Ed.) Maternal Theory: Essential Readings.* Bradford, Canada: Demeter Press. Retrieved from Amazon.com

Anderzen-Carlsson, A., Carvahlo-Lamy, Z., & Eriksson, M. (2014a). Parental experiences of providing skin-to-skin care to their newborn infant – Part 1: A qualitative systematic review. *International Journal of Qualitative Studies on Health & Well-Being,* 9, 1–22. doi:10.3402/qhw.v9.24906.

Arendell, T. (2000). Conceiving and investigating motherhood: The decade's scholarship, *Journal of Marriage and Family,* 62(4), 1192–1207. doi:10.1111/j.1741-3737.2000.01192.x.

Bakewell, S. (2016). *At the Existential Café: Freedom, Being, and Apricot Cocktails with Jean-Paul Sartre, Simone de Beauvoir, Albert Camus, Martin Heidegger, Karl Jaspers, Edmund Husserl, Maurice Merleau-Ponty and others.* New York, NY: Other Press.

Barad, K. (2007). *Meeting the Universe Halfway: Quantum physics and the entanglement of mater and meaning.* London: Duke University Press.

Bartels, A., & Zeki, S. (2004). The neural correlates of maternal and romantic love, *NeuroImage,* 21(3), 1155–1166. doi:10.1016/j.neuroimage.2003.11.003.

Berridge, K. C. (2001). Reward learning: Reinforcement, incentives, and expectations, *Psychology of Learning and Motivation,* 40, 223–278. doi:10.1016/S0079-7421(00)80022-5.

Bowlby, J. (1958). The nature of the child's tie to his mother. *International Journal of Psychoanalysis,* 39, 350–371. Retrieved from www.psychology.sunysb.edu/attachment/online/nature%20of%20childs%20tie%20bowlby.pdf.

Bowlby, J. (1969). *Attachment and Loss: Attachment,* Vol. 1. New York, NY: Basic Books.

Bretherton, I. (1992). The origins of attachment theory: John Bowlby and Mary Ainsworth. *Developmental Psychology,* 28, 759–775. doi:10.1037/0012-1649.28.5.759.

Chae, J. (2015). "Am I a better mother than you?" Media and 21st-century motherhood in the context of the social comparison theory. *Communication Research,* 42(4), 503–525. doi:10.1177/0093650214534969.

Choi, S., & Goo, K. (2012). Holding environment: The effects of group art therapy on mother–child attachment. *The Arts In Psychotherapy* 39(2012), 19–24. doi:10.1016/j.aip.2011.11.001.

Cole-Adams, K. (2009, May 10). My precious burden. *The Sydney Morning Herald Sun.* Retrieved from www.smh.com.au/national/my-precious-burden-20090509-aypm. html.

Csikszentmihalyi, M. (1990). *Flow: The Psychology of Optimal Experience.* New York, NY: Harper Perennial Modern Classics.

Custers, R., & Aarts, H. (2005). Positive affect as implicit motivator: On the nonconscious operation of behavioural goals. *Journal of Personality and Social Psychology*, 89(2), 129–142. doi:10.1037/0022-3514.89.2.129.

De Haan, M., Belsky, J., Reid, V., Volein, A., & Johnson, M. H., (2004). Maternal personality and infants' neural and visual responsivity to facial expressions of emotion. *Journal of Child Psychology and Psychiatry*, 45(7), 1209–1218. doi:10.1111/j.1469-7610.2004.00320.x.

De Marneffe, D. (2007). The "problem" of maternal desire: Essential mothering and the dilemma of difference. In A. O'Reilly (Ed.) *Maternal Theory: Essential Readings.* Bradford, Canada: Demeter Press. Retrieved from Amazon.com

De Mause, L. (1974/1995). The emotional life of nations. Retrieved from http://p sychohistory.com/books/the-emotional-life-of-nations.

Dollard, J. & Miller. N. E. (1950). *Personality and Psychotherapy; An Analysis in Terms of Learning, Thinking, and Culture.* New York, NY: McGraw-Hill.

Dreyfus, H. (2005). Hubert L Dreyfus interview: Conversations with history. Institute of International Studies, UC Berkeley. Retrieved from http://globetrotter.berkeley. edu/people5/Dreyfus/dreyfus-con5.html.

Eagleman, D. (2011). *Incognito: The Secret Lives of the Brain.* New York, NY: Vintage Books.

Edwards, K. (2016, February 1). Why asking women to 'End Mummy Wars' is flawed [Blog post]. *The Sydney Morning Herald.* Retrieved from www.dailylife.com.au/life-a nd-love/parenting-and-families/why-asking-women-to-end-mummy-wars-is-fla wed-20160131-gmhzuj.html.

Elliott, S., Powell, R., & Brenton, J. (2013). Being a good mom: Low-income, black single mothers negotiate intensive mothering. *Journal of Family Issues*, 36(3), 351–370. doi:10.1177/0192513X13490279.

Emmons, R. A., & McCullough, M. E. (2003). Counting blessings versus burdens: An experimental investigation of gratitude and subjective well-being in daily life. *Journal of Personality and Social Psychology*, 84(2), 377–389. doi:10.1037/0022-3514.84.2.377.

Ennis, L. R. (2014) Intensive mothering: Revisiting the issue today. In L. R. Ennis (Ed.) *Intensive Mothering: The Cultural Contradictions of Modern Motherhood.* Bradford, Canada: Demeter Press.

Field, T. (1996). Attachment and separation in young children. *Annual Review of Psychology*, 47, 541–561. doi:10.1146/annurev.psych.47.1.541.

Fitch, W. T. (2008). Nano-intentionality: A defense of intrinsic intentionality. *Biology and Philosophy*, 23, 157–177. doi:10.1007/s10539-007-9079-5.

Fraley, R. C. (2002). Attachment stability from infancy to adulthood: Meta-analysis and dynamic modelling of developmental mechanisms. *Personality and Social Psychology Review, 6*(2), 123–151. doi:10.1207/S15327957PSPR0602_03.

Frankl, V. (1946/2011). *Man's Search for Meaning.* UK: Rider (Random House Group).

Froh, J. J., Sefick, W. J., & Emmons, R. A. (2008). Counting blessings in early adolescents: An experimental study of gratitude and subjective well-being. *Journal of School Psychology*, 46(2), 213–233. doi:10.1016/j.jsp.2007.03.005.

Fuchs, C. (2016). Power in the age of social media. *Heathwood Journal of Critical Theory*, 1 (1), 1–29. Retrieved from http://fuchs.uti.at/wp-content/Power_SocialMedia.pdf.

George, C., Kaplan, N., & Main, M. (1985). *The Adult Attachment Interview*. Unpublished manuscript, University of California at Berkeley. Retrieved from www.psychology.sunysb.edu/attachment/measures/content/aai_interview.pdf.

Goldie, P. (2002). Emotions, feelings and intentionality. *Phenomenology and the Cognitive Sciences*, 1(3), 235–254. doi:10.1023/A:1021306500055.

Goleman, D. (2006). *Social Intelligence: The New Science of Human Relationships*. London: Arrow Books.

Grille, R. (2005). *Parenting for a Peaceful World*. Alexandria, NSW, Australia: Longueville Books.

Hall, A. C., & Bishop, M. J. (2009). Introduction. In A. C. Hall & M. J. Bishop (Eds.), *Mommy Angst: Motherhood in American Popular Culture*. Santa Barbara, California: ABC-CLIO, LLC.

Hall, D., & Kirsten, G. (2008). Kangaroo mother care – A review. *Transfusion Medicine*, 18, 77–82 doi:10.1111/j.1365-3148.2007.00812.x.

Hanley, S. J., & Abell, S. C. (2002). Maslow and relatedness: Creating an interpersonal model of self-actualisation. *Journal of Humanistic Psychology*, 42(4), 37–57. doi:10.1177/002216702237123.

Harlow, H. F., & Zimmermann, R. R. (1959). Affectional responses in the infant monkey: Orphaned baby monkeys develop a strong and persistent attachment to inanimate surrogate mothers. *Science*, 13, 421–432. doi:10.1126/science.130.3373.421.

Hays, S. (1996). *The Cultural Contradictions of Motherhood*. New Haven, USA: Yale University Press.

Hawkes, H. (2016, August 31). Is your busy life killing your oxytocin cuddle chemicals? *Australian Financial Review*, 37. Retrieved from www.afr.com/brand/luxury/how-to-get-more-oxytocin-into-your-life-and-relationships-20160805-gqmbtr.

Heinemann, A-B., Hellstrom-Westas, L., & Hedberg Nyqvist, K. (2013). Factors affecting parents' presence with their extremely preterm infants in an neonatal intensive care room. *Acta Paediatrica*, 102(7), 695–702. doi:10.1111/apa.12267.

Hepach, R., Vaish, A., & Tomasello, M. (2017). The fulfillment of others' needs elevates children's body posture. *Developmental Psychology*, 53(1), 100–113 doi:10.1037/dev0000173.

Heylighen, F. (1992). A cognitive-systemic reconstruction of Maslow's theory of self-actualisation. *Behavioral Science*, 37(1), 39–58. doi:10.1002/bs.3830370105.

Hill, S., & McMahon, C. (2016). Maternal mind-mindedness: Stability across relationships and associations with attachment style and psychological mindedness. *Infant and Child Development*, 25(5), 391–405. doi:10.1002/icd.1947.

Hill, P. L., Turiano, N. A., Mroczek, D. K., & Burrow, A., L. (2016). The value of a purposeful life: Sense of purpose predicts greater income and net worth. *Journal of Research in Personality*, 65, 38–42. doi:10.1016/j.jrp.2016.07.003.

Illingworth, G., MacLean, M., & Wiggs, L. (2016). Maternal mind-mindedness: stability over time and consistency across relationships. *European Journal of Developmental Psychology*, 13(4), 488–503. doi:10.1080/17405629.2015.1115342.

Jung, C. G. (1961/1983). *Memories, Dreams, Reflections*. London: Flamingo Fontana Paperbacks.

Kashdan, T. B., & McKnight, P. E. (2013). Commitment to a purpose in life: An antidote to the suffering by individuals with social anxiety disorder. *Emotion*, 13(6), 1150–1159. doi:10.1037/a0033278.

Katz Rothman, B. K. (2007). Beyond mothers and fathers: Ideology in a patriarchal society. In A. O'Reilly (Ed.), *Maternal Theory: Essential Readings*, Bradford, Canada: Demeter Press. Retrieved from Amazon.com

Kenrick, D. T., Griskevicius, V., Neuberg, S. L., & Schaller, M. (2010). Renovating the pyramid of needs: Contemporary extensions built upon ancient foundations. *Perspectives in Psychological Science*, 5(3), 292–314. doi:10.1177/1745691610369469.

Kerrick, M. R., & Henry, R. L. (2017). "Totally in Love": Evidence of a master narrative for how new mothers should feel about their babies. *Sex Roles*, 76(1–2),1–16. doi:10.1007/s11199-016-0666-2.

Kim, P., Leckman, J. F., Mayes, L. C., Feldman, R., Wang, X., & Swain, J. E. (2010). The plasticity of human maternal brain: Longitudinal changes in brain anatomy during the early postpartum period. *Behavioral Neuroscience*, 124, 695–700. doi:10.1037/a0020884.

Koizumi, M., Ito, H., Kaneko, Y., & Motohashi, Y. (2008). Effect of having a sense of purpose in life on the risk of death from cardiovascular diseases. *Journal of Epidemiology*, 18, 191–196. doi:10.2188/jea.JE2007388.

Koster, M., Ohmer, X., Nguyen, T. D., & Kartner, J. (2016). Infants understand others' needs. *Psychological Science*, 27(4), 542–548. doi:10.1177/0956797615627426.

Kraemer, S. (1996). Betwixt the dark and the daylight of maternal subjectivity: Meditations on the threshold. *Psychoanalytic Dialogues*, 6, 765–791. doi:10.1080/10481889609539152.

Krok, D. (2016). Can meaning buffer work pressure? An exploratory study on styles of meaning in life and burnout in firefighters. *Archives of Psychiatry & Psychotherapy*, 18 (1), 31–42. doi:10.12740/APP/62154.

Ladd-Taylor, M. (1995). *Mother-work: Women, Child Welfare and the State 1890–1930*. Chicago: University of Illinois Press.

Lafrance, A. (2015, January 8). What happens to a woman's brain when she becomes a mother. *The Atlantic*, Retrieved from www.theatlantic.com/health/archive/2015/01/what-happens-to-a-womans-brain-when-she-becomes-a-mother/384179/.

Lanza di Scalea, T., Matthews, K. A., Avis, N. E., Thurston, R. C., Brown, C., Harlow, S., & Bromberger, J. T. (2012). Role stress, role reward, and mental health in a multiethnic sample of midlife women: Results from the study of women's health across the nation (SWAN). *Journal of Women's Health*, 21(5), 581–489. doi:10.1089/jwh.2011.3180.

Lucas, R. E., & Dyrenforth, P. S. (2006). Does the existence of social relationships matter for subjective well-being? In D. Vohs & E. J. Finkel (Eds.), *Self and Relationships: Connecting Intrapersonal and Interpersonal Processes* (pp. 254–273). New York, NY: Guilford Press.

Main, M., Hesse, E., & Kaplan, N. (2005). Predictability of attachment behaviour and representational processes at 1, 6, and 19 years of age. In K. Grossman & E. Waters (Eds.), *Attachment from Infancy to Adulthood: The Major Longitudinal Studies*. New York, NY: The Guilford Press.

Main, M., & Solomon, J. (1990). Procedures for identifying infants as dIsorganised/disoriented during the Ainsworth Strange Situation. In M. T. Greenberg, D. Cicchetti, & E. M. Cummings (Eds.), *Attachment in the Preschool Years: Theory, Research and Intervention* (pp. 121–160). Chicago: University of Chicago Press.

Martela, F., & Steger, M. F. (2016). The three meanings of meaning in life: Distinguishing coherence, purpose, and significance. *The Journal of Positive Psychology*, 11(5), 531–545. doi:10.1080/17439760.2015.1137623.

Maslow, A. (1943). A theory of human motivation. *Psychological Review*, 50, 370–396. Retrieved from http://psychclassics.yorku.ca/Maslow/motivation.htm.

Maslow, A. (1993). *The Farther Reaches of Human Nature*. Middlesex, England: Penguin Publishing.

Max-Neef, M. (1992). Development and human needs. In M. Max-Neef and P. Ekins (Eds.), *Real-life economics: Understanding Wealth Creation* (pp. 197–213). London: Routledge.

Meins, E., Fernyhough, C., de Rosnay, M., Arnott, B., Leekam, S. R., & Turner, M. (2012). Mind-mindedness as a multidimensional construct: Appropriate and non-attuned mind-related comments independently predict infant-mother attachment in a socially diverse sample. *Infancy*, 17(4), 393–415. doi:10.1111/j.1532-7078.2011.00087.x.

Mercer, J. (2011). Attachment theory and its vicissitudes: Toward an updated theory. *Theory & Psychology*, 21(1), 25–45. doi:10.1177/0959354309356136.

Murray, M. (2014). Back to work? Childcare negotiations and intensive mothering in Santiago de Chile. *Journal of Family Issues*, 36(9), 1171–1191. doi:10.1177/0192513X14533543.

Noë, A. (2004). *Action in Perception*. Cambridge, MA: MIT Press.

Ogden, T. (2004). On holding and containing, being and dreaming. *The International Journal of Psychoanalysis*, 85(6), 1349–1364. doi:10.1516/T41H-DGUX-9JY4-GQC7.

Orme, N. (2005). The medieval child. In M. Gubar (project director), *Representing Childhood*. Retrieved from www.representingchildhood.pitt.edu/medieval_child.htm.

O'Malley, A. (2005). The eighteenth century child. In M. Gubar (project director), *Representing Childhood*. Retrieved from www.representingchildhood.pitt.edu/eight eencent_child.htm.

Pascoe, C. M. (1998). Screening mothers: Representations of motherhood in Australian films from 1900 to 1988. Retrieved from https://ses.library.usyd.edu.au/bitstream/2123/385/3/adt-NU1999.0010whole.pdf.

Pearmain, R. (2001). *The Heart of Listening: Attentional Qualities in Psychotherapy*. London: Continuum Books.

Proulx, T., Markman, K. D., & Lindberg, M. J. (2013). Introduction: The new science of meaning. In K. D. Markman, T. Proulx, & M. J. Lindberg (Eds.), *The Psychology of Meaning* (pp. 3–14). Washington, DC: American Psychological Association. doi:10.1037/14040-000.

Riedel, R. (2014). *What is the relationship between Meaning in Life, Purpose in Life and secondary student wellbeing?* Doctor of Philosophy thesis, School of Education – Faculty of Social Sciences, University of Wollongong, 2014. Retrieved from http://ro.uow.edu.au/theses/4412.

Ruddick, S. (1989/1995). *Maternal Thinking: Toward a Politics of Peace*. Cambridge, MA: Beacon Press.

Rutter, M. (1995). Clinical implications of attachment concepts: Retrospect and prospect. *Journal of Child Psychology and Psychiatry and Allied Disciplines*, 36, 549–571. doi:10.1111/m.1469-7610.1995.tbo2314.x.

Sartre, J.P. (1946). Existentialism is a humanism. Retrieved from www.mrsmoser.com/uploads/8/5/0/1/8501319/english_11_ib_-_no_exit_-_existentialism_is_   a_huma nism_-_sartre.pdf.

Seligman, M. E. P. (2002). *Authentic Happiness: Using the New Positive Psychology to Realize Your Potential for Lasting Fulfillment*. New York, NY: Atria Paperback.

Siegel, D. J. (1999). *The Developing Mind: How Relationships and the Brain Interact to Shape Who We Are*. New York, NY: The Guilford Press.

Slaby, J., & Stephan, A. (2008). Affective intentionality and self-consciousness. *Conscious and Cognition*, 17(2), 506–513. doi:10.1016/j.concog.2008.03.007.

Songhorian, S. (2012). Is affective intentionality necessarily irrelevant in social cognition? *Phenomenology and Mind*, 2, 88–96. doi:10.13128/Phe_Mi-19 628.

St Aubyn, E. (2014). *The Patrick Melrose Novels*. London: Picador Classic.

Steger, M. F., Oishi, S., & Kashdan, T. B. (2009). Meaning in life across the life span: Levels and correlates of meaning in life from emerging adulthood to older adulthood. *The Journal of Positive Psychology*, 4(1), 43–52. doi:10.1080/17439760802303127.

Stern, D. (1977). *The First Relationship: Infant and Mother*, 2002 ed. Cambridge, MA: Harvard University Press.

Stern, D., Bruschweiler-Stern, N., & Freeland, A. (1998). *The Birth of a Mother: How the Motherhood Experience Changes You Forever*. New York, NY: Basic Books.

Taormina, R., & Gao, J. (2013). Maslow and the motivation hierarchy: Measuring satisfaction of the needs. *American Journal of Psychology*, 126(2), 155–177. doi:10.5406/amerjpsyc.126.2.0155.

Tay, L., & Diener, E. (2011). Needs and subjective well-being around the world. *Journal of Personality and Social Psychology*, 101(2), 354–365. doi:10.1037/a0023779.

Thurer, S. L. (2007). The myths of motherhood. In A. O'Reilly (Ed.) *Maternal Theory: Essential Readings*. Bradford, Canada: Demeter Press. Retrieved from Amazon.com

Tuomela, R. (2013). *Social Ontology: Collective Intentionality and Group Agents*. Oxford, UK: Oxford University Press.

Ungureanu, C., & Rotaru, I., (2014). Philosophy of skillful coping: Motor intentionality vs. representations for action. *Social and Behavioural Sciences*, 163, 220–229. doi:10.1016/j.sbspro.2014.12.310.

Ussher, J., Charter, R., Parton, C., & Perz, J. (2016). Constructions and experiences of motherhood in the context of an early intervention for Aboriginal mothers and their children: Mother and healthcare worker perspectives. *BMC Public Health*, 16(1), 1–12. doi:10.1186/s12889-016-3312-6.

Warner, J. (2005). *Perfect Madness: Motherhood in the Age of Anxiety*. New York, NY: Riverhead Hardcover.

Warner, J. (2012, July 13). Smother mother: Why intensive child-rearing hurts parents and kids. *TIME*. Retrieved from http://ideas.time.com/2012/07/13/smother-m other-why-intensive-child-rearing-hurts-parents-and-kids/.

Watkins, P. C. (2004). Gratitude and subjective well-being. In R. A. Emmons & M. E. McCullough (Eds.), *The Psychology of Gratitude* (pp. 167–192). New York: Oxford University Press.

Watson, R. A. (1995). *Representational Ideas: From Plato to Patricia Churchland*. Netherlands: Springer Science and Business Media. doi:10.1007/978-94-011-0075-5.

Winnicott, D. W. (1953). Transitional objects and transitional phenomena – A study of the first not-me possession. *International Journal of Psycho-Analysis*, 34(2), 89–97. Retrieved from icpla.edu/wp-content/uplods/2013/02/Winnicott-D.-Transitiona l-Objects-and-Transitional-Phenomena.pdf.

Winnicott, D. W. (1958) *Collected Papers through Paediatrics to Psycho-Analysis*. New York, NY: Basic Books.

Winnicott, D.W. (1960). The theory of the parent-infant relationship. *International Journal of Psycho-Analysis*. 41, 585–595. Retrieved from icpla.edu/wp-content/uploads/2012/10/Winnicott-D.-The-Theory-of-the-Parent-Infant-Relatoinship-IJPA-pdf/.

Winnicott, D. W. (1965/1990). *The Maturational Process and the Facilitating Environment: Studies in the Theory of Emotional Development*. London: Karnac Books.

Woolley, K., & Fishbach, A. (2016). For the fun of it: Harnessing immediate rewards to increase persistence in long-term goals. *Journal of Consumer Research*, 42(6), 952–966. doi:10.1093/jcr/ucv098.

Wong, P. T. P. (2012). Introduction: A roadmap for meaning research and applications. In P. T. P. Wong (Ed.), *The Human Quest for Meaning: Theories, Research, and Applications*, 2nd ed. (pp. xxvi–xliv). New York, NY: Routledge.

Zhang, S. H., Yip, W. K., Lim, P. F., & Goh, M. Z. (2014). Evidence utilization project: Implementation of kangaroo care at neonatal ICU. *International Journal of Evidence-Based Healthcare*, 12(2), 142–150. doi:10.1097/XEB.0000000000000009.

Zimmer-Gembeck, M. J., Webb, H. J., Pepping, C. A., Swan, K., Merlo, O., Skinner, E. A., Avdagic, E., Dunbar, M. (2015). Is parent-child attachment a correlate of children's emotion regulation and coping? *International Journal of Behavioral Development*, 41(1), 74–93. doi:10.1177/0165025415618276.

# 7 Expansion into the mother/child 'us'

## Introduction

Participants conveyed the enormity, intensity, wonder, fullness and meaningfulness of their holding experiences. These qualities described an expanded sense of self, an awareness of self-in-relationship. Felt expansion was not present during every moment of holding but appeared in optimal holding experiences.

At times expansion was engaged deliberately in the service of relational needs, the mother challenged herself, deliberately extended what she felt was possible in order to navigate changes within the relationship. However, experiences of expansion also emerged spontaneously, as a co-creation of mother and child. They described a sensitivity to an altered present moment and they sometimes lingered once the holding was over.

These moments of felt expansion drew our awareness to how the *relationship* can serve as the origin and location of experience and joy for mother and child rather than our traditional understanding of experience located within the individual. These treasured holding moments also led to changes in conceptualisation of what was possible for mother and child within the moment of holding.

Philosopher, Martin Buber (1937) wrote: "all real living is meeting" (p. 9) and noted the embeddedness of identity within relationships: "the I is real in virtue of its sharing in reality. The fuller its sharing, the more real it becomes" (p. 44). In Chapter 6 I looked at how needs and purpose are co-created from within the mother/child relationship during maternal holding. This *Expansion* finding moves the dialogue toward what it *feels* like to experience from a place of intersubjectivity and the powerful benefits of paying attention to experiencing from a place of the mother/child 'us'.

## The felt experience of the mother/child 'us'

> The notion of intercorporeality ... for phenomenology, it is an attempt to embody the intersubjectivity.
>
> (Shogo Tanaka, 2013, p. 62)

DOI: 10.4324/9781003104094-8

Experiences of expansion arose from optimal maternal holding moments and were not everyday occurrences nor did they last for the entire experience. However, they were deeply felt and highly valued, and appeared often enough to warrant this second finding.

Rosanna described what this expansion felt like: "with both of the twins ... there really is this sense of being held by them ... I'm talking about a kind of a flow of energy". This 'flow' represents experiences that shifted participants' awareness of being, from an everyday sense of bounded self to a feeling of self-in-relationship. These were not easy experiences to articulate because the term 'intersubjectivity' is not an everyday term and outside of academia, it does not generally appear in everyday language.

### Expansion: embodiment and interembodiment

Kramer and Gawlik (2003) note that a process of true engagement with others results in an "interhuman wholeness" or "the unfolding of the 'between'" (p. 105). This 'unfolding' captures how awareness of inter-subjectivity can be fleeting and changeable, it is under no individual person's control and is contributed to by both. It is difficult to give language to this awareness as it defies our everyday valuing of self and agency. When these mothers became aware of their intersubjective being with their children it was like they together unwrapped a little of the universe, something precious, not quite known, often unseen and bigger than both of them, and more than a sharing of subjectivities. Participants' descriptions of warmth, connection, compression and release, of emanation, oneness, hugeness, flow and expansion all speak to this 'unfolding of the between'. This phrase served as an access point into my dialogue with literature.

I began with the body as the instantiation of the self in the world, particularly as maternal holding begins and is built upon such an embodied experience. Our immediate response is to speak about the separateness, the individuality of the body. My body is my own. However, an embodied self is porous to the world; the 'self' grows, experiences and relates within the world and includes more than what we imagine as a single self. As Jane Bennett (2010) writes:

> My "own" body is material, and yet this vital materiality is not fully or exclusively human. My flesh is populated and constituted by different swarms of foreigners, we are, rather, an array of bodies, many different kinds of them in a nest set of microbiomes,"
>
> (pp. 112–113)

Our identity as an autonomous and separate body arises from a fundamentally shared existence; our bodies are expressions in and of the world. We invite the world in and cannot do otherwise. We absorb and convert light when we see; we detect and convert waves of sound when we hear; we breathe oxygen into our lungs, and we process weight, texture, balance and smell perceptions (as well as proprioception) to orient our bodies in space.

Tortora (2013) notes that our sense of self is associated with our embodiment. This embodiment is experienced at both "an intrapersonal and interpersonal level" (p. 141). Maternal holding, particularly when the relationship between mother and child is young, is powerfully and primarily physical. As Rothman (2007) writes: "motherhood, (is) the physical embodiment of connectedness," (Chapter 24, Section 3, para. 10).

Our existence is an ongoing process of invitation and opening, sense making and output with the world and others. Merleau-Ponty wrote of the primary embodiment of experience: "I encounter things because I am encounterable to others" (cited in Bakewell, 2016, p. 236). When Leni held her daughter, she knew her presence was a part of her daughter's experience. Leni worried about how her body's state, including her own "need" to hold her daughter impacted upon Lucy, she did not want Lucy to feel that her mother was in any way a "burden" upon her.

Our bodies require "continuing maintenance and improvement" (Lupton, 2013, p. 5). This may appear more striking from birth through childhood and adolescence but continues until our bodies expire. This also includes maintenance and improvement of our bodies *with* others, our bodies in relationship.

Leni regularly interpreted her children's behaviours for clues as to their needs, with or without conscious detective work. For example, she adjusted the way she held her daughter because of Lucy's growing size, she did not want to cause Lucy pain. She recognised the need for changes in the ways that she held Lucy as their shared space and embodiment during holding changed over time. Her detective work occurred in that shared space, it was about the felt experience of mother and child together and not the child alone. Maternal holding, primarily embodied and frequent at the earliest stages of the mother/ child relationship, provides rich opportunities for a focus on the physical qualities of relationship as it unfolds, and this includes awareness of the porousness of each body in relationship.

When I searched for literature about the embodied qualities of significant relationships, I found the term 'interembodiment' (Lupton, 2013). I wondered if the sensual qualities of intersubjectivity might be described by interembodiment. Lupton (2013) writes that interembodiment

> [e]ncapsulates the notion that apparently individuated and autonomous bodies are actually experienced at the phenomenological level as *intertwined*. It is a concept of relation with other people which accepts that individuals' bodies are inevitably lived alongside and in response to others' bodies.
>
> (p. 6)

At the very basis of our experience, embodied encounters with others are interembodied encounters, this speaks explicitly to the physical or sensual qualities of intersubjectivity. Like Kitty's experiences of twining and fit, when positive and welcome interembodied sensations arise into awareness, they can be felt as deeply satisfying moments of connection.

Fusaroli, Demuru and Borghi (2009) note that "one's body and basic sensorimotor skills, which constitute a crucial structure for most of one's cognitive processes, are, in important ways, intersubjectively distributed" (p. 2). To know as a physical, embodied being, is to exist at all times somewhere, somehow, and somewhen in relationship. As Ellsworth (2005) writes "to be alive and to inhabit a body is to be continuously and radically in relation with the world, with others, and with what we make of them" (p. 1).

Participants could only refer to experiences of holding with reference to their children, holding was always about mother and child in relationship; it could only be understood within relationship. Experiences of expansion during holding and on reflection describe conscious instances of Lupton's interembodiment.

Touch provides unequivocal experience of another entity that momentarily *blurs* the boundaries between each, inviting awareness of interembodiment. Untouched by another human being, I might be able to say this is where my body begins and ends but this changes with touch. Tahhan (2014) gives the example of a caress noting that

> [i]n a relational state, the body of the caressing person and the body of the person being-caressed become less clear. There are no clear borders: who is caressing whom is blurred as the positionally defined body of the touching person and the body of the person being-touched can no longer be felt.
>
> (p. 28)

If paid attention to, if valued, touch can alert us to instances of interembodiment. As Kitty said: "we did spend many hours together, we still do. And as Harley got older that sense of holding her, she feels more a part of me today than she did ever … like of my body, than she ever did before, I feel that even stronger now." Spending so much time with Harley, touching and holding, over so many years, has brought Kitty a profound awareness of the ways in which Kitty and Harley's bodies momentarily feel shared. With loving touch, their embodied selves expand so that they feel more than the sum of their individual identities.

The early stages of caring for a child provide for a particular intensity of physical relationship that lends itself to awareness of this interembodiment. As Lupton (2013) writes, bodies are "contingent and dynamic" (p. 4) with our social and biological worlds. She notes: "mothers … act as an ersatz immune system for their infants by attempting to keep out germs" (p. 15). Mothers act as an extended body for their helpless infants, carrying them so that they can move in space, holding them so that they are protected, feeding them so that they survive, cleaning them so that they do not become ill and shielding them from dangerous others or circumstances.

The mother's "bodily boundaries may be experienced as more permeable and fluid" (Lupton, 2000, p. 60) with her child and vice versa. For mothers and children, awareness of their embodied relationship may frequently move along a spectrum of felt autonomy, connection and oneness; from an everyday sense of self to an expansion into 'us'.

Leni commented: "That's how it feels ... mooshy ... lines blurred" when talking about specific moments while holding her children. Kitty provided a description of optimal holding experiences: "There's a calmness and a oneness and sort of like a flow, almost as if there's a musicality to this breathing and rhythm ... this sort of holding is ... very connected, very twining." Imagery like flow, blurring, squeezing, twining, invisible threads, energy shared, and hugeness were all attempts at giving language to a deeply felt experience of self-in-relationship or interembodiment.

There are also times when the feeling of interembodiment becomes overwhelming and difficult for mothers, when, for example, the longing for sleep is thwarted again by a crying baby who also longs for sleep, and the mother's own body responds as if that longing were her own. While the experiences of interembodiment in this inquiry emerged from positive experiences of holding and touch, that does not mean that interembodiment is necessarily or always positive or welcome. Leni found the profound dependence of her infant children confronting; their bodily reliance upon her own body challenged her need for independence and her fear of damaging her children. Awareness of the mother/child 'us' was present at this early stage and avoided. Leni needed to inhabit a space without her children, she did not seek awareness of intersubjective experiences.

If an accessible language existed to describe everyday but meaningful experiences of intersubjectivity, we would be more aware of it, more able to engage in it, and more able to convey our experiences to others. I had a strong embodied and aesthetic sense of the expansion participants described and the expansion I too felt during holding but found this hard to articulate.

I wished to compliment and explore my knowing about the qualities of expansion and maternal holding at this stage in the inquiry by making a series of representations to see what they might reveal. The visual language of flames captured the flow of energy and vitality between bodies described by participants. In the photo I took there were two flames, however their heat intermingled, they danced with one another, their 'embodiment' blurred to represent those precious moments of interemebodiment experienced during holding, the feeling of 'us'.

### Moments of holding invite awareness of interembodiment

The imagery I created to explore expansion illuminated the preciousness and fragility of that 'dance' between mother and child, how deep it can go, how fleeting it can be and how powerfully the heat of living relationship can shape a moment.

All participants were aware of the dependence of their children upon them, particularly the younger their children were. There appeared to be an understanding that in the beginning, a mother is their child's world, her body protects and nurtures their body, and mother and child exquisitely interact to construct their child's sense of self and wellbeing. This was complimented by extensive attachment theory research (as described in the previous chapter) undertaken in the last 70 years since Bowlby (1958) first suggested the term. Attachment theory is so well established and respected in modern society that Cassidy, Jones & Shaver (2013) write:

> Certain large goals of any worthy society – the mental and physical health of its members, the optimal development of each individual's interests and capacities, and a safe environment free of violence and hatred – are likely to be achieved only to the extent that infants and children receive the benefits of what Bowlby and Ainsworth called a safe haven and a secure base, which as far as we can see imaginatively into the future are likely to depend on responsive attachment figures.
>
> (p. 26)

Trevarthen (2009) writes that the infant 'I' is very much a part of a mother/child 'we'. This is an understanding "shared by folk psychologies of mothers the world over" even if "neglected by developmental psychologists seeking more rational and representation-based explanations" (p. 37). He notes that from the very beginning, infants are engaged in intersubjective experiencing and "shared action" (p. 6).

Trevarthen (2009) however takes this beyond the infant/carer relationship: "intentions, interests, and states of internal vitality" (p. 10) must be made available to others in order for *any* coordinated human or animal action to occur. Given that these cooperative behaviours do occur in general, and must occur for infant survival, some of our 'internal' world of thoughts and feelings are available to others. This availability begins with "the natural growth of embodied intersubjectivity" (p. 6). That is, for mothers and their babies, experiences of interembodiment convey vital relational information for both.

Intersubjectivity is a necessary precondition for human relationships and encounters. Teske (2013) writes: "empathy exists in our involuntary and sensorimotor coupling" (p. 779). This 'coupling' occurs without conscious effort and precedes language. It is from direct, shared engagement and passionate involvement that we develop and grow throughout our lives. Our intersubjectivity fuels our traditionally 'higher order' awareness of self, agency and being in the world.

Martin Buber (1937) described self-in-relationship (or what I term 'usness') as an 'I-Thou' (p. 3) way of engaging with the world. It involves an open orientation toward another, a brief shared *encounter* with other in relationship. He described the alternative way of being in the world as an 'I-It' experience, which reflects our everyday way of understanding and interacting with others as entities or conceptual constructs separate from us.

In a reflection on Buber's *I and Thou* (1937), Kramer (2003) notes that: "from the first moment of life, the child reaches out for contact, tactilely and visually confirming otherness. Only later, as the child learns, does the living relationship split into I and It" (p. 28). Prior to this, the child lives in "purely natural combination, bodily interaction and flowing from the one to the other," (Buber, 1937, p. 17). The child is born in an *I-Thou* or 'us' engagement with the world; relationship comes *before* awareness of selfhood and inter-embodiment comes before awareness of embodiment.

Participants were aware of a shared sensitivity to one another's bodies during the moment of holding particularly as their children matured. Mothers were not only sensitive to their children's bodily state, children were also aware of the physicality of their mother and her current state. Rosanna explained of her eldest daughter: "If she sensed a need in me, she would respond to that and you know, hold me in that way". The 'self' of the mother/child relationship continues to develop over time and both mother and child can be acutely attuned to the messages each body conveys about the relationship's wellbeing and identity.

As Springgay (2005) writes, for Merleau-Ponty, "perception must be understood as a reversal, a mode of being touched and touching" just like a fold of fabric: our being in the world exists not solely within our own body but between bodies or environments and in so doing is "intertwined and enmeshed" (p. 37) with others. We begin first with an experience of intersubjectivity and this evolves toward a sense of subjectivity and selfhood. We 'unfold' ourselves from our primary interembodiment as we mature, but that does not mean that interembodiment disappears or cannot be brought into awareness. We simply become used to noticing, conceptualising and valuing ourselves as independent entities (explored in more detail in the *Cultural Contributions* section later on).

Tufnell and Crickmay (2004) evoke the original enactment of this relational folding as it plays out in our lives:

> The growth of an embryo is expressed in a continuous, slow, flux of movements,
> Up, down, and around its axis,
> Curling, uncurling, opening and folding, around the developmental limbs.
> Its movement travels upwards to the developing brain, and downwards towards the tail – movements of growth that begin under the beat of a mother's heart.
> Expressing the flow and impulse of life within us.
> These early movement patterns remain with the body.
> Echoing invisibly within each part of us throughout the days of our lives.
>
> (p. 45)

Bakewell (2016) describes the temporal and fleeting quality of this folding: "[it is] as though someone had crumpled a piece of cloth to make a little nest or hollow. It stays for a while, before eventually being unfolded and smoothed away" (p. 235). These little folds are our encounters with others and other's encounters with us. This brings to mind Leni's description of maternal holding as a "squeeze to release" and Kitty's "oneness". At first glance, these do not seem to be expansive qualities, but rather a form of compression or reduction. And yet these represent compression of two people together, rather than one person alone; the mother, though 'folded', is folded *with* her child and together, as the mother/child relationship, they are larger. This enlargement is described in the experience of expansion. Mothers did not describe a loss of themselves in expansive moments but rather a growth.

Writing about Sloterdijk's *Bubbles* (2011), a philosophical meditation on space and how we inhabit it, Stepnisky (2014) draws our attention to social psychology's neglect (or at least only implicit recognition) of spatiality when looking at social life. He states that it utilises "flat" (p. 413) imagery, it considers individuals as autonomous beings with empty spaces between them but, it ignores the "spatial and atmospheric dimensions of human intersubjectivity" (p. 413). This may appear surprising: when one imagines relationality, one might imagine action, interaction, and three-dimensional beings in space together.

Stepnisky (2014) proposes a "round" social psychology including descriptions and explorations of "shared space" (p. 414). Like Teske (2013), Fusaroli et al. (2009) and Trevarthen (2009), Stepnisky notes "a shared sense of being-in … has an atmosphere, or surrounding texture, that is both constituted by and constitutes our going on with one another in the world" (pp. 414–415). Stepnisky writes that "for Sloterdijk, space is relationship" (p. 417).

A 'round' psychology would pay attention to relational qualities as they are experienced in body and space. For example, Tanaka (2015) describes how moments of shared, non-verbal, embodied understanding reflect a "reciprocal action" (p. 462) between bodies: an embodied empathy that, like Dreyfus' 'skillful coping', does not require conscious thought and deliberation. This empathy, Tanaka notes, "belongs neither to the self nor to the other" (p. 465). It is not an action deliberately and purposefully undertaken by those in relationship but something that organically emerges from being in relationship. The psychology is round because it represents the flow and textures of interembodiment.

Tanaka (2015) notes that a shared intentionality of consciousness (as suggested in Chapter 6) is possible *because* of this shared embodied empathy. For example, "by experiencing the same action: laughing at something, distorting the face for something, reaching toward something" (p. 465) individuals are able to share an experience (like listening to music). Momentarily, intentionality is shared through embodied empathy – both individuals are 'about' the same phenomenon. Thus, if both mother and child in the moment are 'about' holding, then their focus is an intersubjective focus on holding and their awareness will be brought to the interembodied qualities of that holding.

Like Sloterdijk's *Bubbles,* Tanaka (2015) proposes that shared embodied moments may result in "various emotional tones of the interpersonal field"

(p. 467). Mother and child might gain conscious access to an expanded sense of self-in-relationship or 'us' because interembodiment (or intercorporeality as Tanaka terms it) "overrides the individual's intentions and gains its own autonomy," (Tanaka, 2014, p. 265). That is, mother and child may feel their interembodiment as it plays out in the moment. The mother/child relationship becomes the space from which they both feel, their round psychology of' us'.

Feldman Barrett (2017) proposes that unlike our traditional notion of emotions as universal and hard-wired into the brain, emotions are made and every emotion you experience is unique to the moment and its context (external and internal). She writes:

> Our emotions aren't built-in, waiting to be revealed. They are *made*. By *us*. We don't *recognise* emotions or *identify* emotions: we *construct* our own emotional experiences, and our perceptions of others' emotions, on the spot, as needed, through a complex interplay of systems. Human beings are not at the mercy of mythical emotion circuits buried deep within animalistic parts of our highly evolved brain: we are architects of our own experience.
>
> (p. 40)

I would emphasise the contextual 'we' element in our construction of emotions. Emotions that arise during holding are co-constructed by the mother/ child relationship in that moment. If we construct emotion from the present context, as well as prior experiencing, then mothers *participate* in a co-construction of the emotional tone of relationship with their child during holding. The particular qualities of happiness, for example, that manifest in the moment of holding arise from the intersubjective 'us' of mother and child. What happiness feels like for 'us' will be unique to that mother/child relationship both in the moment and over time.

Importantly, emotions are made by the body. Fuchs (2016), like Tanaka, describes interaffectivity as an "intuitive empathic understanding" (p. 196) where "our body is affected by the other's expression and we experience the kinetics and intensity of his emotions through our own bodily kinaesthesia and sensation" (p. 198). Just as interembodied experiences co-create the physical qualities of 'us', interaffectivity describes the emotional atmosphere of 'us'.

When mothers experienced 'usness' during holding, their attention was drawn to instances of the physical (interembodied) and emotional (interaffective) atmosphere of relationship. Exploring these qualities of 'usness' alerted participants and myself to two things:

1  The value of and significance we placed on optimal moments of holding;
2  The way experiences of 'usness' provide signs of the current status of the relationship.

Given how much we all valued our relationships with our children, these relational signs were worth paying attention to. At the same time, paying attention to the state of 'us', left participants increasingly open to and aware of further experiences of expansion or interembodiment.

When Leni said her daughter was "the centre of my world and I think I am the centre of her world"; when Rosanna placed the postcard "I can't live without you" at the centre of her representation and when Kitty said "everything else stands still like it's just her and I in the world" they each articulated how brief moments during holding their children captured qualities of shared space, emotion and body. Words like 'world' and 'centre' are spatial words – 'world' conveys largeness and totality of space, 'centre' conveys the heart of space. Words like 'I can't live without you' reflect survival. These mothers articulated an experience where only a mother/child 'us' existed during moments of optimal holding. These felt qualities and understandings about maternal holding reflected the high value they placed on the interembodied and interaffective space of the mother/child relationship.

Experiences of expansion in body and emotion may also have arisen into awareness because maternal holding left a trace for these mothers; a sense of holding lingered with participants once their child had left their arms. When holding moments ended, sensations, emotions, thoughts and images sometimes remained, not only as memories recalled but as a feeling that lingered after the holding had finished. Like Merleau-Ponty's 'folding' metaphor, when the fabric of the mother/child shared experience smooths out, creases remain. For example, Kitty felt like the holding experiences she shared with Harley "radiated" into her and she felt a "filling out" of herself during and after she held Harley. The creases in the 'fabric' of Harley and herself remained and rippled across her life when she wasn't holding her. For Rosanna the feeling of not being able to hold Deanna lingered within their relationship as a powerfully felt absence and pain.

With the return to 'self' after moments of 'usness', something more is added to maternal experience. I have felt a bittersweet desire for a longer cuddle, a lingering sense of the warmth of the cuddle and a cooling sense of loss, sometimes I've felt shock that the cuddle started and finished so quickly, Leni sometimes felt this too.

Expansion comes with an awareness of self-in-relationship and that awareness can carry on once the actual holding is over. These traces of intersubjective awareness might contribute to the value we placed upon expansion as we reflected upon holding (see Box 7.1). Yong (2016) writes:

> All of us have an abundant microscopic menagerie ... we can't see any of these miniscule specks. But if our own cells were to mysteriously disappear, they would perhaps be detectable as a ghostly microbial shimmer, outlining a now-vanished animal core.
>
> (p. 3)

**Box 7.1 Ariel Moy, *Leaving Traces*, poem.**

Building up,
This moment of us.
Touching,
Being touched,
Antennae entwining,
Unknown territory,
We feel for it all.
When it is gone,
It is still here,
Atom bombs,
Left mid-explosion,
Leaving traces.

Applying this metaphor to maternal holding, we might imagine an echo or an afterimage of the shape of the mother/child encounter: the felt qualities of holding might leave a trace for mothers (and children) once the holding is over. These traces can also let us know how the holding 'went'. As Leni asked: did we "do it right?" This desire to know if the holding went well, if it met her children's needs, draws attention to the intersubjective space of the mother/ child 'us', bringing that space into awareness for examination and evaluation.

While I propose that intersubjective being is fundamental to experiencing and is therefore present during every maternal holding moment (optimal or otherwise), I recognise that we are not usually aware of it. We swim in a sea of intersubjectivity like De Quincey's (2000) 'fish in water'; it is generally not the basis from which we speak, explore or understand nor is it highly valued in our Western culture (which I have explored in more detail below). However, participants in this inquiry were asked to explore and articulate what maternal holding was like for them and, when given the opportunity to reflect upon maternal holding, they all placed a high value on their sense of self-in-rela-tionship, on the 'usness' of mother and child during holding and on reflection. All mothers put a lot of energy, focus and consideration into representing this 'usness' in words and imagery. It was valuable to them even if not a conscious element of every holding experience.

Kitty's imagery of the Big Bang (Figure 4.8) and participants' descriptions of shared energy and flow resonate with Springgay and Freedman's (2009) description of mothering as "a collision, a bursting into being" (p. 25). Leni offered the image of the yo-yo biscuit, the cream that binds the two biscuits together, a metaphor for the sensation of connection between mother and child. Rosanna spoke of the "hugeness of love". These descriptions were attempts to convey the curious, less known, hardly ever spoken about but very much present experience of expanding into the 'us' of mother and child. Becoming aware of intersubjectivity changes what we think of as possible. What was normal, a bounded sense of self, is challenged; what was 'mine alone' can become 'ours', what 'I am' can become 'what we are'.

### Awareness of the mother/child 'us' changes lived space and time

Awareness of our lived body, lived space, lived time and lived relationships (Van Manen's 'fundamental existentials', 1990, pp. 101–102) are all open to experiences of expansion. If an experience like maternal holding provides opportunities for awareness of intersubjectivity in body and relationship, and if bodies constitute space (Springgay & Freedman, 2009, p. 25), that is, they are the way we experience space, then becoming aware of intersubjective experiencing will have implications for how one experiences space and time.

As with an expanded sense of body, emotion and relationship, words describing intersubjective experiences of space and time are not a part of our everyday speech. Participants grappled verbally with different kinds of energetic as well as spatial and temporal metaphors to convey their changing awareness of time and space when experienced from a place of 'us'. Leni's hot and cold, fast and slow imagery in her Representation 3A (see Figure 3.7) conveyed changes in space and time when she held her children: there was a speed to the cuddles which she felt attended to her sense of ticking boxes and doing the hug 'right', but in the middle of cuddling, she also experienced how they "sort of envelop you as well" represented by the wave. Both the speeding up and slowing down of time were welcome elements of the cuddle and not part of her everyday experiencing in general.

Rosanna's final session representation (see Figure 2.8) included photographs that captured the sense of 'us' she had with each daughter at different times over the years; they held thoughts, feelings, sensations and images for Rosanna relevant to each relationship. These photos and drawings showed that when she reflected on holding her daughters, their shared past was also a part of the holding moment, as were a felt sense of the interconnectedness of mother, father, sisters and extended family, what Rosanna referred to as "familial holding"; a holding that extended over time and space.

Bylund and Athanasopoulos (2017) found that over three experiments, Swedish speakers who consider time in long/short *length* spatial metaphors and Spanish speakers, who consider time in much/small *quantity* spatial metaphors were misled as to the duration of time with stimuli that were different than their preferred spatial metaphors. They concluded that: "human temporal cognition is malleable" (p. 3) and that malleability is contributed to by the metaphors we use to understand time and space.

Kitty used scientific and biblical imagery to convey the immensity of her experience; she used embodied "musicality" like the synchronisation of breathing and heartbeats to convey the slowing down and then diminishment of time. Time and space were no longer located within Kitty; time was *theirs* (see Figure 4.3, time is shown in the upper right-hand corner). While she became aware of changed experiencing during mother/child time and space that does not mean these experiences were the *same* for Kitty and Harley. Nevertheless, her sense of temporality, like space and embodiment, were a *product* of the two of them in relationship and not her experiencing alone.

Perhaps in relationship, when there are large changes from movement to stillness, we notice our bodies, we notice our surroundings, and by noticing, we momentarily extend ourselves in time and space and relationship. We move from a series of actions that take us from washing dishes, cooking dinner, shouting instructions, mental check-listing to a full stop (willing or otherwise), to a relational pause, to a *holding*.

Early in her experience of mothering, Kitty deliberately chose to focus her energies, as often as she could, on her relationship with her daughter. Part of that chosen experiencing meant that sometimes Kitty transitioned from the everyday tasks of mothering that included the upkeep of a safe and sane home, to a different speed: the deceleration of holding Harley and being held.

Van Manen (1990) notes that we "do not ordinarily reflect on (lived space)" (p. 102) but it "affects the way we feel" (p. 102). He goes on to propose that in lived space, "we become the space we are in," (p. 102) likening embodied experiences of a cramped elevator or a wide-open space with the myriad yet explicitly different feelings they engender. If mother and child become the space that they are in during the moment of holding, then their interembodied experiencing draws attention to intersubjective or expanded space.

Lived time is also inescapably known via the body as Wittmann writes: "we *are* time" (2016, p. xiii). Pokropski (2015) suggests: "in interaction with the other, the phenomenon of the shared present emerges" (p. 907). Laroche, Berardi and Brangier (2014) write that in certain moments, time is experienced inter-subjectively because individuals share a "dynamical background in which *behaviours* and *experiences* are entangled" (p. 9); in relationship we inhabit a "shared world of significance in which to be together" (p. 11). This includes a shared experience of time (p. 11) and space, in that moment, *we* are time and space.

For Leni, time ticked away behind the scenes in her everyday life but every once in a while, as she held her children, time became a 'wave' slowing her experiences down, a product of their shared time in that moment. For Kitty, time slowed or receded into the background when she held Harley, but she also experienced herself *with* time, emanating out.

From a place of 'us' it is possible that a mother might access, however briefly, qualities of their child's lived time and space as these contribute to the lived time and space of the mother/child relationship. Iris Duhn (2016) reflects on our common understanding of time as an arrow, proceeding into the future in a linear, causal fashion. Equally, we all have an allotted time and must consider how we 'spend' it. However, in Michael Ende's (1973) book *Momo* the child protagonist "finds a way of experiencing time as intense materiality" (Duhn, 2016, p. 381) where "times passes unmeasured and flows freely" (p. 382) and "where new possibilities emerge" (p. 381). Time perception for Momo is shaped within action/experience itself, within space.

Duhn (2016) notes that Momo realises "time lives within her ... an imagination of time as forever changing/becoming, of beauty, vibrancy and variation" (p. 383). This is a young child's sense of time and space, more so than adults. This experience allows Momo to truly 'be' with others, to sit with them, to listen to them, to be a part of their story. If this kind of lived time is brought to a moment of mother/child holding, then it will contribute to the shaping of time and space for the mother from within the relationship. Mothers not only shape children's experiences in moments of holding, children also shape mothers, they both contribute to and receive from something bigger than them both: the mother/child relationship.

In his article *How Infants Grow Mothers in North London*, Miller (1997) noted that the traditional Kleinian view of infant developmental stages might as easily be applied to maternal developmental stages leading to a "construction of a mature parenthood" (Towards maturity, para. 2). He provides the example of the Winnicottian transitional object as an object of power not only for the child but for the mother as well. As with Leni and her daughter's soft cow "Moo", a mother may appear more "frantic at the idea that it may be lost" (Miller, 1997, The depressive position, para. 2) than the child. This may reflect her own stage of coming to accept her child as "other". I would add that it might also reflect a shared experience of attachment to Moo because of what Moo represents.

Database searches including 'impact of children on mothers' and 'role of a child in mother's experience' inevitably come up with a mother's impact on her child or a mother's role in her child's development. As described in Chapter 6, there has been little research undertaken on maternal experiences of holding (outside of kangaroo care, breastfeeding and holding stillborn infants) and significantly, little research on the contributions of children to *mother's* experiences of holding them. However, fiction, memoir and a proliferation of blogs have filled this gap.

It can be a messy, if not impossible task, to try and figure out who contributed what, over time and in space, to mother/child relationships as Shriver's (2003) powerful and distressing novel *We Need to Talk About Kevin* conveys. Describing her response to her psychiatrist's diagnosis of post-natal depression, Eva (the mother of Kevin) writes:

> She also suggested that because Kevin's disinterest in my breast had persisted, I might be suffering feelings of rejection. I coloured. It embarrassed me that I might take the opaque predilections of such a tiny, half-formed creature to heart.
>
> Of course, she was right.
>
> I shouldn't have taken it personally, but how could I not? It wasn't mother's milk he didn't want, it was Mother.
>
> (p. 86)

Given relationships involve more than one person, both mother and child contribute to the mother/child relationship and during the moment of holding, both mother and child contribute (though differently) to what is felt by both mother and child. Perhaps Leni's daughter cuddled quickly because this was a part of her "personality", perhaps she cuddled quickly because those were the kind of cuddles Leni offered or maybe *they* cuddled quickly because that's the kind of cuddle that had grown from their relationship. When Leni described Lucy, she said:

> LENI: I suppose [Lucy is] sort of putting on that face of: I'm having a look, don't approach, I'm just figuring it out.
> ARIEL: [*speaking as Lucy*] Give me my space to process everything.
> LENI: Yes, yes, very much. That's Lucy. That's me [*said softly*].

What was initially ascribed to Lucy as a way of being, may have also arisen from Leni or from that less articulated, in between space of 'us'.

Bergum (1997) writes:

> The vision of mothering as a journey shows a concrete intimacy, in which mother and child journey together, giving and taking, pausing and moving ahead, like dance partners sensitive to the movement and rhythm of each other. The mothering relation, as experienced, blurs the boundaries between mother and child, tending to make them diffuse and flexible, holding close and letting go, being one and then being two. The mother story is the relational story by its very nature.
>
> (p. 169)

Mother and child emotion both contribute to the relationship and thus both contribute to the quality of a mother's (and child's) awareness of space and time during maternal holding. Emotions like boredom or a sense of calm can make us feel as if time is stretching out. If we have a finite number of attentional resources, when we're doing nothing, we have more resources to pay attention to our experience of time. We bring all our attention to bear on the 'paint drying'. We become more aware of our body's sensations and appraisal, we feel ourselves more and feel time more – we experience time as stretching and expanding (Wittmann, 2016). For example, during maternal holding a mother might have to put aside her 'to do' list and simply be with their child in 'child time', as Leni felt compelled to do many times during her children's infancy. On the one hand this can include experiences of frustration, anger or distraction; on the other, if the duration of the holding necessarily extends (for example, if the child falls asleep in her arms), a mother may find herself accepting this new experience of 'child's time' where an endless temporality may emerge.

When Kitty described the synchronization of heartbeats, when Rosanna described holding Lillian as "holding at the deepest level" and when Leni described holding Lucy and Alexander as a moment of "just us", they spoke to a changing awareness of lived space and time. The 'body' of mother/child in the space of 'us' is 'larger' than the body of mother or child alone and thus lived space and time experienced from an 'us' rather than an 'I' also change and expand.

I wondered about how, and even if, time is experienced by infants in the womb. We have no way of telling what time and space are like for us then as we cannot communicate nor recall what it was like, and yet our in-utero beginnings are visceral, primal and universal. As I searched through literature and imagery, I wondered what might have been written or represented about this original 'us' state of mother and infant.

As noted earlier, Buber (1937) wrote that an *I-Thou* encounter is "spaceless and timeless" (p. 19); we emerge from an original I-Thou encounter when we are born and in early infancy. Referring to Sloterdjik's *Bubbles* (2011), Stepnisky (2014) writes: "it is the prenatal With-structure that provides a basic 'feel' for relationship and gives all our encounters their atmospheric quality" (p. 426). That quality is 'spaceless and timeless'. It is possible that maternal holding may re-engage mothers with a fundamental 'usness' or an original I-Thou experience of the world, one first experienced in the womb.

We begin from a relational stance, from an 'usness' and this 'usness' carries through into our future ways of being with others. Both *I-Thou* and *I-It* orientations are natural and necessary consequences of human experiencing, we move between awareness of deep relation and self/other experiences daily, second by second, even if these emerge from a fundamentally intersubjective basis. If a prenatal relationality or *I-Thou* engagement (from the womb and infancy) is carried with us into the world, it may be possible that the mothers in this inquiry re-engaged with their initial 'usness' when they held their child. Maternal holding may have provided them with access to their *own* original *I-Thou* engagement as well as attachment style (as noted in Chapter 6).

Using metaphorical or emotionally laden language and imagery to try and capture a less articulate or understood experience also shaped how those experiences came to be known as our sessions progressed. Kitty's scientific and biblical imagery, Rosanna's felt sense of history with each daughter while holding them and Leni's descriptions of the velocity of holding all built and developed our knowing about expansion into 'us'. Awareness emerged in imagery and then in words, moving back and forth between these to develop our understanding further. We benefitted from moments without language or rather, with a language that was image or sensation-based. These representations sparked language in us, this language in turn helped us share and build our understanding of experiences of expansion during maternal holding as we cycled through ways of knowing.

Finally, the thematic quality of purposefulness may also have had a role to play in the changed experience of time and space during maternal holding. Seneca (4 BC–65 AD) wrote that time well spent was defined as an experience encompassing "a fixed purpose ... (being) at your own disposal; when your face wears its natural expression; when your mind was undisturbed" (2005, p.

4). In these purposeful moments we "know how to use" time (p. 2). Time well spent is recorded as meaningful, and time that is recorded as meaningful can be encoded in memory with richer detail. When we access richer memories, we feel as if those memories represent longer time durations than they may have otherwise (Stetson, Fiesta & Eagleman, 2007). Awareness of the mother/child us in all of its richness, in its changes in body, emotion and relationship, also changes how we experience time and space.

Paying attention and inquiring into the felt qualities of the mother/child 'us' during moments of holding provides a powerful reminder of the satisfying qualities of relationship but also the tangible, visceral experience of deep connection. That connection does not always feel good. After an exhausting night up with her infant, trying to manage a toddler in full tantrum in the middle of the supermarket or facing the closed door of her rejecting teenager once again, mothering can leave women feeling desperate, angry, afraid, confused and terribly isolated. In these moments she's unlikely to feel that she and her child are 'in this relationship together' and yet the strength of both of their emotions, their physical responses, are key indicators that they are very much interconnected. Finding ways of remembering embodied positive moments of interconnection can help mitigate those harder moments and remind mothers they are not alone.

## Cultural contributions to awareness of 'us'

Participants revealed tensions around ideas of individuality and relationship. Kitty questioned whether mothering was a valuable enough "passion", she felt she might be too directed toward her daughter. Rosanna experienced guilt around her belief that she was not available for her children in their teens but also acknowledged the necessity for her to do what she needed to for her own wellbeing as well as the wellbeing of her daughters. Western culture has long valued agency, individuality, personal self-control and responsibility. We consider that we exist within our *own* space and can reach out towards others from our own space, and our sovereignty over our bodies, our minds, and our emotions remains ours alone. Valuing intersubjectivity removes sole agency from a clearly delineated individual and places these experiences and knowing between people.

An underlying tension arises when one experiences intersubjectivity in a society that values autonomy. To complicate matters, many popular images and prescriptions for mothering appear to value self-sacrifice and a full focus on child, almost a giving up of oneself, the opposite of expansion. There appear to be two dominant cultural ideals: maternal autonomy (associated with health of mother and child) and maternal self-sacrifice (for the benefit of the child's health).

In a cultural paradigm of autonomy and/or maternal self-sacrifice, experiencing intersubjectivity might be misunderstood as a kind of 'merging' with mother vanishing or becoming like Kitty's "ghost". However, experiences of expansion were not reductive or dismissive of mother or child, they involved profound pleasure and a sense of something more, something larger.

As Lupton (2013) notes:

> Through touching-being touched, moving-being moved, feeling-being felt, hearing-being heard, the bodies of the mother and infant come close, or bend to each other, and then spread away from each other ... each body's being-in-the-world is shaped by the other's.
>
> (p. 7)

This shaping need not be experienced as a loss of autonomy, it might rather be a felt as a momentary awareness of intersubjectivity or expansion. The individual self can expand to include, for a moment, awareness of a relational 'us'. And participants were left with highly valued traces of that intersubjective experience later.

If pleasure or wonder is found in the experience of the mother/child 'us' then that puts into question dominant cultural values around autonomy as a singular path to wellbeing. Kitty wanted to extend, into adulthood, her relationship with Harley and in particular, their holding of one another (as mentioned in Chapter 4). She considered how that appeared to be frowned upon in Anglo-Saxon culture but more acceptable in Mediterranean cultures.

Cultural ideals dictate that intimate, shared relational space in healthy mother/child relationships should develop towards respectful autonomy as that child matures (Dooley & Fedele, 1999). With terms like 'mama's boy' and 'helicopter parenting', closeness including physical intimacy in these relationships is considered troublesome if not damaging. As Dooley & Fedele (1999) note of the mother/son relationship:

> Faced with cultural pressures that suggest restraint and withdrawal, rather than comfort and nurture, many mothers feel conflicted about their desire to stay connected to their sons. Traditional wisdom cautions that holding on will be damaging and create psychological problems for sons. Faced with this dilemma, mothers often yield to cultural pressures and disconnect from their young sons because they think it's the right thing to do.
>
> (p. 1)

However, Trentacosta, Criss, Shaw, Lacourse, Hyde & Dishion (2011) found that:

> Successful family adaptation to the transitions that characterize this developmental period may require parents and children to maintain relatively high levels of warmth and openness while minimizing and decreasing conflict and coercion in their relationships.
>
> (Conclusions, Limitations and Directions for Future Research, para. 1)

Warmth, presumably including physical warmth, was positively associated with "social competence and socio-cognitive reasoning during adolescence" (Conclusions, Limitations and Directions for Future Research, para. 1) for sons who were part of a warm mother/son relationship. These difficulties may be more salient for mother/son relationships but can nevertheless play out with mothers and their children irrespective of their gender. Physical and mental health need not be associated with a drastic reduction in physical or emotional intimacy.

While all participants were aware of and considered these cultural tensions they still valued and affirmed their experiences of expansion. These experiences did not diminish or sully their relationships with their children despite cultural norms that would challenge these. They did not negate a mother or child's agency. And there were also cultural ideals that affirmed experiences of expansion. As Kitty noted, stories, movies and images of love have attempted to capture that deep connection that can be felt when one is with someone one deeply cares for, including the mother/child bond. She said: "now I can see why there's poetry, and why there's art and why there's Bible stories"; there are cultural artefacts that speak directly to experiences of expansion in a way that celebrates them. From tragedy to comedy, from spoof to deep meditation, experiences of love and expansion are culturally present even if mostly neglected in our everyday language.

Experiences of expansion into self-in-relationship (positive and negative) may appear more often in artistic, religious or mythological expressions rather than everyday language perhaps because of their strangeness and value in the face of dominant notions of individual agency and wellbeing. However, using imagery or poetry to express a less conceptualised but deeply felt experience can send messages about intersubjectivity just as robustly as cultural prescriptions around autonomy and mother/child health. Each participant took from their cultural milieu both concerns around expansion and celebrations of their awareness of embodying 'us' in moments of maternal holding.

## Holding with technology: expanding the ways we hold relationships across distance and time

Participants used technology to convey their experiences of holding but they also used it to hold their children in psychological and emotional ways. When they held their children in this way their focus wasn't on the technology itself but rather on what that technology enabled them to do. This led me to inquire into our relationship with technology, and the ways in which it can slip into and augment our identity and experiencing.

By incorporating Merleau-Ponty's 'body schema' into his theory of 'embodied technology' philosopher Philip Brey (2000) focuses on how the relationship between body and technology is experienced. He suggests that the body as experienced is less about our awareness of its spatial positioning (including our positioning of the tool/technology), and more about its position in regard to meaning and movement. This approach makes more sense of the experience of technology and maternal holding. In this analysis, the technology "becomes a part of one's bodily space" (p. 11). Technology is used meaningfully by extending the possibility of maternal holding over distances and over multiple relationships (for example, communicating with multiple children at once).

We might imagine that the use of technology diminishes our embodied experiencing, this would be particularly relevant to maternal holding that begins in such an embodied way, even as it includes and develops toward more emotional and psychological holding.

However, Springgay (2005) noted that experiences of guilt and forgiveness were "created in the act of an encounter" (p. 44) undertaken *solely* via email. The email exchanges allowed access to each person's "private or personal identity" (p. 41). Springgay writes: "virtual space is understood as dis-embodied, dis-connected and distant ... this sentiment places the body as separate from digital connection" and then asks "instead, how might we begin to consider digital technologies as material, immanent, and inter-embodied?" (p. 45). The use of technology impacts and alters our experiencing, it can extend what kinds of holding or experiences are possible for us.

When we use technology, we can extend or augment our perceptions, for example, visually and verbally across distances or enhancing our ability to examine images up close as well as recording input to reflect upon later. Our experiences of the world with these augmented perceptions can change. For example, Lotto (2017) describes recent experiments conducted by the Magnetic Perception Group (pp. 73–76). He refers to a 2014 study where participants were asked to wear a belt, almost constantly, for seven weeks. The "feelSpace belt" (p. 73) vibrated whenever participants faced magnetic north. Findings included "improved knowledge of where they were" (p. 74) and better visua-lisation of the spatial layout of important personal landmarks. One participant noted: "space has become wider and deeper" (p. 74). Space felt different to participants not just perceptually but emotionally as well. They had adapted to the new information provided by the belt and added new sensory information to their experiencing. Interestingly, even when the belt was no longer worn, a changed sense of how they experienced and oriented themselves in the world remained.

Using her mobile phone, Rosanna experienced an expanded sense of hold-ing. Referring to her installation (Figure 2.3) she said:

> So that (phone) doesn't represent just me and Elaina but all of us and the phone was important because we live in separate cities so we are in con-stant contact through, and we all have iPhones ... (the representation) it's not meant to represent any particular members but the entirety of the holding ... it's *love* really, that's what holds you, that's what binds you and that's what the holding is, it's love.

Using her smart phone (including communication and camera applications) was a means by which Rosanna *experienced holding* and loving all of her daughters at once. Rosanna's embodied experience in that moment included and was shaped by the use of her phone but wasn't *about* her phone. Rather, her phone was incorporated into her sense of embodiment so that she could extend and augment her senses and actions in the service of holding her daughters from a distance. Perhaps this kind of extension feedback into Rosanna's experiencing as a sense of expansion during holding.

Goggin (2006) notes that today mobile technology is "indispensable" (p. 2) and includes a significant role in "a bewildering and proliferating range of cultural activities" including "staying in constant contact … identity-construction, music, mundane daily work routines, remote parenting … surfing the Internet, meeting new people, dating, flirting, loving, bullying, mobile commerce, and locating people" (p. 2). Mothers may use this technology to keep in touch with their children via talking, text or video; they can record memories of their relationship, and search for gifts or articles their children might be interested in, they can even track where their children are. Technology enhances or extends one's "motor and perceptual functions … and skills" (Brey, 2000, p. 11) and, like Springgay (2005), I would suggest one's emotional experiencing as well. Participants referred to their mobile phones, photographs or laptops during our sessions to support their inquiry and share qualities of holding with me. Their use gave rise to emotional, embodied experiencing, returning memories to them, returning feelings to them, in these moments the technology wasn't visible, it was simply an extension of their inquiring.

De Preester (2011) notes how perceptual extensions augment, transform, expand and amplify our senses. For example, glasses and mobile phones enhance what we see and extend our hearing. Additionally, applications like Skype or Zoom "make us perceptually telepresent" (p. 9): we are able to extend ourselves in *space* to (somewhat) appear to others and experience ourselves as present in a space we are not physically present in. However, when one sense is extended (say the auditory sense during a mobile phone call), another sense is reduced (like touch where the engaged other is physically absent). This is an important relational transformation – we can capture some enhanced sense of the other like talking to them or seeing them up close when they are actually far away, but this occurs at the expense of other perceptual information such as touch and smell.

Despite the lack of touch during technological holding, a history of embodied holding is shared between mother and child and this history informs part of the holding experiences they participate in. It is likely that while holding her daughters with technology, Rosanna and her children felt echoes or recollections of their physical holding as well. They also shared in the emotional and psychological holding Rosanna provided and experienced during these moments.

The resulting reduction in some senses with the extension of others via technology is not necessarily a negative given the perceived benefits of the enhancement of other senses. Van Manen (2010) notes that "the more important question is … not just what is lost but also what is gained in the way that technology alters the experience of intimacy, social nearness and distance and personal proximity" (p. 4). For example, he explores the benefits of writing: "in reading the others writing, I may feel addressed, stirred or touched by the written words. I experience a depth in the written words that spoken words may not easily possess, or do not possess in the same manner" (p. 6).

This enhancement of abilities and perceptions with the use of technology also lends itself to empowering individual mothers and children who may experience limits in what they are able to give and receive. Some mothers may not be able to physically hold their children, not just because they may be in different locations, but because they (mother or child) may have physical or psychological conditions that make holding impossible, difficult or painful. Harnessing technology to convey care, affection, concern and intimacy as a form of holding can be of great benefit both when physical holding is possible and also when it is not.

Leni reached out to her network of friends on a social app when she felt 'shocked', confused and hurt by her daughter's changed behaviour – she provided the story as an example of her daughter's changing intimacy behaviours and needs. She sought normalisation, sympathy and support, she sought holding, and she received it. She could not in that moment gather her friends around her for a chat about how she felt. Instead, she used her smartphone, took a photo, wrote a few words, and sent it out into a (luckily) supportive aether. Her lived body, space and relationship were expanded and changed as she reached out to her friends via her phone and these in turn helped her manage a change in her experiences of maternal holding. This provided her with a physically remote but technologically possible holding by her friends as they supported her, and she was then able to bring her own changed emotional atmosphere to how she held Lucy.

Anything that helps us store or shape memory affects how we interpret our memories as well as present experiencing. An increasing reliance on tools and technology like smart phones to return us to memories and navigate the world means that our experiencing increasingly incorporates technology. Losing all trace of precious digital photos may devastate a mother but it might also change her memories of holding her child and that may change her experiencing.

Rosanna's inclusion of photos in her final representation brought together important memories of the making of these photos as well as the times they were taken in order to represent her relationships with her daughters. They also reconfigured elements of the memories they represented. When she reflected on what holding her daughters was like for her, the photos took an active role in shaping that reflection. In a sense, the photos were a part of the layering and enriching of experiences that contributed to what she felt she knew about holding. Again, when memories are particularly detailed, for example, as they are captured in treasured photos, they can appear to have lasted longer than the original event lending them an expansive quality.

Like Brey's (2000) 'embodied technology', Clark and Chalmers (1998) propose a dynamic relationship between human cognition and technology that they term 'extended cognition'. In an example of the "coupling of biological organism and external resources" (p. 18) they refer to Otto (who has Alzheimer's). Otto relies on his notebook to remember for him, it includes directions for him to follow in the place of his own ability to recall directions. In this example, Otto and book are an "extended system". Otto's own memory resides in the book and yet the existence of the book will inevitably shape his memory.

For participants, photos and written accounts contributed to their experiences of holding their children both in the moment and on reflection. As a memory aid, photos might represent more than just the visual qualities of a moment, they also remind/re-create emotions, sensations, sounds, smells and thoughts associated with the moment. Sometimes photos and writing were used as a way of valuing and experiencing a moment *as it occurred* by recording it in order to return to it later or share with others (as Kitty described).

Sometimes photos showed moments of holding that participants couldn't recall but knew must have happened because of photographic evidence. These photos changed what participants re-constructed as memory. Rosanna described how she couldn't recall holding Deanna as a child. This caused her deep pain – "it's really hard to have lost the memories of one of your child's childhoods" – but she believed the photos, she knew she must have held Deanna, and this informed her experiences of holding Deanna in the present.

It is important to note that technological holding does not replace physical holding. Rosanna still needed and wanted to hold her children physically when she had the opportunity. This was particularly the case if there had been a difficulty in their relationship or if her child had experienced something either painful or joyous.

Maternal holding via technology may appear surprising or counterintuitive. However, holding in this inquiry manifested in different ways – sensual, affective and psychological, any one of which may be present to our awareness at any moment. As previously suggested, though we may be aware of one quality in the unfolding of a moment, it does not preclude the presence of other qualities of being. For example, body memory may be activated when holding children via technology across distances or when looking at a photo of one's child as an infant. As some of our senses are augmented with technology, we are able to extend ourselves across distance and relationships. Emotional and psychological holding lend themselves particularly well to an attuned use of technology. It is possible that the use of technology contributed to some experiences of expansion during holding by literally expanding what was possible for mothers and their children beyond the usual limits of our senses and abilities.

Exploring the ways in which technology can enrich and extend holding experiences and tap into optimal moments of expansion benefits the mother/child relationship by providing both with an increased ability to hold across space, relationships and time. Technology can also serve to remind mothers and children of the many positive ways in which they hold and are held.

## Representing the felt experience of expansion

Our language privileges the pairing of self and other, leaving intersubjective experiences languishing in less articulate realms. The expansive qualities of maternal holding were difficult to express and capture for participants and I. Making visual representations of expansion contributed to our growing understanding and ability to articulate what 'usness' felt like.

To explore and represent expansion for each participant, as I understood it, I looked to their use of imagery and metaphor when describing the feeling of 'usness'. Below I include those representations and the poetry that emerged after exploration of each.

### Leni, Lucy and Alexander

*Figure 7.1* Ariel Moy, *A Squeeze to Release*, felt tip pen on paper, 295x210mm.

**Box 7.2 Ariel Moy, *Into Us*, poem.**

I click on my warmth,
Fast then slow and solid.
Feel the natural blue of us;
Quick then easing … everlasting.

We move into stillness:
The light of us.
We move quickly together and apart
time at our edges.
Hot coals sparking, snow calm and waves.
So brief this moment ...
Then out again to Leni
being the time,
apart,
and into us,
and out,
and in,
and ...

*Rosanna, Elaina, Olivia, Lillian and Deanna*

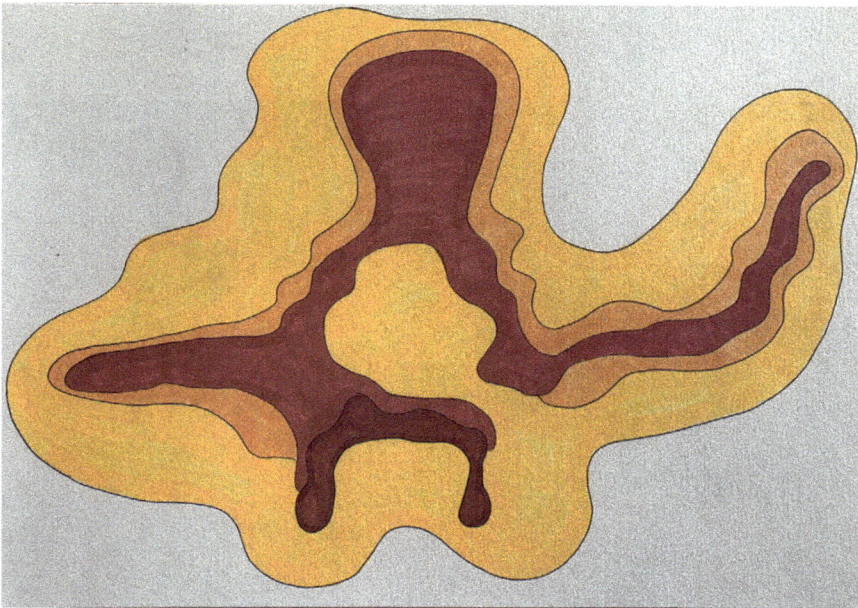

*Figure 7.2* Ariel Moy, *Holding One is Holding All*, felt tip pen on paper, 295x210mm.

**Box 7.3 Ariel Moy, *Expanding the Bubble of Us*, poem.**

We are sunshine and we grow,
Close ...  And far ...
We hold,
across distances and time.
Energy pulsing between us,
The spaces of us are full but free,
We flow through shared history, shared love,
We hold near and far.
I am there beneath you all.
We grow outward,
Expanding into our worlds,
I feel your warmth, you feel mine.
Holding one is holding all.

*Kitty and Harley*

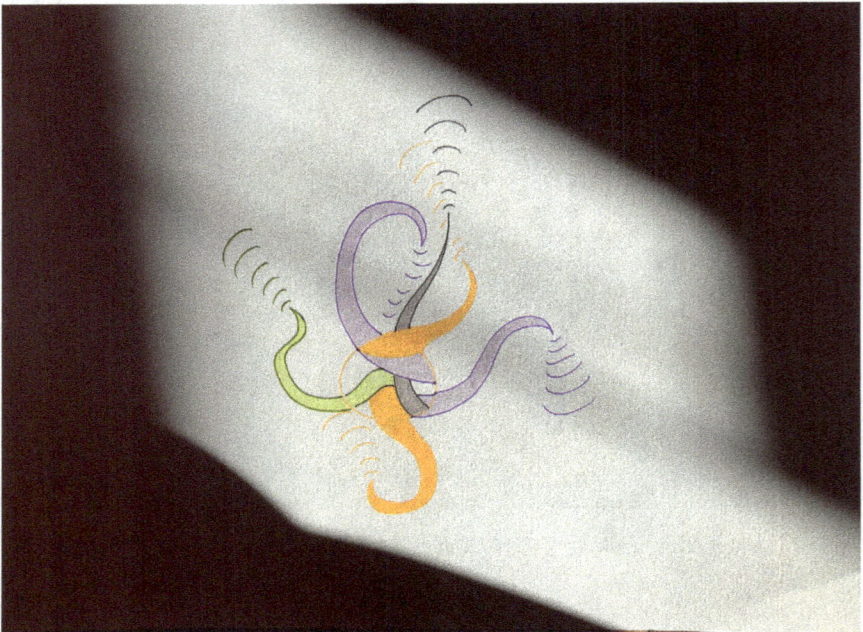

*Figure 7.3* Ariel Moy, *Radiating*, digital photograph.

Box 7.4 Ariel Moy, *A Burst of Energy*, poem.

Swirling. Bursting!
Changing.
Diminishing,
Catching up.
Sometimes two ... Sometimes one.
Radiating into the vastness,
Of you and I.
Limitless and loved,
The rhythms of us,
Are new and unknown,
And enough ...

## Conclusion

In engagement with imagery and literature, I have extended and developed our findings around experiences of expansion during maternal holding. These are summarized below:

1   Mothers make deliberate choices to expand their ways of being and knowing in order to identify, navigate and fulfil relationship needs.
2   A mother can become spontaneously aware of the mother/child 'us' during maternal holding. This experience of intersubjectivity manifests as a feeling of expansion.
3   Maternal holding, primarily physical and frequent at the earliest stages of the mother/child relationship, provides rich opportunities for a focus on the physical and affective qualities of relationship drawing attention to moments of interembodiment and interaffectivity.
4   Experiences of 'usness' may serve as crucial and valued indicators of the current mother/child relational state and its consonance with relational purpose. Experiences of expansion during holding were cherished and left traces behind. Those traces let mothers know how the holding 'went'. When we value these moments of intersubjectivity for the pleasure they bring, as well as the information they provide, we are likely to pay attention to moments of 'usness' in future.
5   Experiences of an embodied and emotional 'us' can also expand mothers' experiences of space and time during holding. Our embodiment shapes the space and time we inhabit, thus experiencing from an 'us' rather than an 'I' enlarges the space and time the mother/child 'us' share. Mothers may also experience some of their young child's 'timelessness'.

6   During the shared moment of maternal holding, mothers may re-engage with an original, intersubjective way of 'being-with' where time is experienced as 'timeless' or as larger than everyday time.

7   Culture can both limit and develop expression and knowing about experiences of expansion into 'us'. The English language tends to value the idea of selfhood at the expense of intersubjectivity, and the felt experience of 'usness' can be difficult to articulate. This is where artistic expression can convey what is deeply felt, valued and known during maternal holding.

8   Technology can expand and modify experiences of maternal holding across lived body, space and time. While this kind of holding is more obviously emotional and psychological, the embodied qualities of holding are present in the memories of that holding that have occurred. With tools and technology mothers can record holding as it occurs and re-engage with those recordings or representations on reflection, thus incorporating technology into how they experience and understand holding. It is possible that the literal extension of sense and ability provided by technology lends, in different ways, an expansive quality to holding.

---

**Box 7.5 Ariel Moy, *Together We Unwrap*, poem.**

Together we unwrap a universe of us.
Unfolding, velvet soft,
We draw breath and hold,
Lean in,
Carefully wonder:
What are we making?
My skin, yours,
We blend and become more,
We fall deep into,
The Night Kitchen,
Brewing ourselves,
Adding and subtracting,
Without words or plans,
Stirring with effort, the feeling,
Of us in our arms, our chests,
We're holding and folding,
Baking us, making us,
More.

Awareness of expansion into a mother/child 'us' was not an everyday occurrence during maternal holding, but it was significant, welcome, valuable and frequent enough to form an essential quality of holding in this inquiry. It is possible that maternal holding might offer an accessible glimpse into our innate 'usness', in particular, a variety of 'usness' that is both *desirable* and *potentially beneficial* to the mother/child relationship.

Above I have included a poem I made in response to this feeling of expansion when I held my son.

## Considerations for therapeutic work

As noted at the end of Chapter 6, and described in more detail in Chapter 1, begin with an arts-based therapeutic inquiry into a holding experience from a place of curiosity and openness. In this case, see if your client can represent what a moment of holding feels like. As you begin exploring the representation together, you and your client may focus in on potential experiences of expansion into the mother/child 'us'. Each of the questions below can be directed towards both your client's selected moment and the artistic expression made:

- Return to that particular moment of holding, attending to the embodied qualities of it as much as possible.

  Where do you stop, and your child begin in a moment of touch/holding? How would you describe your sense of self and other in an optimal moment of holding? Is there a sense of where a sensation or feeling arises as you hold your child?

- What do you notice, if anything, about experiences of time or space during that moment?
- What feels good/difficult/not quite known about that moment?
- Has your holding experience told you something about the state of your relationship at the time? Did this change the way you were with your child afterward?
- Did anything of the holding experience linger after the holding was over?
- If we asked your child what holding was like for them in that moment, what do you think they would say?
- What, if any, other voices impacted upon your experience of self and relationship as you held your child in that moment, or in other moments?

  Do these voices match what you experienced? Are they in harmony or discord?

- In what way, if any, do you think you use technology to hold your child?

  Do you send texts or photos to show your child you're thinking of them? What would it be like to hold in this way? How do you think your child feels (or might feel) receiving these?

Do you look through photos or recordings to recollect memories of closeness?

How do you feel these contribute (or would contribute) to your relationship with your child and your holding experiences?

- You may suggest that your client pay attention to the next time/s they're holding their child – this may be physical, emotional and/or psychological holding. They might attend to the holding as it happens or immediately afterward on reflection. Ask them to consider the following for the next session:

*Try to empty your mind of thought, allow the experience to remain in the body and attend only to the sensations of what is happening/happened for you and your child in the moment of holding. Afterward, see if you can write a few words about what that felt like, focusing on the sensations and feelings that arose. Put aside any thoughts or ideas for now. Bring those notes to your next session for exploration.*

## References

Bakewell, S. (2016). *At the Existential Café: Freedom, Being, and Apricot Cocktails with Jean-Paul Sartre, Simone de Beauvoir, Albert Camus, Martin Heidegger, Karl Jaspers, Edmund Husserl, Maurice Merleau-Ponty and others.* New York, NY: Other Press.

Bennett, J. S. (2010). *Vibrant Matter: A Political Ecology of Things.* Durham, NC: Duke University Press.

Bergum, V. (1997). *A Child on Her Mind: The Experience of Becoming a Mother.* Conneticut, USA: Bergum & Garvey.

Bowlby, J. (1958). The nature of the child's tie to his mother. *International Journal of Psychoanalysis*, 39, 350–371. Retrieved from www.psychology.sunysb.edu/attachment/online/nature%20of%20childs%20tie%20bowlby.pdf.

Brey, P. (2000). Technology and embodiment in Ihde and Merleau-Ponty. *Metaphysics, Epistemology, and Technology. Research in Philosophy and Technology*, 19, 1–14. London: Elsevier/JAI Press.

Brown, P. (2015). *Golden Son: Red Rising Trilogy 2.* London: Hodder and Stoughton. Retrieved from Amazon.com.

Buber, M. (1937/2013). *I and Thou*, London: Bloomsbury Academic.

Bylund, E. & Athanasopoulos, P. (2017). The Whorfian time warp: Representing duration through the language hourglass. *Journal of Experimental Psychology: General*, 146(7), 911–916. doi:10.1037/xge0000314.

Cassidy, J., Jones, J. D., & Shaver, P. R. (2013) Contributions of attachment theory and research: A framework for future research. *Development and Psychopathology*, 24(402), 1–39. doi:10.1017/S0954579413000692.

Clark, A., & Chalmers, D. (1998). The extended mind, *Analysis*, 28, 10–53. Retrieved from http://consc.net/papers/extended.html.

De Preester, H. (2011). Technology and the body: The (Im)possibilities of re-embodiment. *Foundations in Science*, 16(2-3), 119–137. doi:10.1007/s10699-010-9188-5.

De Quincey, C. (2000). Intersubjectivity: Exploring consciousness from the second-person perspective. *The Journal of Transpersonal Psychology*, 32(2), 135–155. Retrieved from http s://pdfs.semanticscholar.org/5e82/60991d22fa36011c9ec904d308ef7443f6a.pdf.

Dooley, C., & Fedele, N., (1999). *Mothers and Sons: Raising Relational Boys.* Work in Progress Publication Series, Jean Baker Miller Training Institute at the Wellesley Centers for Women. Retrieved from www.jbmti.org/pdf/84sc.pdf.

Duhn, I. (2016). Speculating on childhood and time, with Michael Ende's *Momo* (1973). *Contemporary Issues in Early Childhood*, 17(4), 377–386. doi:10.1177/1463949116677922.

Ellsworth, E. (2005). *Places of Learning: Media, Architecture, Pedagogy.* New York, NY: Routledge Falmer.

Ende, M. (1985). *Momo.* Middlesex, UK: Puffin Books.

Feldman Barrett, L. (2017). *How Emotions are Made: The Secret Life of the Brain.* New York, NY: Houghton, Mifflin, Harcourt Publishing Company.

Franzen, J. (2015). *Purity.* London: Fourth Estate.

Fuchs, T. (2016). Intercoporeality and interaffectivity. *Phenomenology and Mind*, 11, 194–209. doi:10.13128/Phe_Mi-20119.

Fusaroli, R., Demuru, P., & Borghi, A. M. (2009). The intersubjectivity of embodiment, *Journal of Cognitive Semiotics*, 4(1), 1–5. doi:10.1515/cogsem.2009.4.1.1.

Goggin, G. (2006). *Cell Phone Culture: Mobile Technology in Everyday Life.* New York, NY: Routledge.

Kramer, K. P. with Gawlik, M. (2003). *Martin Buber's I and Thou: Practicing Living Dialogue.* Mahwah, NJ: Paulist Press.

Laroche, J., Berardi, A. M., & Brangier, E. (2014). Embodiment of intersubjective time: Relational dynamics attractors in the temporal coordination of interpersonal behaviours and experiences. *Frontiers in Psychology*, 5, 1–17. doi:1-.3389/fpsyg.2014.01180.

Lotto, B. (2017). *Deviate: The Science of Seeing Differently.* London: Weidenfeld & Nicholson.

Lupton, D. (2000). "A love/hate relationship": The ideals and experiences of first-time mothers. *Journal of Sociology*, 36(1), 50–63. doi:10.1177/144078330003600104.

Lupton, D. (2013). Infant embodiment and interembodiment: A review of sociocultural perspectives. *Childhood*, 20(1), 37–50. doi:10.1177/0907568212447244.

Miller, D. (1997). How infants grow mothers in North London. *Theory, Culture & Society*, 14(4), 67–88. Retrieved from www.ucl.ac.uk/anthropology/people/academ ic-teaching-staff/daniel-miller/mil-1.

Pokropski, M. (2015). Timing together, acting together. Phenomenology of intersubjective temporality and social cognition. *Phenomenology and the Cognitive Sciences*, 14 (4), 897–909. doi:10.1007/s11097-0149386-7.

Rothman, B. K. (2007). Beyond mothers and fathers: Ideology in a patriarchal society. In A. O'Reilly (Ed.), *Maternal Theory: Essential Readings.* Bradford, Canada: Demeter Press. Retrieved from Amazon.com.

Seneca (2005). *Seneca on the Shortness of Life: Life is Long if You Know How to Use It.* New York, NY: Penguin Books.

Shriver, L. (2003). *We Need to Talk About Kevin.* New York, NY: Harper Perennial.

Sloterdijk, P. (2011). *Bubbles: Spheres,* vol. 1. Los Angeles, CA: Semiotext(e).

Springgay. S. (2005). Thinking through bodies: Bodied encounters and the process of meaning making in an e-mail generated art project. *Studies in Art Education: A Journal of Issues and Research*, 47(1), 34–50.

Springgay, S., & Freedman, D. (2009) M/othering a bodied curriculum: Sleeping with cake and other touchable encounters. *Journal of Curriculum Theorizing*, 25(2), 25–37. Retrieved from journal.jctonline.org/index.php/jct/article/view/SPFRM

Stepnisky, J. (2014). Social psychology from flat to round: Intersubjectivity and space in Peter Sloterdijk's *Bubbles*. *Journal for the Theory of Social Behaviour* 44(4), 413–435. doi:10.1111/jtsb.12060.

Stetson, C., Fiesta, M. P., & Eagleman, D. M. (2007). Does time really slow down during a frightening event? *PLoS ONE*, 2(12), e1295. doi:10.1371/journal.pone.0001295.

Tahhan, D. A. (2014) *The Japanese Family: Touch, Intimacy and Feeling*. New York, NY: Routledge.

Tanaka, S. (2013). The notion of embodied knowledge and its range. *Encyclopaedia: Journal of Phenomenology and Education*, 37, 47–66. doi:10.4442/ency_37_13_03.

Tanaka, S. (2014). Creation between two minded-bodies: Intercorporeality and social cognition. *Akademisk Kvarter*, 9, 265–276. Retrieved from www.academia.edu/10505185/Creation_between-two-minded-bodies.

Tanaka, S. (2015). Intercorporeality as a theory of social cognition. *Theory & Psychology*, 25(4), 455–472. doi:10.1177/0959354315583035.

Teske, J. A. (2013). From embodied to extended cognition. *Zygon: Journal of Religion and Science*, 48(3), 759–787. doi:10.1111/zygo.12038.

Tortora, S. (2013). The essential role of the body in the parent-infant relationship: Nonverbal analysis of attachment. In J. E. Bettmann and D. D. Friedman (Eds.), *Attachment-based Clinical Work with Children and Adolescents* [Essential Clinical Social Work Series] (pp 141–164). New York, NY: Springer Science+Business Media.

Trentacosta, C. J., Criss, M. M., Shaw, D. S., Lacourse, E., Hyde, L W. & Dishion, T. J. (2011). Antecedents and outcomes of joint trajectories of mother-son conflict and warmth during middle childhood and adolescence. *Child Development*, 82(5): 1676–1690. doi:10.111/j.1467-8624-2011.01626.x.

Trevarthen, C. (2009). Embodied human intersubjectivity. *Journal of Cognitive Semiotics*, 4(1), 6–56. doi:10.1515/cogsem.2009.4.1.6.

Tufnell, M., & Crickmay, C. (2004). *A Widening Field: Journeys in Body and Imagination*. Alton, Hampshire: Dance Books.

Van Manen, M. (1990). *Researching Lived Experience: Human Science for an Action Sensitive Pedagogy*. Ontario, Canada: State University of New York Press.

Van Manen, M. (2010, March 24). The pedagogy of Momus technologies: Facebook, privacy and online intimacy, *Qualitative Health Research Online First*, 2010, 1–10. doi:10.1177/1049732310364990.

Wittmann, M. (2016). *Felt Time: The Psychology of How We Perceive Time*. Cambridge, MA: MIT Press.

Yong, E. (2016). *I Contain Multitudes: The Microbes Within Us and a Grander View of Life*. New York, NY: Harper Collins.

# 8 Stories of us

## Introduction

Storytelling emerged as the primary vehicle of communication, both verbal and visual, for participants in this inquiry. Even when I explicitly attempted to inquire into experiences by looking at discrete non-contextualised qualities of maternal holding, participants quickly placed this data within a narrative.

Story is intimately linked to the 'aboutness' or intentionality I referred to in Chapter 7. Dan McAdams (2001) has spent decades researching and formulating a theory of narrative identity, he writes: "human intentionality is at the heart of narrative, and therefore the development of intentionality in humans is of prime importance in establishing the mental conditions necessary for storytelling and story comprehension" (p. 102). Having explored the significant presence of a mother/child relational intentionality in holding, I further develop this understanding in relation to story.

Both visual and verbal storytelling are relationship focused. Stories shown and narrated are given to an audience to shape their knowing about the story's experiences and themes. In turn, storying shapes the storyteller's knowing as they craft what they understand into something communicable to an audience. Stories of maternal holding were for and about the mother/child relationship as well as for and about participants and I, as storytellers and audience.

In order to explore maternal storying of memories, I engaged with literature and imagery that spoke to the consequences of conveying memory in narrative as well as the benefits and limitations of storying for the mother/child relationship.

Importantly, these mother/child stories of 'us' need not be experienced in the same way by mother and child, they need not be factually 'accurate', but their content is always formed by, about and for the mother/child relationship both in the moment of holding and on reflection.

I will suggest that maternal holding may offer special access to and awareness of mother/child story construction, navigation and meaning. These stories of 'us' can be profoundly powerful for mothers, children and their relationships because they explain and structure what mothers feel has happened, their understanding of relationship and what they believe is possible for their relationship.

DOI: 10.4324/9781003104094-9

# The storying of memories and maternal holding

## *Memory reconstruction and making sense of experiences*

Memories of holding, approached and reconstructed via multiple ways of knowing, comprised the initial data for this inquiry. These re-constructed memories were not discrete, they were deeply intertwined with other memories, intermingled with what was happening in the present, with our environment, our relationships and with our ideas about our relationships. This inquiry involved reflecting on past experiences and working with those past experiences in the present moment. When articulated and shared, these memories were not conveyed as phenomenological, factual snapshots but rather as visual and verbal stories.

When I wrote about one of my first holding experiences in my journal (see Introduction) I was describing what I felt within minutes of holding my son. I conveyed the feeling of warmth and weight, the visuals of his tiny toes and black hair but I reconstructed these experiences after they occurred. This reconstruction included so much more than I may have been aware of in the moment of holding. I was already telling a story of 'us'. I was writing of my hopes and fears for us, I was imagining our future, I was including memories of a friend's comments, and an albeit brief history of our new relationship. And I did this in the form of a narrative making sense of events for myself as audience; shaping what I recalled in a way that aligned with my understanding of and hopes for us. The original holding experience immediately accreted stories and was itself to form an 'event' in an ongoing and larger story of 'us'.

As a part of a new relationship, I had begun weaving and being woven into fresh, tentative understandings about who I was, who my son was and who we were and perhaps might be, together. This wouldn't have happened if the events of my son's birth or my initiation into motherhood hadn't mattered. These experiences mattered profoundly, and I needed to make sense of them. I also needed to navigate our imagined future and this little story already conveyed a sense of structure and purpose for me as well.

An important means of understanding memories is by storying them. When Rosanna described a new kind of holding with her daughter Elaina, her understanding of it was intimately entwined with her past experiences of holding her:

> I didn't realise until I got back and thought about it, that ... it's different now, which is really good, she now has a baby that *she* can hold and that's what she's wanted.

This description was embedded in a brief experience in time − what holding was like then and now and the differences in the needs navigated in the past and the present. Rosanna felt that a deep need for holding Elaina had previously shared with her mother, was now being met by her own experience of motherhood. This holding moment conveyed in story captured multiple memories as well as Rosanna's meaning making around those memories.

When we construct event memories or scenes "many of the details are likely to be drawn from your general knowledge" (Rubin & Umanath, 2015, p. 6), from the knowledge you have gleaned from multiple personal experiences including those that involve movies, books, and interactions with other's experiences. As described in Chapter 1, memory encoding, processing and retrieval are activities that are powerfully shaped by context, relationships and needs in the present moment. Event memories can also include scenes that are "real or imagined, for the past or the future" (p. 2). Rosanna's storied memories may have included her general understanding around needs and the changes that can occur when a woman has her first child.

There is a great deal of research on memory but for the purposes of this exploration of storying memory, a few qualities stand out. As described in Chapter 1, memory is malleable and adaptive. We 'reconstruct' those memories that are more likely to help us in the present moment. For example, Öner and Gülgöz (2017) found that recalling an autobiographical memory appeared to regulate its emotional tone to reduce the intensity of negative emotions originally associated with the experience like anger or fear. Levine, Lench, & Safe (2009) note that the "ability to remember past emotions (and) … the ability to forget and update such memories" (p. 1072) are both important. While the under or overestimation of an experience's emotional intensity when recalled has traditionally been considered a negative outcome and memory accuracy has traditionally been considered of prime importance, Levine et al. (2009) propose a different view: If the function of memory is reconsidered as an adaptive feature that enables "goal-directed behaviour" (p. 1070) then changing the emotional tone of that memory to serve a goal, is beneficial. A class example of this is the tendency for women to forget the exquisite pain of childbirth.

The tools and processes we use to re-engage and work with memory also shape memory selection and reconstruction. I asked participants to bring in something that they associated with the experience they wished to recall. When Leni chose Moo to represent her daughter in the moment of holding, the soft toy activated a network of memories, associations and understandings about holding that Leni related to both Moo and Lucy (see Figure 3.4) and these served as the building blocks for the stories Leni conveyed about holding Lucy.

Nader, Schafe and Le Doux (2000) noted that "reactivated and new memories exist in similar states" and refer to Lewis's (1979) distinction between active and inactive memory rather than short term and long-term memory. These different labels highlight that when memories are in an *active* state, that is, are currently being engaged with, they can be 'curated' in order to meet our current requirements.

Memory re-construction tells us what's worked in the past and what might work in the future; we can select or adapt strategies employed in similar past experiences to meet anticipated needs in the now. For example, Kitty was able to identify and manage needs in her changing relationship with Harley as she held her, and she did this by engaging in the moment with her prior experiencing and knowledge, both explicitly and implicitly.

The goal of our inquiry, to explore and understand maternal holding, and the collaborative nature of our inquiry, provided ample opportunity for the shaping of experiencing and memory into story. The act of returning to a memory or memories in order to explore them required some level of coherence and sense making of those memories – both hallmarks of story.

I recognised the ways in which the inquiry's methodology and values might encourage the storying of memory but was nevertheless surprised and intrigued by just how powerfully and quickly story appeared as data. In the first instance, this led me to encourage our return, again and again, to discrete imagery, movement and curiosities in the visual representations in order to access aesthetic and non-conceptual knowing separate from story. But, as with Rosanna's installation, the representations themselves *told a story*. We could focus on elements of the representation but each of those elements also held and evoked a story.

For our inquiry into maternal holding, memory reconstruction invariably manifested as story. It was the dominance of visual and verbal stories as data that led me to wonder about the ways in which narrative affects memory reconstruction. The reconstruction of memories to suit the constraints of story would shape those memories in particular ways. Further, the 'curation' of memory would have implications for our understanding of maternal holding experiences, and I explore these below.

### Story curates memories

---

**Box 8.1 Ariel Moy, *A Tale of Us*, poem.**

A tiny speck of us,
Thickened with time,
Growing limbs, feet,
Hands to help,
Shape the felt,
Into a tale of us,
In space, over time,
And into the future,
Bit by tiny bit,
The heat of experiences shared,
Accrete and we expand,
Sharp and precise,
The only 'us' in the universe.

---

Once a memory has been storied (visually or verbally) it is no longer the same, it is now a memory *including* the story of it. It includes imagery, language, other memories and associations, understanding and ideas added to the memory. The memory is no longer simply for oneself but for another, an audience, and it is oriented toward that audience; even if that audience is oneself. The above poem written to try and describe those first instances of holding my infant son also conveyed my understanding of holding after conducting this inquiry, memories were storied in albeit unconscious but particular way that spoke to my meaning-making in the present moment.

Smorti and Fioretti (2016) highlight the intimate and ongoing mutual relationships between autobiographical memory, autobiographical narrative and the storyteller's relationship to the audience. Their model captures how "memory influences narrative and narrative influences relational situations" and "the relational situation ... affects narrative and from there, memory" (p. 313). Story comes with an audience, and even if that audience is the storyteller, a story needs to make some kind of sense. Smorti & Fioretti (2016) note that "cohesion and continuity" (p. 308) are essential qualities of narrative structures. While disparate memories do not need to make sense, once they are storied, qualities of 'cohesion and continuity' reshape those memories.

As described in previously, Rubin & Umanath (2015) recognized that reconstructed memories can include data both real (in the sense that the data reflects an event that actually occurred to the person remembering) and imagined. In order to create a coherent story, what we know about something and what we have experienced of something (real or imagined) both come into play. Obtaining story coherence often requires the filling in of gaps from other re-constructed memories or general knowledge. A story, like re-constructed memories, is not a direct telling of events but rather a creative and active reconstruction of events with other sources of information geared towards making sense. This requirement of story changes and adds to already re-constructed memories.

Smorti and Fioretti (2016) write that when a memory is given narrative structure it also encourages increased complexity of feelings: I may recall sadness in an event but if I relay that memory to another, I may note longing as well as sadness or a mix of happiness and sadness. They write that: "new feelings and new points of view about the past life event" (p. 313) can be added to recollections when shaping a memory into words and relaying it to another, even if that other is a private diary. Storying memories allows for an expanded point of view on those memories and their emotional complexity.

By storying memories, we make choices about those recollected plot points we do and do not want to include. We have some influence over what memories we might like to consolidate, elaborate or even diminish and gloss over as we can choose the contents of our stories. While we have not yet entered the era of memory eradication as seen in movies like *The Eternal Sunshine of the Spotless Mind* (2004) at each moment we can potentially, consciously or unconsciously, change the emotional tone, plot points or themes of our storied memories.

Polkinghorne (1991) describes storytelling and understanding stories as "ultimately grounded in the general human capacity to conceptualise - that is, to structure experiential elements into wholes" (p. 142). Storying memory in speech or visual representation brings discrete experiences into 'wholes', into a shape we can make sense of conceptually but also aesthetically. For example, Kitty found deep satisfaction in many of the representations she made because they showed us meaningful stories about what it felt like to hold Harley. Her representation needed to make sense to her aesthetically, she needed to feel the "clarity" of her experiences and she did so by developing those experiences into a visual, and then later, verbal story.

Verbal and visual narrative structures applied to memory can also impose a *temporal* structure upon them. In order to make sense of memories via story we often refer to events in time. We show and/or tell an audience how this led to this, which led to this (like in a comic strip). We tell stories of experiences in time. We can leave a trail of cause and effect in our stories. But experiencing in the moment is not necessarily as neat as cause and effect. If, for example, I had explored maternal holding as it occurred with participants, if they had been able to make a representation in the moment of holding or verbalise in the moment, perhaps what they conveyed would not have emerged in the shape of a story with a temporal structure. However, our inquiry was explicitly undertaken on reflection, and therefore included reconstructed memories as data, and that data was conveyed in stories. As those stories imposed a temporal structure upon the reconstructed memories, participants and I made sense of maternal holding experiences by placing those experiences in time.

This linking of past and present events "lifts them from their temporal surroundings and yields a whole that is internally articulated into its contributing parts" (Polkinghorne, 1991, p. 140). By plotting events into a story, we can identify causality and develop meaning. Importantly, this plotting is unfinished and continually open to reconstruction and re-interpretation in the light of the present moment, including the impact of the audience and a hoped for or anticipated future. Plotting, like memory reconstruction, is adaptive. As we plot our stories in the moment, we are also weaving them within important meta-stories and goals.

It is possible that one of the reasons why experiences of expansion were felt to be so strange and difficult to articulate is because experiences of time changed during expansion – time elongated or vanished all together. Recollections that do not obey the generally accepted rules of everyday time confound the person reconstructing them in order to make meaning. They're a little harder to put into verbal narrative as they trouble our normal conceptualisations of time. This is where making creative representations might allow for some wiggle room when it comes to the constraints of storying memories. In a visual space, we can see everything at once in relationship, while in verbal or written narrative, information is relayed in a linear fashion. We can still, like Kitty, obtain a satisfying sense of clarity with the making of a visual story as we represent what we know about experiencing.

Storying autobiographical memory can also simplify it around themes that speak to identity. In his narrative theory of identity McAdams (2001) conveys that autobiographical memories provides the ingredients for a life story, but a life story involves curating memories around themes. It is these curated memories or life story that "constitute identity" (p. 117).

Stories often serve and represent a larger narrative sense of self, and in the case of this inquiry, this *larger narrative self was about the intersubjective mother/child 'us'*. For example, during our sessions, Leni described a story of her trip to Queensland with her children to represent how she came to understand the differences in what her children noticed and appreciated and what she had expected them to notice and appreciate on holiday. This story served to convey and make sense of a more generalised understanding of her relationship with her children and how it had evolved over time: she came to notice what her children enjoyed, she incorporated that into her understanding of how to be with her children, and she came to value some of the simpler things they valued. This story served Leni and her children's 'us', it touched on a theme of shared enjoyment and Leni's development with her children in the mother/child relationship.

Story not only shapes memory, by providing coherence and structure, it provides meaning or a space to make meaning of events. For example, it is extremely valuable for many grieving parents to accumulate memories of their babies in order to create meaningful stories of their relationship with them, however brief that relationship was. The increasing availability of cuddle cots and bereavement photography are testament to this need for story and meaning making. These opportunities provide experiences as well as memory objects (like photos and video) for bereaved parents. Ramirez, Bogetz, Kufeld and Yee (2019) found that parents: "valued professional photographs for a number of unique reasons, including validation of the experience, permission to share, creation of a legacy, creation of positive memories, and moving forward" (p. 10). Neimeyer and Thompson (2014) note that narrative processes help us make meaning of loss, or as they write, the ways in which we "knit together the torn fabric of our lives" (p. 5). Memories of the relationship between parent and child, shaped into stories, lend meaning to events that may at first defy meaning.

Perhaps given the way stories develop, generate meaning and shape identity it is unsurprising that we can be highly selective about the memories and stories we convey to others and ourselves. As journalist David Carr (2008) wrote:

> as a member of a self-interpreting species, one that fights to keep disharmony at a remove, I'm inclined to mention my tender-hearted attentions as a single parent before I get around to the fact that I hit their mother when we were together.
>
> (p. 24)

Social network sites and apps are all explicit platforms for the curation of memory into stories around themes of identity that the authors wish to tell.

However, Carr (2008) also points to the fundamentally shared nature of memories: "what I learned from two years of reporting, investigation and writing (his autobiography) is that you can't know the whole truth. But if there is one, it lies in the space between people" (Helsel, 2015, para. 7). The meaning of any relational story involves both members of that relationship, it can never be fully conveyed or grasped by one member alone, these storied memories are always in reference to the relationship and if any 'truth' is to be divined it will be conveyed the intersections of stories, in this case, between mother and child.

The clarity, coherence and meaning gleaned from and shaped by stories of maternal holding spoke to the mother/child relationship. These stories expressed and developed our understanding about our relational identity with our children. Stories of the mother/child 'us' brought clarity, coherence and meaning to the mother/child relationship. In the 'object' of a visual or verbal story we had the opportunity to notice, examine and explore the strange but deeply felt 'us'.

In session, mothers told stories about their relational experiencing without their children present and yet they regularly imagined and incorporated what their children may (or may not) have said about some of their stories, reflexively modifying their stories as they made sense of their shared experiencing. For example, when exploring Rosanna's experiences of holding Elaina she noted:

> What I think and I hope is that she found it comforting when I held her, but I never actually asked her … but the things she's written to me do seem to indicate that she feels very loved and, and all of that, but I think it would be best to send you … her words.

Rosanna later showed me a card she received from Elaina though I did not include it in the inquiry as it had identifying information on it. Significantly, Rosanna understood the importance of her daughter's voice in the story of their holding, this was mirrored by the other participants. As mothers conveyed their stories, they reflexively incorporated what they imagined their children might say, feel or think. These maternal stories of holding could not be created, communicated or considered without reference to their children because they ultimately represented memories of relationship.

Maternal memories reconstructed into stories of relationship were not necessarily about accuracy or exhaustively communicating past experiences even if that were possible. These stories served certain functions: they promoted clarity and they served the mother/child relationship. Participants stories were usually positive and/or served a positive purpose for their relational identity. Those stories that had negative content nevertheless tended to 'end well' as the mother and child developed and adapted over time together to avoid or successfully navigate that particular kind of negative experience in future.

When Leni first experienced Lucy's rejection on the train she was upset, when she recalled those memories however, the pain of that moment was less intense. Many experiences had intervened, but Leni also explicitly included in her story of that experience, how she had reached out to her friends at the time for support and sense-making. Leni's story of that rejection was less painful than it had been at the time because the reconstruction of that memory changed over time in order to support the ongoing positive qualities of her relationship with Lucy. This speaks to the ways in which holding was experienced as purposeful: The storied curation of memories can reduce the intensity of negative emotions to support (in this case) the relational goals of the mother/child 'us'.

It appears that a 'storying' self was active during our inquiry into past experiences of holding: Memories 'retrieved' or reconstructed were almost all shaped into story. In Chapter 1, I described how the 'remembering' self was active in the present moment. I would also suggest that the 'storying' self is most likely active in holding *as it occurs*. Just as memories inform experiencing, those memories that have been storied inform experiencing. When I held my son and wrote that first journal entry (Box 0.1) stories were already forming about our relationship, some were already formed, and they shaped how I understood that holding in the moment. It is likely that the ways in which participants made sense of their holding experiences (carried by stories of shared history and relational patterns of being) also informed how they held their children in the moment. I suggest that the remembering self *and* the storying self are present in moments of holding. Like implicit memories, these stories need not have been explicitly present in awareness in order to contribute to that moment. This speaks to the power of the stories we 'write' about our relationships; they can shape our experiencing and our meaning-making.

Storying of memories in the inquiry served our aim of exploring maternal holding as participants and I wished to make sense of our experiences. However, storying memories also served other important functions. Story promoted clarity around the unusual but deeply felt mother/child 'us' and storying allowed for replotting of memories around significant mother/child goals. It is quite possible that stories of 'us', like memories, were active in the moment of holding as well as upon reflection. In the following section I explore the possibility that maternal storying of holding experiences also invited the mother/child relationship into our awareness in order to promote relational agency.

### *The power of maternal holding stories: sharing and shaping understanding*

Storytelling appears to be a unique and fundamental human practice. It developed explicitly with other essentially human practices: artmaking and language. Linguist Daniel Dor (2015) highlights two relevant qualities of verbal language for this inquiry: Firstly, "language is a social entity … it resides *between* speakers, not *in* them" (p. 1) and secondly, language is a "communication technology … the first communication technology we ever invented" (pp. 1–2). Boyd (2017) writes that "narrative arose from an adaptive predisposition for sociality, social monitoring, and information-sharing in our hominin forebears that found much richer expression after the invention of language" (p. 12). I suggest that visual representations are also a language or communication technology.

Describing language or art as a social communication technology raises the question of its function and purpose. Dor (2015) proposes that language is "dedicated to the systematic *instruction of imagination*" (p. 2). Language and art enable people to engage others not only with what they personally experience, but also with what they might imagine. This fundamentally changes the interaction between humans. As Dor writes: "First we invented language. Then language changed us" (p. 4). Language, art and story expand our awareness beyond our own experiencing into an awareness of our experiencing with others and in the material world. Once shared, story intrinsically draws attention to its topic. It places that topic in third space 'between speakers' where it might 'instruct' or intermingle with the imagination of its audience as well as its narrator.

Storytelling can take what is unsaid, amorphous, fragile and temporary and bring it into the tangible world. While our aim for the inquiry was to explore *maternal* experiences of holding, the storied memories that emerged were entirely about the mother/child relationship. Like their stories of expansion; when participants storied their memories of relational patterns and shared history, they brought the mother/child 'us' into our awareness. They turned a spotlight on shared mother/child experiences so that we could explore them. When those plot points, images, feelings, thoughts and sensations of mother and child together were articulated in story, what might have been tacit became explicit in the shared space of storyteller and audience.

Storytelling seeks to engage us across multiple modes of being – physically, emotionally, conceptually, aesthetically and relationally. In a 2009 study, Speer, Reynolds, Swallow & Zacks found the same areas of the brain that 'light up' for our own real-world observations or actions also light up when those observations or actions are read about. While we can usually tell the difference between a story that we're told, or read, watch or participate in (like virtual reality) this overlap of neurological activity expresses how deeply engaged with story we are – our own stories or stories of others. In the act of storytelling and engagement, we enter into the story with storyteller and audience. We can, for example, respond neurologically to the story of another's pain as if their pain was ours (Singer, Seymour, O'Doherty, Kaube, Dolan & Frith, 2004; Bernhardt & Singer, 2012).

When Rosanna told her story of not holding Deanna as a child, I *felt* the pain and intensity of her story; when Leni recalled the way her son launched into her arms, I felt some of the joy and surprise she conveyed. I brought my own experiences to participants stories; I entered them and imagined myself there too. My experience of their stories did not 'instruct my imagination' in precisely the way participants experienced them, but instead gave me a richer, more complex and deeply felt sense of their experience. I was able to understand experiences through the lens of our shared space, through my experience as listener to their visual and verbal stories, and through my own stories. I could consider what was the same and what was different from my own experiences, what I needed to ask about to clarify my understanding, and what questions or responses I might offer participants to support our inquiry into their understanding. Their stories were powerful in that they captured our attention and imagination and shaped our understanding of holding.

Story can be so engaging that it can serve as a proxy for real-world relationships. At the Mar Lab in Toronto researchers have explored how attachment styles relate to narrative responses and found that those with attachment anxiety and avoidant attachment appear to become more emotionally involved with story; they are 'transported' by the narrative and its characters (Rain, Cilento, MacDonald & Mar, 2017). Rain et al. suggest that it is possible these readers "desire social interaction but fear or mistrust it and so they can enter into a relationship of sorts with fictional characters" (p. 69).

Stories shared between participants and I, and stories explicitly shared between participants and their children, were shaped in the telling of them by narrator and listener. The sounds of story are literally absorbed by both listener and narrator but more than that, the space between storyteller and listener is, at times, shared, it is a space of shaping and being shaped by the relationship in the moment of storytelling. Author Ursula Le Guin (2004) writes:

> Listening is not a reaction, it is a connection. Listening to a conversation or a story, we do not so much respond as join in – become part of the action.
>
> (p. 196)

She later adds:

> Words are events, they do things, change things. They transform both speaker and hearer, they feed energy back and forth and amplify it. They feed understanding or emotion back and forth and amplify it.
>
> (p. 199)

When we 'instruct' another's imagination with our story, their stories change too. Kitty told a story about her relationship with Harley:

> When I cry, I touch her hand to my tears and say "that's to go to your heart", so when I'm crying … for school and everything, I tell her "it's happy tears [she's just started prep]" and I say "here, take my happy tears and then know how happy I am".

Kitty's story was instructional; she didn't want to hide her emotions from Harley, but she also wanted to make sure that Harley understood particular qualities of those emotions even if there was more to her tears than happiness. In this moment, both Kitty and Harley have the opportunity to become aware of 'their' story but are also mutually engaged with that story as it unfolds. Keiser (2017) wrote: "our linguistic expression of experience, therefore, can determine the experience of another; such conditioning of another's experience extends upon levels of inter-subjectivity" (p. 127). In sharing her story with Harley, Kitty deliberately entered into an intersubjective moment with her daughter where both may leave changed, imaginations instructed by one another. In sharing her story with Harley, Kitty brought both of their awareness to important qualities of their relationship – that Kitty can feel something beautiful for Harley and that Harley can hold onto those feelings as well. In the sharing of this story Kitty was not fixing Harley's experience so that it would be the same as Kitty's, but she was given the opportunity to contribute to how Harley understood her mother's tears.

All participant stories conveyed the relational landscape of mother and child, its past, its present and its imagined future even if not all of these stories were about holding in particular but rather contextualised holding experiences. They contributed to our increasing awareness of the qualities of relationship present in holding and shaped our understanding in their telling.

## Co-created stories of us

Participants' memories of holding appeared as stories. Those stories brought our awareness to significant qualities of the mother/child 'us'. In our inquiry the relationship between mother and child was conveyed by the mothers alone, their children were not present and yet these stories did not seem to be entirely of the mother's making. Similarly, the stories of holding my son that arose for me and evolved throughout the inquiry did not feel mine alone.

At every stage, these stories of our shared history and relational ways of being together responded to and evolved within our relationship. I could never 'read' or 'write' my stories the same way twice; I as reader and author always came to them from within an everchanging relationship with my son. So too, participants' stories evolved with their children; from session to session, from minute to minute we encountered, 'read' and 're-storied' those stories ever so slightly differently in response to whatever was happening within the mother/child relationship at that stage (as well as our relationship as co-inquirers).

On examination we could convey a timeline on the emergence of specific events relating to a story and describe events that followed. We could narrate or represent 'character' actions or mood shifts over time. However, these stories of relationship were alive. Their vitality arose from the co-creative space of mother and child together. There were no stories of mother and child without mother *and* child 'writing' and 'reading' them simultaneously. This did not mean that stories of 'us' were experienced or understood in the same way by mother and child, only that in terms of authorship, the generation of stories was always in response to the lived experience of the relationship in the moment. These stories were effectively written by the relationship.

This experience of co-creative authorship in our mother/child stories, like expansive experiences of intersubjectivity, was a difficult quality to pin down and articulate. I felt it had something to do with the ways in which stories can form and act in relationship implicitly as well as explicitly. This is similar to the way memories can be alive in a present moment in an implicit or explicit fashion.

Daniel Stern (2004) notes that:

> In narratives, there is a two-way traffic between the implicit and explicit. Images, feelings, in the implicit domain must get rendered into the verbal explicit domain by the speaker. And in the opposite direction, words must get rendered into images, feelings, and intuitions by the listener. The implicit (the intersubjective field) also has a role in creating the "right" context to permit explicit material to emerge. And telling and listening, as an act in themselves, combine elements of both implicit and explicit.
>
> (p. 187)

Stern's identification of the implicit in storytelling as 'the intersubjective field' captured my felt sense that mother and child stories of relationship were co-created. This did not require explicit co-construction of story, rather, in the implicit space of mother and child together stories are woven from their physical, emotional and imaginal interactions.

We noticed and explored these shared stories of relationship on reflection; we could imagine how they were co-created by mother and child by understanding that there was no 'us' story without reference to both mother and child. However, co-created stories of 'us' are also involved in the moment of holding in an implicit way, just outside of awareness, as they shape and are shaped by the moments mother and child share together in affection and touch. The implicit interactions that form the stuff of relational stories are intersubjectively felt and intersubjectively shape and are shaped by the moment.

In 2012, art-therapist Dr Michal Bat Or worked with mothers creating clay sculptures of maternal holding of preschool aged children. Both the sculptures and phenomenological interviews with the mothers were qualitatively analysed to reveal participant's knowing about holding their children as a "caregiving representation" (p. 118). For each mother, her behaviours, cognitions and emotions emerged from her evolving relationship with her child as well as her own experience of care when she was a child. Bat Or found that holding manifested on a continuum from mothers actively and protectively holding their children through to mothers holding their children more symbolically as they became increasingly autonomous. This reflected the changes these mothers constantly made as they adapted to their evolving relationship's needs, and it illustrated the ongoing "preoccupation" or "primary relatedness" (p. 123) mothers experienced with their children beyond infancy. Representations of holding were about mother and child relational patterns of being together.

In Bat Or's (2012) study representations of holding were viewed through the lens of attachment theory as these styles capture dominant patterns of being in relationship. In the present inquiry, I attempted to look at holding through a less theoretical lens, guided by inquiry values (as described in Chapter 1). Bat Or's research however highlighted the "great effort" (p. 123) and the "continuous adjustment to the growth of her child" a mother makes as her children grow. I would suggest that the mother's sculptural stories of their holding experiences were implicitly at play as they held their children, these stories were generated from within the relationship and were about the relationship. During holding mother *and* child responded to one another as their relational needs intermingled with their individual needs for intimacy and touch. When arising within a mother/child holding moment, these individual needs manifested and became *about* mother/child needs. A mother not only 'adjusted' to her child, her child also adjusted to the mother and these relational adjustments were a part of their active story of relationship. The mother was not alone in experiencing change in holding, together both mother and child exerted 'effort' and grew.

Relational patterns can be implicit and unspoken, and yet they are lived out in the relationship. Like attachment styles, these patterns are themselves significant stories of relationship. Patterns of being together, even if unarticulated, 'instruct' the imaginations, behaviours, feelings and, on reflection, conceptualisations of what it is to be in the mother/child relationship. For Bat Or's (2012) mothers, their stories of holding, represented in sculpture, instructed both mother and child's imaginations of what it was like to hold and be held. Kitty, Rosanna and Leni were all aware, though to differing degrees, of the power of their own relational stories and all wished to story their relationships with their children in new ways, explicitly different from their own experiences of being mothered.

Fuchs (2016) points out that since the 1970s, our interpretation of others has been considered an internal, representational, cognitive process of inference. However, in our personal experiences of interacting with others and divining their emotions or intentions, we don't perceive these kinds of representational processes. Emotions, according to Fuchs, do not reside within the individual so much as between individuals, in the "intercorporeal" (p. 196) or inter-subjective space of 'us'. It is in this interaction or 'bodily resonance' that we perceive other's emotions and intentions as they relate to us. Empathy and social cognition, building blocks of relational stories, are pre-reflective, implicit, embodied and emotional rather than representational; they arise from the intersubjective 'us'.

In keeping with findings around attachment, Fuchs (2016) proposes that patterns of behaviour and emotion shared as an infant with a primary caregiver are stored in memory and these patterns significantly contribute to the child's later understanding of and interaction with others. These implicit memories are "based on an intercorporeal memory" (p. 196) and can become, if reflected upon, explicit stories of 'us'.

I wondered about the embodied quality of relational stories, how deeply they can be felt, how true and static they can appear, how strange and magical they may seem as they emerge from and return to somewhere not quite bounded by an individual. This speaks to the implicit power of relational stories.

Making a drawing in order to explore the power of implicit stories, I noticed the intensity of energy exchanged in the moment of touch. We implicitly 'read' relational stories through our embodied and emotional encounters. Though implicit, these stories are profoundly felt and have enduring effects.

During early attachment processes, the infant has no verbal language, but they communicate and 'read' their relationships with their mothers; a non-verbal, non-conceptual, embodied learning takes place over and over again as they interact. Mothers 'read', 'write' and respond to developing stories of relationship with their infants as well as they figure out what does and doesn't work for them together and over time. As Kitty relayed, a crying sleepless infant doesn't work for either mother or child. If she'd listened to "what felt good for us" rather than others "stupid advice" she would have co-slept with Harley as that calmed them both and their first year together "would have been easier". She made choices around what stories to pay attention to and in this instance, those stories were cultural and familial messages rather than Kitty and Harley's own.

Stories of 'us' that are explicitly shared can also be powerful in the mother/child relationship. Leni for example, spoke about the power of her mother's stories about Leni, which were, on reflection, very much stories about their relationship – her mother's wishes for Leni and Leni's desire to make her mother happy. Leni had been "very much ruled by what other people think, I've always been like that, very, very self-conscious about what other people think". She responded implicitly and explicitly to what her mother thought of her. Their stories from Leni's childhood still held enormous power for her as an adult, she had incorporated the significance of other people's voices into her earliest holding experiences with her children. These explicit stories were a co-creation of mother and child: Leni's mother deliberately or unintentionally attempted to live out her own dreams through her daughter. Leni responded by attempting to live those dreams out for her mother but also could not ignore an abiding tension, an inner sense that she simply was not good at foreign languages nor was she interested in them. This story of 'us' was fraught and took decades to for Leni to realise, interpret and question.

So powerful are stories as an indicator of relational health, the ways in which they are conveyed can alert us to the function and wellbeing of an individual's fundamental patterns of relating to others. Siegel (1999) notes that the way adults describe and narrate their own childhood experiences can be a significant indicator as to their adult attachment styles. Writing about Main and Goldwyn's (1998) adult attachment interviews he says:

> The most critical aspects of the process of interview analysis rest upon the speaker's ways of presentation and evaluating his history. It is here that the AAI offers a unique perspective on the relationships among attachment, memory and narrative.
>
> (Siegel, 1999, p. 79)

Parents who had made sense of their own childhood experiencing and conveyed a coherent life narrative were able to engage in healthy relationships and cultivate "sensitive and nurturing parenting" (p. 312), necessary for secure attachment style. Adult life narratives that were discordant and disorganised were associated with insecure childhood attachment styles and "intergenerational transmission of suboptimal parenting" (p. 312).

However, life story coherence can be "earned" (Siegel, 1999, p. 313): with the intervention of therapy or the presence of another significant person in their lives as children or adults. This enables "parenting behaviour to be sensitive and empathic" (p. 313) and thus the "transmission of insecure forms of attachment to the next generation can be prevented" (p. 313).

It is how we make sense of our early childhood experiences that matters more than the actual experiences themselves; how we story our earliest caregiving memories has a profound impact on how we then provide care to our own children and we do this storying within relationship. As Siegel (1999) writes:

> The capacity for self-integration, like the processes of the mind itself, is continually created by an interaction of internal neurophysiological processes and interpersonal relationships. Resilience and emotional well-being are fundamental mental processes that emerge as the mind integrates the flow of energy and information across time and between minds.
>
> (p. 314)

Relational stories affect our physiology. Manczak, McLean, McAdams and Chen (2015) described the relationship between 'parental scaffolding', parent/adolescent relationship quality and physiological reactivity (including blood pressure and heart rate). They explored "the ways that parents use conversations to help shape how their children understand challenging life events" (p. 529). Parental scaffolding is defined as behaviours that support or negate children's understanding and relating of experiences. They found that the "effects of parental scaffolding depend on the relational context" (p. 528) as the kinds of positive or negative scaffolding provided by parents differed in outcome depending on the relationship quality. As expected, adolescent's physiological reactivity increased when their stories were undermined by their parent. Parental diastolic blood pressure also increased in these circumstances, no matter how the quality of the relationship had been rated. When the parent facilitated the conversation with encouraging behaviours both parental and adolescent reactivity decreased irrespective of the rated relationship quality. What was important in these scenarios was the relationship quality over time *and* in the moment.

Interestingly, reiterations (a positive scaffolding behaviour where the parent repeats what the adolescent has said rather than elaborates on it) resulted in higher reactivity in good quality ('higher-nurturance dyads') and lower reactivity in lower nurturance dyads. Manczak et al. (2015) suggest that

> it is possible that children who are accustomed to high levels of caregiving behaviours may interpret repetition as departures from more sophisticated scaffolding. Within low nurturance dyads, however, these reiterations may be interpreted as a sign of attention or interest.
>
> (p. 529)

This points to the incredible and unspoken sensitivity of adolescents and mothers to the quality of their relationship.

This study demonstrated that when children and parents share a conversation (that is, tell stories) about challenging past events (experienced together or alone) both parent and child's physiological reactivity changes depending on the quality of relationship and interaction behaviours. Though the study looked at how the kinds of scaffolding behaviours a parent provides an adolescent during conversations interacted with physiological reactivity, I would suggest that the kinds of responses the adolescents provide in return would also affect the dyad's physiological reactivity. The sharing of stories between mother and child occurs within relationship, and as this study showed, relationship quality mediated physiological reactivity to different parental behaviours. The ultimate factor that contributed to outcomes in terms of physiological reactivity was the *relationship*.

The ability of mother/child stories to shape present experiencing cannot be underestimated. McLean (2016) writes:

> Family stories can be particularly confining … one of the reasons it can be hard to go home for the holidays, a reason people are motivated to move away in the first place, a reason to branch beyond those confines, and to create a new self, a new story.
>
> (p. 62)

The "imposition of others' stories on the self" (p. 63) can be devastating. This speaks to the power imbalance of the mother/child relationship and how stories of these relationships are also shaped by this power imbalance. Stories, while intersubjectively co-created, are contributed to in different ways by mother and child particularly so when the child is young. For example, the mother has conceptual knowing and language at her disposal as well as a social network to share with and reinforce the mother/child stories in a way that young children do not. Children can and do question the relational stories built with their parents when they were young (like Leni did with her mother) but this is not immediately present in their relationship nor necessarily easy to navigate within the relationship as it matures. Relational narratives can be beneficial, or they can tell a disruptive, condemning or painful story, the variations are only limited by the mother and child's experiences as well as relational patterns of being together.

Bretherton and Munholland (1999) drew attention to how children understand themselves in relationship with their parents, explaining that when a child has a secure working model of a parent, they view themselves as "valued and competent" (p. 5) and a working model of a "rejecting or ignoring" parent appears coupled with a view of self as "devalued and incompetent" (p. 5). This illustrates how "the developing complementary models of self and parents taken together represent both sides of the relationship" (p. 5). I suggest it is also possible that parents who have a secure model of their relationship with their child view themselves as 'valued and competent' and those who have a 'rejecting or ignoring' relationship with their child may 'devalue' themselves and feel 'incompetent' precisely because mother and child are forming an identity of themselves within that relationship. Bat Or (2012) noted that interest in studying a mother's "mental world" (p. 118) has developed mainly during the last two decades. Like her study, and my research, it would be beneficial for a richer picture of mother/child relationships if we turned our inquiring gaze onto women's understanding of self in relationship with their children as much as children's understanding of themselves in relationship with their parents.

McLean and Pasupathi (2011) explored the construction and retention of stories shared by university students engaged in a new, intimate romantic relationship. They found that narrative identity develops (in new romantic relationships) through shared and agreed upon meanings with their significant others (termed "shared connections", p. 140). This may be applied to mother/child relational stories as it points to how relational stories are co-constructed: in the sharing of these stories implicitly through behaviours and emotional atmosphere or explicitly through the telling of stories, any agreement between mother and child (again implicit or explicit), will reinforce those stories for mother and child. The mother/child narrative identity is built and reinforced by agreement between mother and child on important stories of 'us'. That does not necessarily mean that the stories are positive or beneficial to the relationship, only that they are agreed upon by both.

Kitty captured a sense of narrative agreement between mother and child on a highly valuable story of 'us'. She shared stories about how Harley always used to sit on or near her at home and when they were out. They both explicitly enjoyed this behaviour. Kitty made a representation of the "physical and emotional side of" this kind of holding and intimacy. She entitled it 'The Interconnectedness of Reciprocity' describing the sensation as "enmeshed … like a biofeedback". It captured her experience of the "in and out, ebbing and flowing" of their emotional and physical states in these moments of closeness, particularly seen in the central point of her representation (see Figure 4.4).

Sensitivity to how a personal story might be received by mother or child was also at play in participants' narratives. Rosanna spoke about knowing what personal stories to share and not share in terms of her individual relationships with her daughters. A 2013 study by McLean & Morrison-Cohen looked at how mother/child conversations about past events affect maternal development. They examined the emotional vulnerability mothers were willing to share with their children as they each told their stories. They found that the older a child was, the more that mothers communicated vulnerability in their stories. They also found that the stories mothers shared served three functions: modelling narrative coherency, developing the separation of mother and child as the child matures and developing intimacy via the sharing of vulnerability. When it came to the explicit and deliberate sharing of personal stories, a sense of how the mother/child *relationship* would receive the story was the deciding factor, that is how mothers and children both would cope with a story shared.

Rosanna didn't just protect her daughters from certain personal stories, she protected their relationship because it would be their relationship that would change in response to those stories.

In our inquiry, stories were not set in stone as they were continually co-constructed between mothers and their children over time as well as between participants and I during and between sessions. Our stories of holding were alive in relationship with our children and the world. These stories emerged from the shared physical, emotional and psychological space of mother and child during holding.

Expressing and working with these malleable and adaptive stories helped us become aware of what we felt we knew about maternal holding at that moment in time. It also gave us the opportunity to explicitly develop that knowing and bring it into our relationships with our children. This will be explored below.

### Stories of us bring relational purpose into awareness, allowing for story development and increased relational agency

All participants told stories of how they adapted to changing relational circumstances, how they learned from difficulties, and celebrated and nurtured what they enjoyed in their relationships. Our inquiry also contributed to this adaptability. For example, Leni described how participating in the inquiry changed the way she considered maternal holding and gave her some measure of relief that her children "do not have my shit". This relief was consciously present in some of her holding encounters with her children between and post sessions. Rosanna and Kitty also noted that storying their memories and developing understanding brought with them new conceptualisations of holding that played out in their relationships with their children.

Expression and awareness of important mother/child stories provided mothers with the opportunity to reflect upon, challenge, cherish, develop and *re-story* those narratives. They could bring their developed knowing into their holding experiences and thus provide their children with the possibility of change as well.

I recognized that the general functions of these co-created stories (coherence, meaning making) and the possibilities of increased relational agency would be immensely valuable to maternal holding. However, the data appeared to suggest that there was something particular to these co-created stories of 'us' and holding that played out in a specific kind relational agency. I just couldn't quite 'put my finger on' what that was.

I took an arts-based approach and wandered my house in search of clues. Keeping my question in mind, I picked up objects that felt as if they had something meaningful to say about participants stories of 'us'. Piling them on top of one another, I slightly obscured the photo of my son and opened up the books to add text. I darkened the image to make it less distinct, the brilliant red of our stories not yet visible.

I noticed that most of the space was taken up with an unfolding of blank dark red shapes and black and white text. There was only one recognisable human face looking beyond the books and text to something or someone. Key words arose including 'directed gaze', 'looking to the light', 'I don't see 'us' and 'missing centre'. This representation attended to 'stories' but the words were not our own and I hadn't yet figured out what kind of agency emerged from these stories.

I rearranged the objects. A lighter red now covered most of the representation and light appeared on three faces. I saw us at the centre of the image, partially covered in books without text. This time the direction of my son's gaze felt directed toward something. Our relationship felt safe, nested in and protected by our stories.

The stories were about us, but the stories were also *for* us. The relational agency that emerged from these stories spoke to mother/child purpose; it was not only about the choices made available by our stories in order to empower us, it was about choices relevant our relational purpose. Stories of shared history and relational patterns of being returned us to questions of needs and their navigation.

Stories of us served as possible guidelines for how to navigate needs and purpose in future, as models for how *not* to navigate needs and purpose in future and as stories that might be re-framed so that ultimately relational purpose was served. By storying what had occurred within the mother/child relationship relevant to holding, participants brought into awareness and made sense of mother/child relational needs and relational purpose. This is perhaps unsurprising given that storied memories formed the primary vehicle for data in this inquiry and a key finding was that holding was purposeful.

The power of participant's storying for the navigation and shaping of relational purpose was evident throughout. Images, ideas and sensations arising from story were powerfully felt and often surprising: Rosanna was shocked by the presence of herself as the red postcard in the middle of her final representation (Figure 2.8) and its message: "I can't live without you". She understood that she was a part of the moment of holding her daughters but now also saw that her needs were co-existent with theirs. This shifted her understanding of maternal purpose toward recognizing that both mother and child's needs were present and that that was "a part of loving".

When Leni looked back at the difficulties she experienced while holding her children as infants, she knew something felt wrong at the time, she remembered she felt conflicted and concerned. When we worked together to explore her understanding of those storied memories, a different narrative emerged between us around dependence and fear. From that story, Leni gained a sense of the meaning of what had happened back then and an awareness of the purposeful acts she had undertaken since then. Memories were reconstructed into a different story to "make narrative sense" (McAdams & McLean, 2013, p. 233) of Leni's experiences: in re-storying her memories, in making sense of them in a different way, Leni gained a nuanced and beneficial understanding of them; she re-framed her storying of past purposefulness in light of her new interpretation of events.

The openness and malleability of storying supports the constant adaptation to changing needs and their contribution to purpose within the mother/child relationship. Stories can be revised in the light of new information, emotional tone may change, the roles of each character may change and anticipated actions in future may change. For example, when stories of the past were in accord with what occurred in present holding and relationship, they worked to reinforce what participants knew about their relational purpose and elaborated on what participants valued about their relationship and what was nurtured. Leni picked little stories that repeatedly conveyed qualities of 'just us' like shopping expeditions, being together at parties and sitting on the couch together.

When old stories were not in accord with experiencing in the present moment (experiences were now challenging, difficult or new) those stories were brought into question. Participants sometimes recognized the validity of the old story while beginning to write a new 'chapter'; at other times they stuck with the old story and attempted to continue old ways of relating by reframing their current experience so that it fit the old story and at other times the old story was no longer relevant. For example, Kitty wanted to continue holding Harley beyond her childhood years. She was aware of a difficulty with this desire because she felt that the society in which she lives frowns upon ongoing affection between mother and child and championed independence in opposition to this affection. From this point of view, maintaining intimate embodied relationship might be damaging or infantalising for Harley. Kitty had a story of intense embodied intimacy that was highly valuable to her and she did not wish to lose that, that kind of embodied intimacy was a part of her relational purpose.

In response to a perceived cultural story that would promote disconnection from Harley, Kitty curated and storied her memories in a way that reinforced their togetherness: she felt Harley was a "part of my body". She felt that with this kind of connection: "I won't ever lose her in time or space or anywhere". Kitty's story of their shared history reflected her present concern with wanting to maintain affection and relationship with Harley and her hopes for an emotionally and physically affectionate future with her. She hoped that future 'chapters' would be 'co-written' around forms of intimacy in keeping with this purpose. Kitty 'wrote' and would continue to 'write' a shared history of maternal holding and affection with Harley that attended and responded to *their* values, their purpose and not necessarily those of society.

Working together, Kitty and I elected to co-contribute to the shaping of their story in a way that would maintain a sense of their physical affection both emotionally and practically. This was also a way of preparing for change and developing different 'chapters' in the story about what constituted intimate holding. It also included applying different levels of value to holding in the story so that she would pay more attention to the little moments of touch or brief moments of holding as they potentially diminished over time. Kitty would not impose her will upon Harley if her daughter should not wish to engage in as much physical affection as she matured. Kitty would instead pay more attention to the holding that did occur in order to enrich her memories and stories of it and recognise other ways of holding that met her needs both in relationship and outside of the relationship.

Dooley and Fedele (1999) suggest that Western culture promotes "restraint and withdrawal, rather than comfort and nurture" (p. 1) between mothers and sons. Motherhood has been coupled with stories of successful psychological and biological development as a series of separations (Silverstein and Rashbaum, 1995) from children, both sons and daughters. Psychologist Carol Gilligan (1982/1993) writes:

> Theories of psychological development and conceptions of self and morality that have linked progress or goodness with disconnection or detachment and advocated separation from women in the name of psychological growth or health are dangerous because they cloak an illusion in the trappings of science: the illusion that disconnection or dissociation from women is good.
>
> (p. xxvii)

Kitty explicitly did not want this kind of separation and did not feel it was healthy for her relationship with Harley. However, given she was already experiencing some separation she attempted to *re-story* her present, and potentially her future experiences of holding, by valuing those moments where they *did* hold. This served the wellbeing of the relationship so that Harley's needs for affection elsewhere were not hampered by Kitty's need to hold as often and as intensely as she had when Harley was younger. This was a new kind of story about holding that continued to serve an ongoing relational purpose around affection, enabling relational agency.

Relational and personal stories are not the only stories we 'live by' (McAdams, 1993). As evidenced by Kitty's story above, cultural narratives affect the stories of 'us' that shape meaning, purpose and relational identity as well. McAdams and McLean (2013, p. 236) note: "narrative identity is exquisitely contextualised in culture". When Rosanna said that to understand parts of what were valuable for her about holding, she referred not only to her personal experiences but also to her nationality, stating that we'd need to "take into account … I'm very English". She was not limited by her cultural heritage, but she was aware of the part it played in the stories she built, re-shaped and shared with her daughters.

Hammack (2008) notes that his "longitudinal research (since 2003) with youth suggests a strong tendency to reproduce a master narrative of identity" (p. 238). Referring to his 2006 research into Israeli and Palestinian adolescents, Hammock found that Jewish Israeli youth "tend to construct personal narratives that assume a redemptive form" while Palestinian youth "tend to construct life stories that assume a tragic or contaminated form". For these youth their experiencing and identity were shaped by cultural stories, but they did not unquestioningly assume these narratives as their own.

In this inquiry, most participant's stories were positive or moved from difficulty to a positive ending. It is possible that their stories reproduced master narratives around fulfilling maternal purpose and the satisfaction that goes with it. Daniel Klein (2015) writes:

> Over the centuries, virtually everyone in England has developed "tea consciousness." That is not because absolutely everyone there, drinks tea, but because a sufficient number did and do, and their resulting consciousness becomes the norm. The culture born of tea consciousness informs daily language and personal interactions; it becomes part of the process of successful socialisation.
>
> (pp. 19–20)

Perhaps a culturally prescribed 'maternal purpose consciousness' existed for participants and their children as explored in Chapter 6. However, in sharing their stories, participants were also able to hear them and question assumptions underlying them, tailoring them to their specific mother/child needs. Leni did this regularly in our sessions as she challenged the influence of "other voices" in her relationship with her children. Participants did not swallow their 'cultural tea' wholesale as their sense of purpose returned again and again to their unique shared history and relationship with their child.

In our day-to-day functioning we are often unaware of the intimate intertwining of relational or cultural assumptions with our own stories of self, other and relationship. As Christof, the master puppeteer behind *The Truman Show* (1998) says: "we accept the reality of the world with which we are presented" (Niccol, Rudin, Feldman, Shroeder & Weir, 1998). The personal, familial and cultural stories we tell ourselves are our world, and it takes something that confronts, questions, illuminates or champions those stories to bring them into awareness where they may be re-engaged with and re-shaped.

Relational agency exists in the plotting of our stories. In a "subjective and reflective process" (McLean, Syed & Shucard, 2016, p. 357) story brings together a reconstructed past "and imagines the future in such a way as to provide a person's life with some degree of unity, purpose, and meaning" (McAdams & McLean, 2013, p. 233). Story plotting, as Polkinghorne (1991) notes, recognizes our temporality and acknowledges the 'ongoingness' of action. When storying our experiences, we plot what has happened, what is happening and what may happen in the future; plotting serves a purpose and in the case of maternal holding and stories of relationship, *plotting serves co-created mother/child purpose directed toward the relationship*.

When plotting, we take what is meaningful and valued in our previous 'scenes' or 'chapters' and imagine what we might want for the future or we re-story an older narrative to suit a desired or understood present state. McAdams (2001) writes: "autobiographical memory is contoured by the person's current goals and anticipations of what future chapters and scenes are likely to bring" (p. 117). Narrative structure demands movement in time with qualities of causality and coherence: there is a problem, there is some conflict and there is a resolution; all made meaningful by their relationship with purpose and all open to change depending on the present moment and hopes for the future. Storying memories inherently includes purpose.

Even if the story is 'resolved', for example, holding for now may be ideal or acceptable, there can still be a sense of wanting that kind of holding to remain in the future, of wanting the next chapters to unfold in a way that suits our hopes or wanting old chapters to shift slightly in keeping with a different present view of relational purpose. Leni and Kitty both wanted their intimacy to continue with their children (to varying degrees), they both wanted their children to feel that they had built a history of intimacy with their parents. Rosanna was aware of the changing qualities of her shared holding experiences as her children had children of their own, she wanted to continue developing how she held her daughters and her grandchildren. Their relational purposes changed and so did their storying of relational purpose for both past experiences and potential future scenarios.

Historian Yuval Noah Harari (2016) proposes that what makes humans unique is our ability to make meaning of and shape the world by the application of story. He provides an example:

> The practical work of administering Egypt was left to thousands of literate officials … the biological pharaoh was of little importance. The real ruler of the Nile Valley was an imagined pharaoh that existed in the stories millions of Egyptians told one another.
>
> (p. 159)

What was imagined held more sway than what was real, the story of the pharaoh was more meaningful and powerful than the actual pharaoh. Harari writes: "Sapiens use language to create completely new realities" (p. 150) and this language is shaped and conveyed by story. Language and story may be verbal but may also be symbolic and visual as the image of the Pharaoh conveys. Even more so than the 'facts' of experience, the way we shape those facts into story possesses more power than what was originally experienced.

Story makes sense of the world we live in and shapes that world. Storying the mother/child relationship makes sense of it and also shapes it according to relational purpose. In the evolving, long-term and meaningful moments of maternal holding, I suggest that powerful stories of 'us' are continually constructed and re-constructed around the needs of the relationship. The ongoing storying of that relationship constantly brings relational purpose into awareness along with the opportunity for the reinforcement, revision, development and challenge of that purpose.

Mothers storied their memories in this inquiry and those stories often constellated around relational purpose. However, I was still curious as to why these stories of 'us' emerged from an inquiry into maternal holding. While I do not have a definitive answer to this question, I have generated a possible reason based on function and benefits.

I suggest that maternal holding may offer special access into guiding stories of 'us' because:

a   Holding creates a *pause* in the mother/child relationship. It may be a quick check-in like Leni's holding or a longer sense of embodied and emotional 'fit' like Kitty's holding. Within those moments, mothers and children have the chance to notice interembodied experiences, to feel *from* within the mother/child relationship. This includes sensing the current status of the relationship.

b   'Golden' or optimal moments of holding are so valuable they are implicitly and/or explicitly recorded into memory in a rich and powerful way. They serve to consolidate and develop positive stories of 'us'. These valued memories can then be more easily accessed/reconstructed, reflected upon and developed at a later date.

c   As suggested in Chapters 6 and 7, and in the two points above, positive experiences of relationship are beneficial to that relationship. Returning to them supports the relationship during harder times and over the long term. Treasured experiences of 'usness' and an insight into the current state of the relationship promote relational reward and relational agency.

By bringing into awareness valuable stories of 'us' and the current relational state, maternal holding contributes to relational agency and wellbeing. I considered again Klein's (2015) 'tea consciousness' and attempted to describe in poetry the 'consciousness of us' that maternal holding can provide (see Box 8.2).

## Box 8.2 Ariel Moy, *Steam, Tea, Cup*, poem.

Steam slips curiously up,
Tales thickening in the air,
But bounded by their origins:
The shape of mother and child.
Our stories cool and reappear,
Perched droplets on history told,
They constellate upon firmer ground,
The structure that we are.
What we tell in transformation,
Returns to us.
Leaves expand, breath deepens,
The heat that travels within.
What we share now,
Is who we are,
Life softening, warming,
Brewed anew, strange but known to 'us'.

Stories of 'us' that are accessed and constellate around holding are powerful; they shape relationship and are also shaped by relational experiencing and understanding. In their ability to make sense of, provide structure, and create meaning of relationship, and their malleability in service of relational purpose, stories of 'us' are profoundly important indicators of and means of change for healthy mother/child relationships.

## Conclusion: maternal holding and stories of us

Dan McAdams (2001) writes: "Stories live to be told to others. Life stories therefore are continually made and remade in social relationships and in the overall social context provided by culture" (p. 118). Stories of maternal holding were made and remade within the intersubjective space of the mother/child relationship and within the intersubjective space of our sessions. Re-constructed memory and prior knowing were communicated in open-ended stories that structured, supported and made sense of the mother/child 'us' while at the same time allowing for change, purposeful narrative and structure, and relational agency.

Below I provide a summary of the ideas around story and maternal holding that emerged from this inquiry:

1   Stories of 'us' are built upon re-constructed relational memories.
2   Stories *curate* memory providing coherence and meaning. Stories of maternal holding simplify experiencing around shared history and relational patterns of being together. Like memory, stories are malleable and adaptive allowing for open-ended plots and re-storying; they allow for awareness of emotional complexity; verbal stories in particular can impose a temporal structure upon experiencing; stories require an audience and have the ability to deeply engage that audience.
3   The storying of memories in our inquiry served our aim of exploring maternal holding as participants and I wished to make sense of their experiences, but it *also* promoted understanding of the strange experience of the mother/child 'us' and allowed for replotting of memories around significant mother/child goals.
4   Stories of 'us' are both implicitly and explicitly shared and powerfully contribute to the mother/child relationship. Exploring these shared stories brings the experience and understanding of relational patterns of being and shared history into awareness. These represent significant stories of the mother/child relationship. In the moment of holding and on reflection, memory, story and present experiencing actively intermingle as they shape the experience of holding and the relationship.
5   Mother and child co-create stories of their holding when they are apart and when they are together in an ongoing, reflexive, curation of shared implicit and explicit memory and experience that always references the relationship. These co-created stories of 'us' will continue to evolve for as long as the mother/child relationship exists.

6  Storying of relational patterns and shared history constellated around purpose. Stories about what happened in the relationship in the past spoke to how needs and purpose had been navigated, they also served as possible guidelines for how to navigate needs and purpose in future, as models for how *not* to navigate needs and purpose in future, and as instances of stories that might be re-framed so that ultimately relational purpose was served.

7  Awareness of stories of 'us' encourages relational agency; mother and child together have the chance to deliberately co-author and re-author their stories.

8  Maternal holding might provide special access to powerful, precious, rewarding, guiding and insightful stories of 'us' because it creates a pause in time and being; it enables the potential for awareness of experiencing from a place of 'us' and the value placed upon these 'golden moments' enables rich recording of experiences into memory. Rewarding and insightful stories of relationship support that relationship during the harder times inevitable in any significant and long-term bond.

McNeill (2016) writes in *The Beginning Woods*:

> You look at me now, and you think you see me. But you do not … You see a person that you have created, that has nothing to do with me, nothing at all. You see a story. Just as your parents, looking at you, saw a story.

(p. 364)

*Figure 8.1* Ariel Moy, *Our Stories, For Now*, 295x210mm.

When mothers hold their children and reflect upon holding their children, they return to significant stories of relationship that represent not only holding but the plot, character and atmosphere of their unique mother/child 'us' over time. They see a story of their relationship that is as real for them as it is possible to see. Mothers may see a story of their child, but the story is intimately interwoven with themselves, the story of their child is the story of their *relationship* with their child; it is a collection of evolving stories of 'us', the only reality it is possible to know about the mother/child relationship.

McNeill's 'person that you have created' speaks to the intersubjective knowing arising from an experience of two people; any tensions or harmonies, difficulties or joys emerge from and return to that relationship, we only ever see the story of that relationship because we are a part of it, we cannot be or see otherwise. Accessing these stories of 'us' and working with them provides the mother/child relationship with an increased ability to author meaningful and adaptive stories of 'us'.

## Considerations for therapeutic work

As with previous suggestions for therapeutic work around Purposefulness and Expansion, you can use an arts-based approach to inquire into a holding experience in general before focusing in on elements of storying that arise.

If stories do appear you might consider some of the following questions:

- In what ways does your client convey or manifest their story?

  Is it visual, written, spoken, in movement or sound?
  Is it a particular musical piece or a movie/character they feel relates to them?
  Is it in the form of a sand tray or a series of photos?
  Attending to the many different ways in which a client communicates their current understanding of their relationship with their child provides rich, often unexpected or not yet fully digested information.

- Is this story easy to understand? Does it make sense? Or is this story scattered and difficult to communicate?

  This may speak to underlying adult attachment styles or patterns of being that impact the present mother/child relationship. Exploring your client's childhood experiences as a 'life narrative' will give you both valuable information about how these experiences play out in their current relationship with their child.

- What is the plot of this story? Does it describe a single event or is it representative of many holding experiences? Is it about holding? Shared relational patterns? Shared history? Or something else?
- What does the story tell us about the characters? Are the main characters the mother and child or are there other characters that are necessary to the story?

- What is the environment like in this story? Is it, for example, protected or threatened? Orderly or chaotic?
- What is the mood, colour, texture, movement of the story? That is, what feeling tones populate this story and are they desirable or would your client like these to change?
- What values are at play in this story? What does your client feel is important for their relationship?
- In what way does your client feel this story shapes their holding experiences and/or their relationship with their child? What do these stories make possible for the relationship?
- Does your client feel that their story is fair? Helpful? Representative or an aberration?
- What does your client imagine their child might say, add or subtract, about this story?
- Do your client have any precious stories of holding they might share?

Is there an image/sound/smell/texture that they associate with this kind of story about holding and their relationship? This image etc. can be used as a short cut to the story, a quick reminder of what cherished and known about the relationship in times when the relationship feels difficult.

As described in Chapter 6, perhaps you and your client can develop their story and any 'short cuts' to that story together as a touchstone to support your client through the more difficult moments in their relationship.

## References

Bat Or, M. (2012). Non-verbal representations of maternal holding of preschoolers. *The Arts in Psychotherapy*, 39, 117–125. doi:10.1016/j.aip.2012.02.005.

Bernhardt, B. C., & Singer, T. (2012). The neural basis of empathy. *Annual Review of Neuroscience*, 35, 1–23. doi:10.1146/annurev-neuro-062111-150536.

Boyd, B. D. (2017). The evolution of stories: From mimesis to language, from fact to fiction. *Wiley Interdisciplinary Reviews: Cognitive Science*. doi:10.1002/wcs.1444.

Bretherton, I., & Munholland, K. (1999). Internal working models in attachment relationships: A construct revisited. In J. Cassidy & P. Shaver (Eds.), *Handbook of Attachment: Theory, Research, and Clinical Applications* (pp. 1–34). New York: Guilford Press. Retrieved from www.researchgate.net/publication/232515342_Internal_working_model_in_attachment_relationships_A_construct_revisited.

Dooley, C., & Fedele, N. (1999). *Mothers and Sons: Raising Relational Boys*. Work in Progress Publication Series, Jean Baker Miller Training Institute at the Wellesley Centers for Women. Retrieved from www.jbmti.org/pdf/84sc.pdf.

Dor, D. (2015). *The Instruction of Imagination: Language as a Social Communication Technology*. Oxford, UK: Oxford University Press.

Carr, D. (2008, July 20). Me and my girls – The night of the gun. *The New York Times Magazine*. Retrieved from www.mobile.nytimes.com.

Fuchs, T. (2016). Intercoporeality and Interaffectivity. *Phenomenology and Mind*, 11, 194–209. doi:10.13128/Phe_Mi-20119.

Gilligan, C. (1982/1993). *In a Different Voice: Psychological Theory and Women's Development*. Cambridge, MA: Harvard University Press.

Hammack, P. L. (2006). Identity, conflict, and coexistence: Life stories of Israeli and Palestinian adolescents. *Journal of Adolescent Research*, 21(4), 323–369. doi:10.1177/0743558406289745.

Hammack, P. (2008). Narrative and the cultural psychology of identity. *Personality and Social Psychology Review*, 12(3), 222–247. doi:10.1177/1088868308316892.

Harari, Y. N. (2016). *Homo Deus: A Brief History of Tomorrow*. London: Harvill Secker.

Helsel, P. (2015, February 13). David Carr, New York Times Media Columnist, Dead at 58. *NBC News*. Retrieved from www.nbcnews.com/news/us-news/david-carr-new-york-times-media-columnist-dead-58-n305516.

Keiser, D. L. (2017). Teaching (and) being we (and) not me. In O. Gunnlaugson, C. Scott, H. Bai, & E. W. Sarath (Eds.), *The Intersubjective Turn: Theoretical Approaches to Contemplative Learning*. Albany, New York: State University of New York Press.

Klein, D. (2015). *Every Time I Find the Meaning of Life They Change It: Wisdom of the Great Philosophers and How to Live*. Melbourne, Australia: Text Publishing.

Le Guin, U. K. (2004). *The Wave in the Mind: Talks and Essays on the Writer, the Reader and the Imagination*. Cambridge, MA: Shambhala Publications.

Levine, L. J., Lench, H. C., & Safer, M. A. (2009). Functions of remembering and mis-remembering emotion. *Applied Cognitive Psychology*, 23(8), 1059–1075. doi:10.1002/acp.1610.

Lewis, D. J. (1979). Psychobiology of active and inactive memory. *Psychological Bulletin*, 86(5), 1054–1083. doi:10.1037/0033-2909.86.5.1054.

Main, M., & Goldwyn, R. (1998). *Adult Attachment Scoring and Classification System*. (Version 6.3). Unpublished manuscript, University of California at Berkeley.

Manczak, E. M., McLean, K. C., McAdams, D. P., & Chen, E. (2015). Physiological reactivity during parent-adolescent discussions: Associations with scaffolding behaviours and relationship quality. *Annals of Behavioral Medicine*, 49(4), 522–531. doi:10.1007/s12160-014-9680-1.

McAdams, D. P. (1993). *The Stories We Live By: Persona Myths and the Making of the Self*. New York, NY: The Guilford Press.

McAdams, D. P. (2001). The psychology of life stories. *Review of General Psychology*, 5(2), 100–122. doi:10.1037/1089-2680.5.2.100.

McAdams, D. P., & McLean, K., C. (2013). Narrative identity. *Current Directions in Psychological Science*, 22(3), 233–238. doi:10.1177/0963721413475622.

McLean, K. (2016). *The Co-authored Self: Family Stories and the Construction of Personal Identity*. New York, NY: Oxford University Press.

McLean, K., & Morrison-Cohen, S. (2013). Moms telling tales: Maternal identity development in conversations with their adolescents about the personal past. *Identity*, 13(2), 120–139. doi:10.1080/15283488.2013.776498.

McLean, K. C., & Pasupathi, M. (2011). Old, new, borrowed, blue? The emergence and retention of personal meaning in autobiographical storytelling. *Journal of Personality*, 79(10), 135–163. doi:10.1111/j.1467-6494.2010.00676.x.

McLean, K. C., Syed, M., & Shucard, H. (2016). Bringing identity content to the fore: Links to identity development processes. *Emerging Adulthood*, 4(5), 356–364. doi:10.1177/2167696815626820.

McNeill, M. (2016). *The Beginning Woods*. London: Pushkin Press.

Nader, K., Schafe, G. E., & Le Doux, J. E. (2000). Fear memories require protein synthesis in the amygdala for reconsolidation after retrieval. *Nature*, 406, 722–726. doi:10.1038/35021052.

Neimeyer, R. A., & Thompson, B. E. (2014). Meaning making and the art of grief therapy. In B. E. Thompson and R. A. Neimeyer (Eds.), *Grief and the Expressive Arts: Practices for Creating Meaning* (pp. 3–13). New York: Routledge.

Niccol, A., Rudin, S., Feldman, E. S., & Schroeder, A. (Producers), & Weir, P. (Director). (1998). *The Truman Show* (Motion Picture). US Paramount Pictures.

Öner, S., & Gülgöz, S. (2017). Autobiographical remembering regulates emotions: A functional perspective. *Memory*, 26(1), 15–28. doi:10.1080/09658211.2017.1316510.

Polkinghorne, D. E. (1991). Narrative and Self-Concept. *Journal of Narrative and Life History*, 1(2 & 3), 135–153. doi:10.1075/jnlh.1.2-3.04nar.

Rain, M., Cilento, E., MacDonald, G., & Mar, R. A. (2017). Adult attachment and transportation into narrative worlds. *Personal Relationships*, 24(1), 49–74. doi:10.1111/pere.12167.

Ramirez, F. D., Bogetz, J. F., Kufeld, M., & Yee, L. M. (2019). Professional bereavement photography in the setting of perinatal Loss: A qualitative analysis, *Global Pediatric Health*, 6, 1–12. doi:10.1177/2333794X19854941.

Rubin, D. C., & Umanath, S. (2015). Event memory: A theory of memory for laboratory, autobiographical, and fictional events. *Psychological Review*, 122(1), 1–23. doi:10.1037/a0037907.

Siegel, D. J. (1999). *The Developing Mind: How Relationships and the Brain Interact to Shape Who We Are*. New York, NY: The Guilford Press.

Silverstein, O., & Rashbaum, B. (1995). *The Courage to Raise Good Men: You Don't Have to Sever the Bond with your Son to Help Him Become a Man*. New York, NY: Penguin Books.

Singer, T., Seymour, B., O'Doherty, J., Kaube, H., Dolan, R. J., & Frith, C. D. (2004). Empathy for pain involves the affective but not sensory components of pain. *Science*, 303, 1157–1162. doi:10.1126/science.1093535.

Smorti, A., & Fioretti, C. (2016). Why narrating changes memory: A contribution to an integrative model of memory and narrative processes. *Integrative Psychological and Behavioral Science*, 50(2), 296–319. doi:10.1007/s12124-015-9330-6.

Speer, N. K., Reynolds, J. R., Swallow, K. M., & Zacks, J. M. (2009). Reading stories activates neural representations of visual and motor experiences. *Psychological Science*, 20(8), 989–999. doi:10.1111/j.1467-9280.2009.02397.x.

Stern, D. (2004). *The Present Moment In Psychotherapy and Everyday Life*. New York, NY: W. W. Norton & Company.

# 9 Endings and beginnings

## Endings and beginnings

Much of the research looking at the mother/child relationship has done so from the perspective of the well-being, development, malleability and vulnerability of the child. Our research explicitly explored and developed understanding of *maternal* remembering and meaning making about this significant relationship through the lens of holding.

In her final session, Leni noted that she had experienced:

> A *big* learning curve ... from such an innocuous little word ... cuddle. 'I just give them a cuddle, I just do it', but no ...

The three mothers and I moved along that learning curve together, developing our knowing about seemingly small, everyday interactions between mother and child with an arts-based therapeutic approach. What we discovered was that holding is a form of love we give to ourselves and our children; that together, mother and child are their holding experience.

We learned that holding can be physical or built upon a shared history of physical holding. It can be emotional and psychological, and we can hold across distances, multiple relationships and time with the use of technology.

In the stories that capture those holding experiences we become aware of significant relational patterns of being and meaningful shared history. These stories are built by both mother and child. With the expression of these stories we have the chance to rewrite unhelpful narratives and create new beneficial chapters, to see what is possible for us as we develop relational agency.

Holding illuminates our sense of purpose as it manifests in mother/child relational needs. Knowing these empowers our relationship, providing us with the opportunity to identify and navigate what we deem essential to relational flourishing. Our attention is drawn to the ways in which mother and child together co-create needs and their satisfaction. As mothers, we begin to notice, not only what we give, but what we receive from our children and how what we perceive as our own needs, or our child's needs, are unique to this relationship; these needs arise from the particularity of our mother/child 'us'.

DOI: 10.4324/9781003104094-10

Further, much has been explored within the domain of attachment studies looking at the formation of attachment styles and the impact of these styles on both adults and children. I suggest that in the mother/child relationship it is not only the child who is developing an attachment style, it is possible that the mother too is evolving her own attachment patterns within her significant and meaningful relationship with her child.

If we pay attention to and explore it from unexpected angles, holding can provide us with an experience of deep interconnection, of self-in-relationship or what I call mother/child 'usness'. These cherished moments are often outside of our everyday awareness and yet can be experienced in the simple act of holding.

With an arts-based approach to therapy you can inquire into what is pre-reflective, ambiguous, metaphorical, symbolic and felt in the moment. This yields rich and complex material we can bring to language and conceptualisation. The privileging and use of arts and experiential modalities, and present moment embodied awareness, allows clients and therapists to stay with what emerges as significant in the now, to explore what is felt but not quite understood, and allow for suspension of judgement.

This approach develops and strengthens the therapeutic alliance by creating a space where the not quite known, confusing or troubling has room to breathe before we begin to make sense of it. Between therapist and client, there is a third object, the representation or creative expression as well as the experience, that we can co-explore. This helps reduce some of the intensity of experiencing around maternal holding and the mother/child relationship by moving that depth of feeling and inquiry onto the object, for a time.

The arts-based approach also applies to therapist's ways of exploring and making meaning of their work with clients, by allowing experiential and presentational knowing their 'time in the sun' before moving on to conceptual knowing, now grounded in these other forms of knowing. We give ourselves the chance to stay radically open to just what the client and we bring to our work together.

With arts-based therapy we can also create 'shortcuts' to previous moments of 'usness', developing with mothers a tangible connection back to moments of deep love and reward with their children. Sometimes having a touchstone in the form of a photo, a smell, a small object or image to remind us of what is important and valuable in our mother/child relationship can be the difference between exhaustion and despair or hope and recollection of meaning.

The rewards that can arise in part from an awareness of co-created purpose, in part from the deep pleasures to be found in the unusual experience of expansion into self-in-relationship and from meaningful stories of 'us', can support the relationship through the harder times. With increased awareness of the intersubjective 'us' come enhanced opportunities to *savour* the good times and appreciate the co-creation of relationship by mother and child.

In our final session, Kitty and I reflected on our shared inquiry so far. She noted:

KITTY: Today I got a real clarity about it … it's been very moving and very touching to see it all like this [*all of her representations together*] and to explore it all, incredibly moving, and it's given me an insight that I didn't, that wasn't there for me before … we all know the importance of touch and everything but to see … the actual profound impact it has and the profound importance it has in my relationship with Harley and the blessing of it. Because I hadn't really thought much about it before.She continued:

KITTY: So, I think about it a lot more. Even this morning I was thinking about it when she came into our bed and I was holding her, and I thought "you haven't done this for such a long time" – but to feel it, and remember it, and the importance of it.

ARIEL: Really appreciating it … And focusing on it when it happens.

KITTY: Which I don't think I had that before we were doing this.

The benefits of savouring include increased positive emotions in general as well as a temporary elevation of a person's mood (Jose, Lim & Bryant, 2012). Bryant, Smart, and King (2005) found that the more often a person reminisced about a positive event and the more vivid the memory, the more the person's happiness was impacted. Conversely, Bond and Borelli (2017) explored the relationship between insecure maternal attachment styles and decreased savouring of the mother/child relationship. They suggested that *not* engaging in savouring responses could contribute to less maternal satisfaction in their relationship with their child. Kitty savoured her positive memories of holding and also reported savouring her positive holding experiences as they occurred. Attending to holding brought more joy and appreciation into her relationship with Harley.

Over many years the mother/child relationship can harbour the hurt and distress, as well as the joys and meaningfulness of mother and child together. For mothers, and most likely children, there are many moments when we can feel desperately alone. New mothers, in particular, can experience profound isolation but so can mothers of children now off to school, mothers of teens who begin pulling away, and mothers whose children have left the family home.

As our child grows our relationship changes and we also grow. At any point in the mother/child relationship we can feel helpless or hopeless, afraid or angry, overwhelmed, exhausted, ashamed and utterly isolated. Bringing mother's attention to holding and its precious, rewarding, revealing and inter-subjective qualities can result in incredibly beneficial outcomes:

1    Mothers discover through lived experience that they are *not alone* in their relationship with their child.
2    Their responsibilities, experiences and understanding may be different from their child's, but whatever they feel about their mother/child relationship arises from and returns to that relationship; together they co-create their relational purpose, what is given and received, relational rewards and significant stories of 'us'.

3   Attending to experiencing from within relationship also gives us the chance to notice the current status of the relationship: what is working well, what we are unsure about and what we'd like to change.

4   Mothers learn that because significant patterns of being together and shared history are co-created by mother and child in the form of stories of 'us', those stories are always open to re-interpretation and development as they are inherently malleable and adaptive and *of* the relationship.

5   Experiencing and making sense from a place of the mother/child 'us' ultimately provides *relational agency*.

This inquiry highlights the value of exploration into and arts therapeutic work with mother's experiences of holding their children. When we engage

*Figure 9.1* Ariel Moy, *A Final Representation of Holding … For Now*, felt tip pen on paper, 210x295mm.

with qualities of maternal holding such as a sense of co-created purpose, experiences of expansion and co-created stories of relationship, we have the opportunity to deeply enjoy, savour, develop and strengthen mothers' relationships with their children.

From this emerges a grounded and practical relational agency incorporating awareness of responsibility and also reward. Mothers have the chance to really feel that they're not alone, a particularly beneficial outcome when they're holding their wailing child at 3am in the morning, carrying their exhausted arm-flailing toddler out of the supermarket or placing a gentle arm around their less than enthused teenager.

Maternal holding can take us to visceral experiences of love (see Figure 9.1), confronting us with our relational needs and status, our sense of self-in-relationship, our fears, purpose and possibilities. In that moment of raw meeting we can and do consolidate, develop and imagine what is possible for our relationship. In the significant and life-long relationship that is the mother/child 'us', engaging in arts therapeutic work with experiences of maternal holding can help us attend to, understand, evolve and strengthen our relational bonds and wellbeing.

## References

Bond, D. K., & Borelli, J. L. (2017). Maternal attachment insecurity and poorer proficiency savoring memories with their children: The mediating role of rumination. *Journal of Social and Personal Relationships*, 34(7), 1007–1030. doi:10.1177/0265407516664995.

Bryant, F. B., Smart, C. M., & King, S. P. (2005). Using the past to enhance the present: Boosting happiness through positive reminiscence. *Journal of Happiness Studies: An Interdisciplinary Forum on Subjective Well-Being*, 6(3), 227–260. doi:10.1007/s10902–10005–3889–3884.

Jose, P. E., Lim, B. T., & Bryant, F. B. (2012). Does savouring increase happiness? A daily diary study. *Journal of Positive Psychology*, 7(3), 176–187. doi:10.1080/17439760.2012.671345.

# Index